Adobe Photoshop
CREATIVE TECHNIQUES

Adobe Photoshop

CREATIVE TECHNIQUES

Denise Salles
Gary Poyssick
Ellen Behoriam

Hayden
Books

Photoshop Creative Techniques

Library of Congress Catalog Number: 94-73186
ISBN: 1-56830-132-4

97   96   95   4   3   2   1

Interpretation of the printing code: the rightmost double-digit number is the year of the book's printing; the rightmost single-digit number is the number of the book's printing. For example, a printing code of 94-1 shows that the first printing of the book occurred in 1994.

This book was produced digitally by Macmillan Computer Publishing and manufactured by Shepard Poorman Communications Corporation, Indianapolis, Indiana.

Credits

Publisher
Don Fowley

Acquisitions Manager
Karen Whitehouse

Acquisitions Editor
Oliver von Quadt

Development Editor
Marta J. Partington

Technical Editors
Michael J. Partington
Stephen Graham

Copy Editor
Jyoti Weaver

Production Editors
Steve Mulder
Kathy Simpson

Publishing Coordinator
Rosemary Lewis

Interior Designer
Barbara Kordesh

Cover Designer
Karen Ruggles

Manufacturing Coordinator
Paul Gilchrist

Production Manager
Kelly Dobbs

Production Team Supervisor
Laurie Casey

Production Team
Troy Barnes, Dan Caparo, Kim Cofer, Trudy Coler, Joe Millay, Erika Millen, Beth Rago,
Gina Rexrode, Christine Tyner, Marvin Van Tiem, Karen Walsh, Robert Wolf

Composed in
AGaramond

Acknowledgments

Much appreciation to Kate O'Day for her perseverance and precision in editing and working with many of the tips in this book.

Many thanks to all the fine artists who allowed us to use their artwork in the pages of this book. Without their work, this book would not have been possible. Please refer to the artist listing in the back of this book if you are interested in purchasing artwork from any of these artists.

Contents

A. Before You Begin: Configuring the Photoshop Environment

Configuring the Photoshop Environment 1
Customizing the Commands Palette 2
Managing the Floating Palettes 3
Managing the Screen Display 4

B. Selection Tools and Methods

The Lasso Tool 5
Adding to and Subtracting from Selections 6
The Marquee Tool 7
The Magic Wand Tool 8
The Color Range Command 9
Saving Selections 10
Creating a Quick Mask 11
Creating Selection Borders..12
Removing Unwanted Pixels 13

C. Painting

Selecting Colors..14
Using the Brushes Palette..15
Custom Brushes..16
Using a Grid to Place Art 17
Sketching and Inking..18
Using the Rubber Stamp Tool 19
Twirl Filter..20
Applying the Spherize Filter..21
Creating Lighting Effects..22
Creating Simple Gradients..23
Gradient Masks 24
Shearing and Pinching..25
Creating Basic Textures 26
Wave and Zigzags 27
Coloring Line Art 28

Floating Selections 29
Lighting Effects Filter (Part 1) 30
Lighting Effects Filter (Part 2) 31
Simulating a Color Halftone 32
Ripples in the Water 33
Pointillize and Crystallize Filters 34
Facet Filter 35
Mezzotints 36
Clouds Filters 37
Textures on Layers 38
Replacing Colors 39
Posterize 40
Using Quick-Edit 41

D. Painting Modes

Normal 42
Dissolve 43
Multiply 44
Screen 45
Overlay 46
Soft and Hard Light 47
Darken and Lighten 48
Difference 49

E. Working with Layers

Defining Layers 50
Creating Drop Shadows 51
Creating a Rainbow Effect 52
Type on Layers 53
Adjusting the Color of Placed Images 54
Global Color Adjustments 55
Creating a Lens Flare Effect 56
Grouping, Merging, and Flattening Layers 57

F. Working with Channels

Saving Selections 58
Managing Channels 59

Channel Selection Method 60
Creating a Fade Effect 61
Creating a Vignette Mask 62
Importing Custom Masks 63
Using Channels to Create Shadows 64

G. Resolution

Resolution and Image Size 65
Canvas Size 66
JPEG 67
Resolution and Screen Frequency Requirements 68
Creating Cool Icons 69

H. Retouching Images

Scratches and Flaws 70
Using Filters to Clean Images 71
Blur Filters 72
Sharpen Filters 73
Unsharp Masking 74
The Dodge, Burn, and Sponge Tools 75
Descreening 76

I. Image and Color Corrections

Adjusting Tonal Ranges 77
Creating a Scale of Grays 78
RGB versus CMYK 79
Brightness and Contrast 80
Curves 1 81
Curves 2 82
Adjusting Shadows 83
Adjusting Midtones 84
Adjusting Highlights 85
Hue and Saturation 86
Removing Casts 87
Using Variations 88
Adjusting Single Ink Sets 89
Selective Color 90

Duotones 91
Four-Color Black and White 92
Enriching CMYK Colors 93
Adjusting Nature's Colors 94

J. Color Management

Creating Color Wheels 95
Complementary Colors 96
Creating Color Targets 97
Custom Swatch Palettes 98

K. Type Treatments

Importing Type from Adobe Illustrator 99
Neon Type 100
Reflections in Type 101
Metallic Type 102
Cut Stone 103
Smoked Glass 104
Glowing Type 105
Embossed Type 106
Anti-Aliasing 107
Antiquing and Distressing Type 108
Putting Images into Type 109

L. Drawing

The Pen Tool 110
Planning Paths 111
Managing Paths 112
Converting Paths and Selections 113
Exporting Outlines 114
Importing and Exporting Paths 115

M. Prepress

Understanding Continuous Tone Images 116
Line Screen Angles and Dot Shapes 117

Dot Gain and Transfer Functions 118
UCR and GCR 119
Gamut Restrictions 120

N. File Formats

Photoshop 3.0 File Format 121
EPS 122
DCS (Desktop Color Separations)..123
TIFF 124
Using the Photo CD Disk 125
Opening Photo CD Images 126

About This Book

There are several components to each two-page spread:

Artwork/Artist
The artwork is shown on the left side of the page. Since the samples provided by the individual artists naturally spanned a broad spectrum of sizes, shapes, and substrates, the images that you see have been somewhat standardized. Therefore, these images have been scaled up or down to fit the space allocated by the book's designers. The name of the artist responsible for the piece is shown under the artwork. An appendix provides contact information about each artist.

Comments
The Comments section discusses global issues concerning the technique found on that page.

Studio Usage
The Studio Usage section provides specific instances where a particular solution might be considered—in practical terms. This helps you connect a particular technique to other projects you might be involved in at the time.

Related Techniques
Each of the individual art tiles has been chosen to help you visualize the steps required to achieve a specific effect. In reality, though, each of the individual files has been constructed using dozens—even hundreds—of individual techniques used in concert with one another to achieve the desired end-result. This list provides a "pointer" to tips and solutions that either enhance or expand on the issues being discussed.

Steps
Wherever possible, each tip is broken into three or more specific steps that you can apply within Adobe Photoshop to achieve the effect in question. Some solutions are conceptual or theoretical in nature, and therefore provide information in steps to build and reinforce a specific idea. By looking closely at the artwork and reading the steps (or, better yet, practicing them on your own projects), you will begin to see how the artists approached particular graphic problems, and how they solved them using Photoshop's built-in functionality. Often, they found methods not discussed in the program's manuals.

Bonny Lhotka

Comments

To accurately replicate the techniques in this book, it will be helpful to begin by setting up your Photoshop environment to correspond with the one used in this book.

Studio Usage

In order to work efficiently, it is helpful to configure your Photoshop settings, called *preferences,* according to the project. For example, if you're retouching an image using a painting tool, you may want to view the brush at actual pixel size instead of viewing the brush icon.

Related Techniques

Customizing the
Commands Palette   2

Managing the
Floating Palettes   3

Managing the Screen Display   4

1 | Open the General Preferences Dialog Box

Choose File→Preferences→General (⌘-K). The General Preferences dialog box appears, which controls the display of the painting and editing tools, as well as a number of other general display options.

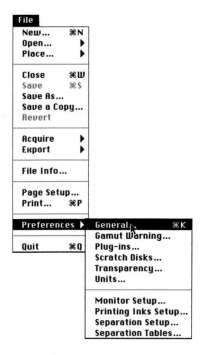

2 | Set the Display for the Painting Tools

Painting tools can be displayed in three ways: the Standard option displays the tool as it appears in the toolbox; the Precise option displays the tool as a crosshair with a single pixel at the intersection of the crosshairs for precise control; and the Brush Size option displays the painting tool at its actual size in pixels. Make sure that the Brush Size option is selected for the painting tools; this option is used throughout the book.

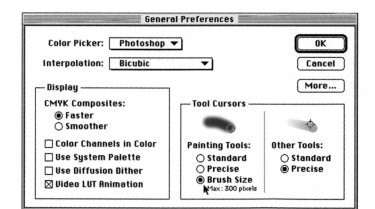

3 | Change the Display of the Editing Tools

The editing tools may be displayed as Standard or Precise. The default tool icons work well, but they don't provide the same degree of accuracy as the Precise setting. Almost all the pros use the Precise setting for the editing tools. Make sure that the Precise option is selected for the other tools.

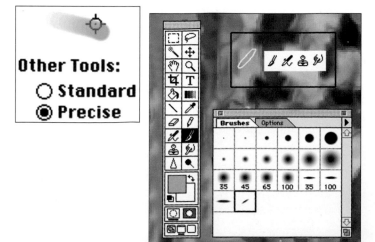

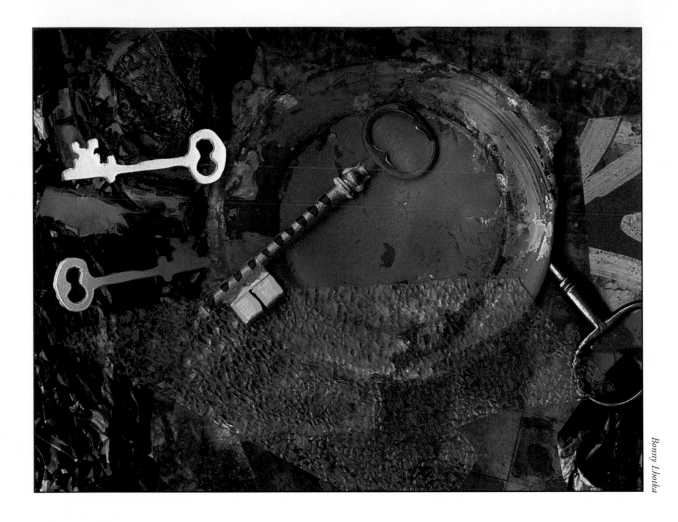

Bonny Lhotka

Comments

Adobe Photoshop provides a Commands palette that lets you select frequently used commands with a single click of the mouse or by pressing a Function key. You can customize the Commands palette to fit your individual preferences. Before you begin experimenting with the techniques in this book, you may want to set your Commands palette to match the Commands palette in this book.

Studio Usage

You'll be more productive if you customize the Commands palette to contain all your frequently used commands. You can assign colors to like commands, and you can also save a number of different Commands palette configurations to suit individual projects.

Related Techniques

Configuring the
Photoshop Preferences   1

Managing the
Floating Palettes   3

Managing the
Screen Display   4

1 | Open the Commands Palette

Choose Window→Palettes→Show Commands. The Commands palette appears with the default settings.

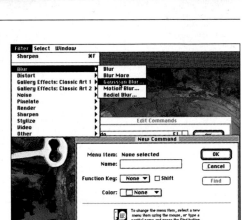

2 | To Add a Command

Choose New Command from the palette pop-up menu (the black triangle to the right of the palette's name.) Choose the desired command from the appropriate menu to place the command name in the Name field. If desired, assign a function key to the command using the Function key pop-up menu. To assign a color to a command, choose the desired color from the Color pop-up menu. Click OK to add the command to the Commands palette.

3 | To Edit a Command

Choose Edit Commands from the palette pop-up menu. To change the order of the commands, drag the command name in the list of commands. As you drag, a hand and a black horizontal line indicate where the command will be placed when you release the mouse button. Click OK to apply the change.

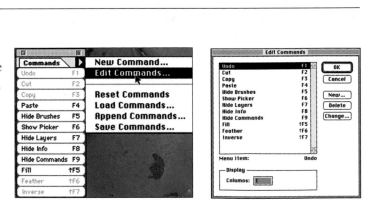

4 | To Save, Load, Reset, or Append a Command Palette

You can save, load, reset, or append command files. To perform any of these tasks, choose the desired option from the Commands palette pop-up menu. (It is helpful to create a separate folder in which to store the command files you create.) Several alternative Commands palettes are included with the Adobe Photoshop software—to select an alternate palette, locate and open Goodies folder, select and open the Command Sets folder, and then choose an alternate palette from the list of available palettes.

Phil Howe

Comments

The Adobe Photoshop software contains ten palettes. When you start the Adobe Photoshop program for the first time, eight of the palettes, arranged in three groups of similar functions, are displayed. There are two additional palettes that are not initially displayed—the Info palette, which provides information about the current tool, and the Commands palette, which you can use to select frequently used commands.

Studio Usage

Organizing your floating palettes is an effective way to reduce screen clutter and do away with the necessity to repeatedly choose palettes from the Window menu. After you've organized your palettes on the desktop, they remain in the same position each time you open Photoshop.

Related Techniques

Configuring the Photoshop
Environment 1

Customizing the
Commands Palette 2

Managing the
Screen Display 4

1 | Select the Default Palettes

Before you begin this tip about working with palettes, make sure that the default palettes are displayed. To select the default palettes, choose File→Preferences→ General (⌘-K), click the More option, and then deselect the Restore Palette & Dialog Positions option. A message box appears; click Yes to reset the default palettes. Click the Restore Palette & Dialog Positions option so that your palette settings will be restored in future sessions. Click OK twice to exit the Preferences dialog box. The default palettes appear onscreen.

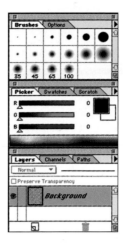

2 | To Select Palette Submenus

All the Adobe Photoshop palettes have submenus that contain the active palette's options. To display a palette's submenu, select the black triangle to the right of the palette name.

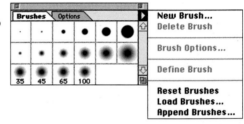

3 | To Select, Move, and Size Palettes

To select a palette, click the palette tab. To move a palette, drag the gray bar at the top of the palette. As you drag, you'll notice that the palette "snaps" to an invisible grid on the screen. Drag the palettes to a convenient location onscreen and leave them open while you work. To increase your work space, you can collapse palettes. To collapse a palette, click the zoom box; to collapse the palette to only its titles, Option-click the zoom box. To close a palette, click the close box at the top of the palette. To display a palette that has been closed, choose the palette name from the Window menu.

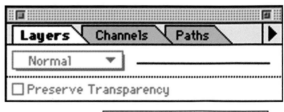

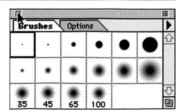

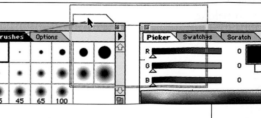

4 | To Rearrange Palettes

You can rearrange or separate palettes by dragging the palette's tab. To move a palette into another palette, drag the palette tab to the desired palette and release the mouse button. To create a new, separate group, drag the palette's tab anywhere outside the palette and release the mouse button.

Paul Watson

Comments

Three icons at the bottom of the Adobe Photoshop toolbox represent document viewing options. The standard option displays the screen with the artwork, the menu bar, and the scroll bars. The full screen with menu option displays the artwork in a full screen with the menu bar, but without scroll bars. The full screen option displays only the artwork, without the menu bar or the scroll bars.

Studio Usage

Previewing artwork onscreen can be difficult if you're distracted by screen elements. By selecting a viewing option, you can preview artwork in a way that best suits your visual preference.

Related Techniques

Configuring the Photoshop
Environment 1

Customizing the
Commands Palette 2

Managing the
Floating Palettes 3

1 | Standard Option

Three view icons are located at the bottom of the Photoshop tool box; an underline appears under the currently active view icon. Click the leftmost icon (the default view) to display artwork in Standard view, which displays the artwork—including all the scrolling and sizing options. In this view, you can see any open windows from other applications behind the active Photoshop window.

2 | Full Screen with Menu Option

Click the middle icon to display artwork in Full Screen with Menu view, which displays the artwork in a full screen with a menu bar, but without scrolling and sizing options. Although other open documents are hidden when this view option is selected, you can bring any open document to the front of the screen by choosing its name from the Window menu.

3 | Full Screen Option

Click the rightmost icon to display artwork in Full Screen view, which displays only the artwork without the menu bar or scrolling options. In Full Screen view, any open palettes are also displayed. To hide all open palettes, press the Tab key; press the Tab key again to show the palettes.

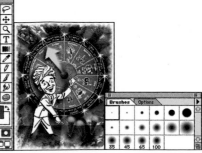

Selection Tools and Methods *The Lasso Tool*

Oko & Mano, Inc.

Comments

In order to edit portions of images, you must first select the area that you want to affect. Photoshop provides several ways to select parts of images. Depending on the type of selection and the degree of precision required, you can use the Marquee tool, the Lasso tool, the Magic Wand tool, and the Color Range command. After you have selected part of an image, only the area within the selection border can be edited.

Studio Usage

The ability to make precise selections is one of the most important aspects within Photoshop. Because Photoshop is a pixel-based program, the accuracy with which you make a selection determines the quality of the finished artwork. Selections are used for a variety of techniques including color correction, applying filters, and creating composite images from a variety of artwork files. The Lasso tool is most commonly used for freehand selections.

Related Techniques

Adding to and
Subtracting from Selections 6

Saving Selections 10

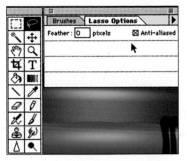

1 | Setting the Lasso Options

Double-click the Lasso tool in the tool box to display the Lasso Options palette. (Most of the Photoshop tools have an option palette that can be selected by double-clicking the tool in the toolbox.) To practice with the Lasso tool, make sure that the Feather amount is set to 0 and the Anti-aliased option box is selected. Anti-aliasing produces a smooth edge by partially selecting pixels that fall only partially within the selection border.

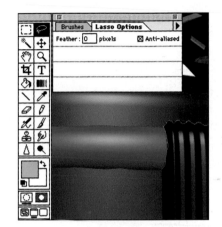

2 | Drawing Freehand

Drag the Lasso tool in a continuous motion to draw a freehand outline around an object. Make sure that you start and end the selection at the same point—if you don't, the Lasso tool averages the distance between the starting and ending point and draws a selection line between them, which can result in an inaccurate selection. For areas requiring precise selection, use the Zoom tool to magnify the selection area. It may be easier to draw a freehand outline with a precise cursor instead of the Lasso tool. Press the Caps Lock key to change the pointer from the Lasso to a precise cursor.

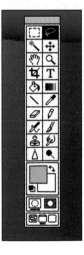

3 | Drawing Straight Lines

To draw straight lines with the Lasso tool, hold down the Option key and click the Lasso tool to define end points. Each time you click the Lasso tool, the straight line follows the lasso to the next point. If you are making a transition from a straight line to a freehand lines, do not release the mouse button when you make a transition from one type to another.

4 | Hiding and Showing a Selection Border

A selection marquee appears around an object when you release the mouse button. If you edit the selection and want to turn off the selection border to preview any editing you've done within the selection, choose Select→Hide Edges (⌘-H). To make the selection border visible again, press (⌘-H). If you don't like the effect of your editing, choose Edit→Undo (⌘-Z).

Selection Tools and Methods *Adding to and Subtracting from Selections*

Anne S. Barrett

Comments

Intricate selections can be developed using a variety of selection tools. For example, you might use the Marquee tool to select a large portion of an image and then add to the initial selection using the Lasso tool or the Magic Wand tool. To add to and subtract from a selection, use the Shift and Command keys in conjunction with the appropriate selection tool.

Studio Usage

Building custom selections is done in stages. Begin by determining which tools are appropriate to the type of selection and then create a rough outline around the area. For example, to select an item that contains many color variations but has a consistent background color, you use the Magic Wand tool to select the background color and then invert the selection to select the object.

Related Techniques

The Lasso Tool   5

The Marquee Tool   7

Saving Selections   10

1 | Create a Selection

To begin a complex selection border, draw a basic outline around the object using a selection tool. Don't worry if the selection isn't perfect the first time; you can add to the selection or subtract from the selection using the Shift and Command keys.

2 | Adding to a Selection

To add to a selection, hold down the Shift key and drag the Lasso tool around the pixels you want to add to the selection. (To see the individual pixels surrounding a selection area, it's helpful to use the Zoom tool to magnify the view of the area.)

3 | Subtracting from a Selection

To subtract from a selection, hold down the Command key and drag the Lasso tool around the sections of the image that you want to eliminate.

4 | Inverting a Selection

If you have started a selection by choosing the area opposite the desired selection (see Studio Usage), use the Inverse command to invert the selection marquee. Choose Select→Inverse; the area opposite the original selection marquee becomes the active selection.

Sanjay Kothari

Comments

Using only the Lasso tool to make selections can be tedious. The Marquee selection tool, which can take the shape of a rectangle or an oval, can be helpful in initially selecting a large area of an image. After you've selected a large area of the image, you can use other selection tools to add to or subtract from the basic shape.

Studio Usage

To select large areas of an image, you can use the Marquee tool. The Marquee tool shape can be either a rectangle or an ellipsis. The same basic functions that apply to the Lasso tool also apply to the other selection tools—expect to use all of them when developing complex selections.

Related Techniques

The Lasso Tool   5

Adding to and
Subtracting from Selections   6

Saving Selections   10

1 | Select the Marquee Tool

Click the Marquee tool. The Marquee can be shaped either as a rectangle or as an ellipsis. To select the ellipsis shape, hold down the Option key and click the Marquee tool in the toolbox; holding down the Option key toggles between the rectangular and elliptical tool. To select the Marquee Options palette, double-click the Marquee tool.

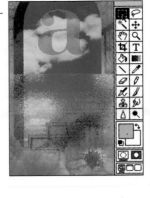

2 | To Move a Selection Border

To move a selection border without affecting the underlying pixels, hold down the Command and Option keys, position the pointer just inside the selection border, and then drag to move the selection border. Release the mouse button and then release the Command and Option keys.

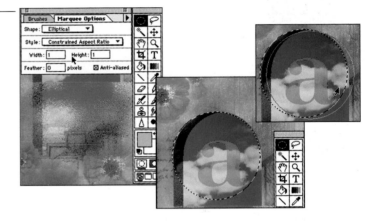

3 | To Add to and Subtract from Selections

Use the Shift Key in conjunction with either Marquee tool to *add* portions of an image to your selection. Use the Command key in conjunction with either Marquee tool to *subtract* portions of a selection.

4 | To Select Marquee Options

To create a selection marquee of a fixed size, select Fixed size from the style pop-up menu in the Marquee Options palette and then enter a size in pixels. When you click the Marquee tool in the document window, the fixed-size selection border appears.

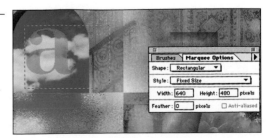

Phil Howe, Photographer; Ed Lowe ©Microsoft 1995

Comments

The Magic Wand tool selects areas based on color and the similarity in color of adjacent pixels. The Magic Wand tool contains an additional option, called *tolerance*, that allows you to specify how many levels of color to select, as in light green to dark green. You can also use the Shift and Command keys with the Magic Wand tool to add to or subtract from a selection.

Studio Usage

Some images are difficult to select, due to their proximity to other objects or to their complexity. The Magic Wand tool also works well to select a background of a consistent range of color, which can then be inverted to select the desired object.

Related Techniques

The Lasso Tool   5

Adding to and Subtracting
from Selections   6

The Marquee Tool   7

Saving Selections   10

1 | Select the Magic Wand Tool

Click the Magic Wand tool in the toolbox. To select the Magic Wand options palette, double-click the Magic Wand tool.

2 | Set the Tolerance

In the Magic Wand options palette, the Tolerance level determines the range of color the Magic Wand tool selects. The default setting is 32, which selects colors that are 16 levels higher (darker) and 16 levels lower (lighter). The smaller the number you enter in the Tolerance field, the fewer colors selected.

3 | To Select Large Color Ranges

To select a wide range of color, increase the value in the Tolerance field of the Magic Wand options palette. For example, if you enter a value of 255 in the Tolerance field, the Magic Wand tool selects the entire image because every color in the spectrum is represented, from black (0) to white (255). To add pixels to a selection, hold down the Shift key and click the Magic Wand tool; to subtract pixels from the selection, hold down the Command key and click the Magic Wand tool.

4 | To Apply the Grow and Similar Commands

You can use the Grow and Similar commands from the Select menu to add pixels to a selection. The Grow command selects *adjacent* pixels that are similar in color, and the Similar command selects pixels *anywhere* in the document where pixels of similar color are detected.

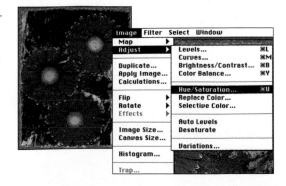

Bonny Lhotka

Comments

The Color Range command is one of Photoshop's most powerful selection methods. You can select colors within existing selections or within an entire image. Unlike the other selection tools, the Color Range command can work within existing selections, allowing you to choose subsets of colors. You can choose from a list of preset single colors, or you can sample colors from your image to create a selection.

Studio Usage

Making complex selections based on color or density has long been a standard function on high-end retouching systems. The Color Range command works very well for making complex selections. It's also an excellent way to select and shift or change a color range in an image when used with the Hue and Saturation commands.

Related Techniques

The Magic Wand Tool 8

Adjusting Shadows,
Midtones, Highlights 83,
84, 85

Hue and Saturation 86

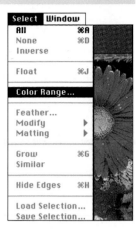

1 | To Create a Selection Using Sampled Colors

Open an image for experimentation purposes. The image of the daisies is an excellent example of an image requiring more than average selection techniques. Choose Select→Color Range to open the Color Range dialog box. At the top of the dialog box, the Select pop-up menu provides the method by which the selection is made. When Sampled Colors is selected, the selection is based on colors that you choose in the image. The Fuzziness slider below the Select pop-up menu works like the Tolerance slider with the Magic Wand tool. The higher the Fuzziness value, the greater the range of color selected.

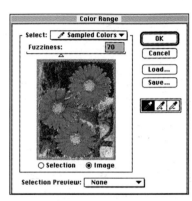

2 | To Select, Add, and Subtract Colors

You use the Eyedropper tools in the Color Range dialog box to select colors or ranges of colors. When you open the Color Range dialog box, the preview window is black if nothing in the document is selected. Click Image to see the preview image. Move the pointer into the preview area and then click the color that you want to select. To add colors to the selection, click the eyedropper with the plus sign and either click additional colors or drag to select a range of colors. To subtract colors from a selection, click the Eyedropper tool with the minus sign and click the colors that you want to remove, or drag to remove a range of colors.

3 | To Preview a Selection

To see where the selection border will be created, either click the Selection button under the preview image, or hold down the Control key to see the image in Selection mode. The white areas are where the image will be selected. You also can preview the results of the selection by choosing an option from the Selection Preview pop-up menu; the preview is displayed in the original document window.

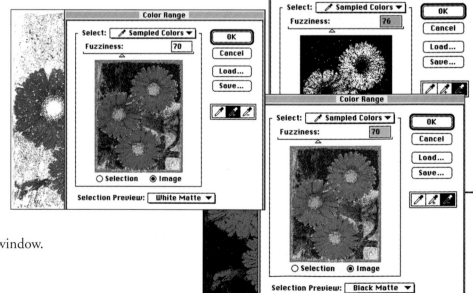

4 | To Change Specific Colors Globally

To change the hue or saturation of a specific color in an image, choose Select→Color Range, select one of the preset single colors (red, green, blue, cyan, magenta, yellow, or black) from the Select pop-up menu, and then click OK. Choose Image→Adjust→Hue and Saturation (⌘→U). Drag the Hue slider to change the hue of only the selected pixels. This is an ideal way to change a specific color in any image. You can also use the Color Range command to select specific tonal ranges (highlights, midtones, and shadows)—an invaluable technique for color correction.

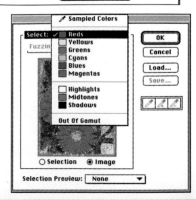

Lisa Rivard

Comments

After you have created a selection, you can save it and then load it whenever you want to work with it. When you save a selection, you don't have to reselect an area each time. Selections are saved in *channels*, which function as storage areas for individual selections. You'll learn more about channels and other uses for channels in later tips.

Studio Usage

Photoshop images are composed of channels. For example, an RGB image has four channels—red, green, blue, and a composite, or combined channel that displays the image in full color. In addition to using channels to save selections, you can apply filters and special effects to individual channels to create extraordinary effects in your artwork.

Related Techniques

Managing Channels   59

Creating a Vignette Mask   62

Importing Custom Masks   63

Using Channels to
Create Shadows   64

1 | Create a Selection

Use the selection tools to create a selection marquee around the area you want to isolate and save.

2 | To Save a Selection

Choose Select→Save Selection. The Save Selection dialog box appears. The default name for the selection is *New*, which you can change in a later step. Click OK to save the selection. Because saving selections is one of the most frequently used commands, it's a good idea to put the Save Selection command into the Commands Palette. Choose Select→None (⌘-D) to deselect everything in your document.

3 | To Load a Selection

Choose Select→Load Selection. The Channel pop-up menu now contains the name #4, which is the number of the channel where the selection has been saved. You'll rename this channel later. Click OK to load selection #4; the selection marquee appears in your document.

4 | To Name a Selection

Click the Channel palette tab to display the Channel palette; then click the zoom box in the top right corner of the palette to see all the channels in the document. At the bottom of the list, you'll notice your selection, named #4. You'll also notice that the composite channel and the red, green, and blue channels are numbered from 0 to 3. Each time you save a selection, it is numbered in ascending order with the next available number. To rename the selection, double-click channel #4; type a name in the Channel Options name field; then click OK to rename the channel.

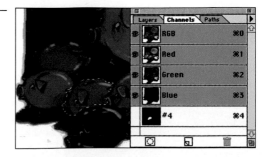

Peter Martin

Comments

The Quick Mask mode displays a colored overlay, called a *mask*, over the unselected parts of a document. Areas of the document that have been selected are see-through, much like a cutout stencil. In addition to the many selection methods available in Photoshop, you can add to or subtract from a selection by painting with the overlay color or by erasing the overlay color while in Quick Mask mode.

Studio Usage

Although Photoshop has tremendous selection capabilities, there are times when a Brush tool is your best option for painting masks. This technique can be used to create new masks or fix existing ones that may have been made using the dozens of automatic methods available to you. This is a good skill to master and remember—it often works when nothing else will.

Related Techniques

Adding to and Subtracting from Selections 6

Saving Selections 10

Custom Brushes 16

1 | Display the Image in Quick Mask Mode

Open a document and make a rough selection of the area that you want to isolate; then click the Quick Mask icon on the right in the toolbox to enter the Quick Mask mode. When you click the Quick Mask icon, a red overlay covers all but the selected area. The mask color indicates the area of the image that is *not* selected. You'll refine the selection by "painting" and "erasing" with the Brush tool to edit the mask.

2 | Paint the Mask

To add or subtract from the mask make sure that the default foreground and background colors, black and white, are selected in the tool box. Black "paints" red and white "erases" red. To add to the mask, select a painting tool and paint with black (red); to erase areas of the mask, select a painting tool and paint with white (transparent). Because painting a mask often involves intricate areas, it is helpful to choose a small brush for painting.

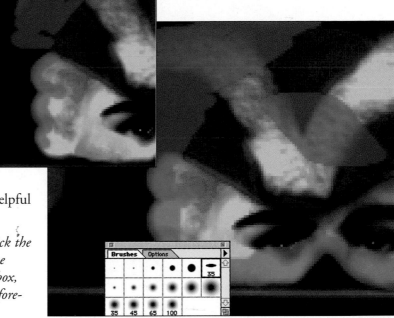

Note: *To paint with white (to erase the mask) click the double-headed arrow in the top right corner of the foreground and background swatches in the tool box, which reverses the swatches and makes white the foreground color.*

3 | To View and Save the Mask

After you've completed the mask, click the left icon in the toolbox to return to a normal view. The transparent area becomes the selection—if you still need to make adjustments, click the Quick Mask icon and adjust the mask; then return to the normal view. Quick Masks are not automatically saved; choose Select→Save Selection to save the results of the Quick Mask in a separate channel.

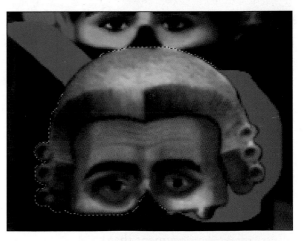

4 | To Create a Partial Mask

You can create a partial mask by painting with a shade of gray. The percentage of gray represents the percentage of protection (masking). To create a partial mask, click the Quick Mask icon, select a gray swatch from the Swatches palette, choose a painting tool, and then paint on the image with the gray (light red) color. Return to the normal view and then press the Delete key. Areas outside of the partial mask are deleted and part of the masked area is retained.

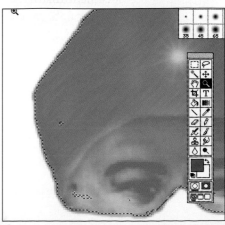

Lisa Rivard

Comments

Blending selections into new backgrounds often requires retouching and patching the edges of the selection. After a selection has been made, creating a selection border around the object can aid in the retouching effort that may be needed.

Studio Usage

This technique can be used for a number of effects, but it is probably most effective when used in conjunction with one of the Blur filters to blur the border's edges. By selecting and blurring the border of the object, you can easily retouch the border area by using the painting tools or filters.

Related Techniques

Adding to and
Subtracting from Selections 6

Saving Selections 10

1 | Make Selection

The illustration uses three color gradients to show how Add Noise reduces banding. Select the entire gradient by using the Rectangular Marquee.

2 | To Define the Border

Choose Select→Modify→Border. Enter a figure in pixels to define the width of the border selection. Click OK.

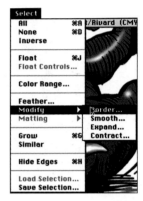

3 | To Blur the Selection Border

Choose Filter→Blur→Gaussian Blur and slightly blur the border of the image. Note the change in the pixel value across the entire width of the selection. Previously, half of the border overlapped the selection while the other half hung out into the white background. Now there are pixels in the entire border. This blurring technique *mixes* the value of pixels inside the border selection.

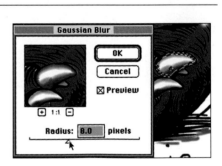

4 | To Fill the Selection Border

Choose Edit/Fill and fill the border with 100% black. Because the border contains a range of tonal value, the edge of the filled region is soft—creating an almost stained-glass effect. Experiment with the different fill modes in the Fill dialog box. For example, selecting the Overlay mode only slightly darkens and accentuates the border of the image.

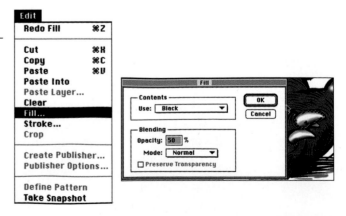

Phil Howe

Comments

No matter how carefully you create a selection, some of the pixels surrounding the selection border are included in the selection, which may cause a fringe or halo around the selection's edges when it is moved or pasted onto a new background. The Matting options remove these unwanted pixels to create a smooth transition between the pasted object and the background.

Studio Usage

When creating composite images using a number of moved or pasted objects, the quality of the final output is greatly determined by how well objects are blended against the background. For example, if a figure is pasted into a background for a special effect in a movie, the border of the person (selection) must be seamless in order to create a realistic effect.

Related Techniques

Saving Selections 10

Creating a Quick Mask 11

Creating Selection Borders 12

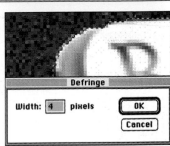

1 | To Create Smooth Borders for Composite Images

First, open the document containing the background and then open the document containing the object or objects that you want to move into the background document. Select an object; then position the pointer within the selection and drag it to the document window containing the background. This method of moving objects between windows is called drag-and-drop. (You can also copy and paste an object if desired.) While the selection is still active, you can drag the selection to the desired position.

2 | To Examine the Selection's Edges

Use the Zoom tool to zoom in on the edge of the moved or pasted image—a light fringe or halo usually appears around the selection. Press ⌘-H to hide the selection border to make it easier to examine the selection's border. If the fringe, or halo, extends into the selection border, choose Select→Matting→ Defringe and enter a value in pixels that is about equal to the area affected by the halo. Click OK to see the results and then choose ⌘-H to display the selection border around the object.

3 | To Select Black and White Matte Options

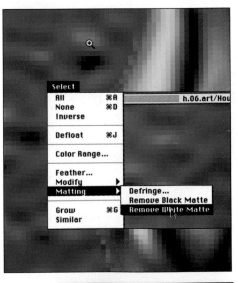

If you move or paste a white (or light) object onto a dark background, choose Select→Matting→Remove White Matte to remove the lighter pixels from the selection border. If you move or paste a black (or dark) object onto a light background, choose Select→Matting→Remove Black Matte to remove the darker pixels from the selection border. Although the Matting options work well most of the time, there may be cases when you'll need to use other retouching tools to blend the pixels along the edge of the selection.

4 | When All Else Fails

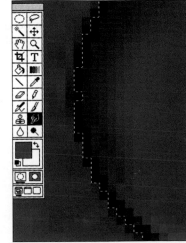

If the matting options do not eliminate all the unwanted pixels around a selection, you can use the Smudge tool to correct the unwanted pixels. First, drag a marquee with the Zoom tool to magnify the edge that requires retouching; then deselect the object by choosing Select→None ⌘-D. Choose a very small brush size (one pixel) from the Brushes palette; then select the Smudge tool and position it within the area containing a correctly colored pixel. Drag from the correctly colored pixel into the unwanted pixel to smudge the desired color into the unwanted pixel. Repeat this process around the edge of the object until all the edge pixels are corrected.

Painting *Selecting Colors*

Dorothy Krause

Comments

In Photoshop, the foreground color is used to paint, fill, or stroke a selection. It is also used as the beginning color for gradients. The background color is used to fill selections, to replace erased pixels, and to fill in areas when non-floating selections are moved or cut. The background color is also used as the ending colors in gradients. By default, the foreground color is set to black and the background color is set to white.

Studio Usage

There are several color models you can use in Photoshop. Most people create and edit their images in the RGB (red-green-blue) model and then convert their images to the CMYK (cyan-magenta-yellow-black) model when they're printing four-color separations. The RGB gamut (or range of colors) is wider than the CMYK gamut; therefore, some colors that you can display on your screen can't be printed using CMYK process inks.

Related Techniques

RGB versus CMYK   79

Custom Swatch Palettes   98

Gamut Restrictions   120

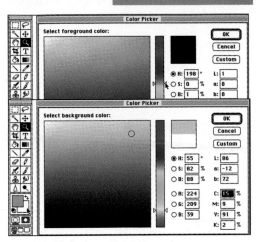

1 | Use the Color Picker

The color swatches in the toolbox represent the foreground and background colors. Click the foreground (top) color swatch. The Color Picker appears. Drag the sliders along the vertical strip to change the colors displayed in the color field and then click the color field to locate the exact color you want to use. The color you choose appears in the top of the color swatch to the right of the vertical bar. The previous foreground color appears in the bottom of the color swatch. Click OK to choose the foreground color. Then click the background (bottom) color swatch in the toolbox and choose a new background color.

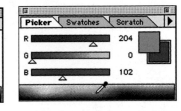

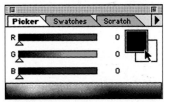

2 | Use the Picker Palette

To display the Picker palette, choose Window→Palettes→Show Picker. In the Picker palette, click the foreground color swatch to select it. A double frame appears around the selected color swatch. Drag the R, G, and B sliders to mix a foreground color. Click the background color swatch and drag the sliders to create a new background color. (Click only once when switching between the color swatches—if you double-click, you'll display the Color Picker.) You can also click the color bar to pick new foreground or background colors. The colors you select in the Picker palette also appear in the toolbox.

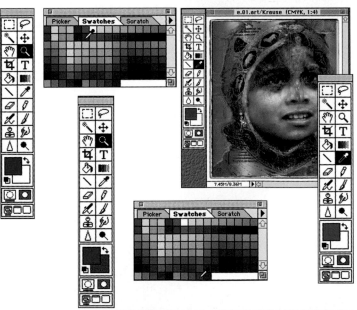

3 | Use the Swatches Palette

Click the Swatches tab to display the Swatches palette. The Swatches palette contains the color palette associated with the image (most often the System palette). Move the pointer over a swatch and it becomes an eyedropper. Click a color to choose a foreground color. Press Option and click to choose a background color. You can also use the Eyedropper tool to change foreground and background colors. Select the Eyedropper tool, move it over a color in any open image, and click to choose a foreground color. Option-click to choose a background color from an image.

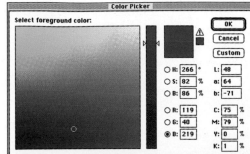

4 | Out-of-Gamut Warnings

When you're working in the RGB color model and you pick a color that is out-of-gamut (that is, can't be printed using CMYK inks), Photoshop displays an Alert triangle with an exclamation point. These Alert triangles appear in the Color Picker dialog box and in the Picker palette. The color swatch that appears next to the Alert triangle displays the closest CMYK equivalent to the color you're choosing. To substitute the CMYK equivalent, click the triangle or the color swatch.

Painting *Using the Brushes Palette*

Bonny Lhotka

Comments

Many of Photoshop's tools require that you select a brush before you begin using the tool. Photoshop comes with several different sets of brushes that you can display in the Brushes palette. You can also create new brushes and modify existing brushes. You can then add them to the Brushes palette.

Studio Usage

The brush you choose depends on the image you're working in and the effect you want to achieve. For example, when you're retouching, you might use soft-edged, angled brushes to blend changes into the existing pixels. Scratches and hairline corrections, however, often require hard-edged brushes. The brush shape refers to the size and shape of the painting or editing cursor tip. Photoshop can represent brush shapes in three ways: as the standard tool icon, as a cross-hair pointer for precision, or as an icon representing the brush size in pixels.

Related Techniques

Using the Rubber
      Stamp Tool   19

Scratches and Flaws   70

Custom Swatch Palettes   98

1 | Opening the Brushes Palette

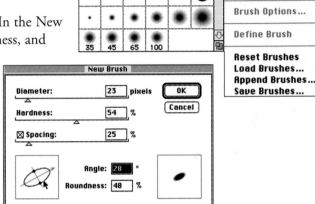

The bottom eight tools in the toolbox use the Brushes palette. To display the Brushes palette, choose Window→Palettes→Show Brushes or click one of the tools in the toolbox. If the Tool Options palette is on top, click the Brushes tab to bring the Brushes palette forward. Each tool has a default brush. After you select a brush for a tool, that brush remains in effect until you choose a new brush. The default Brushes palette contains one row of hard-edged brushes and several rows of soft-edged brushes. The number under each of the larger brushes indicates its diameter in pixels.

2 | Creating and Deleting Brushes

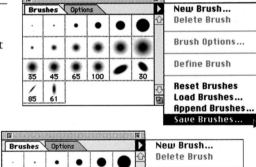

Choose New Brush from the Brushes palette pop-up menu. In the New Brush dialog box, drag the sliders to set the Diameter, Hardness, and Spacing options. In the lower-left box, drag the axis to set the Angle. In the same box, drag the dots around the circle to set the Roundness. The preview box at the lower-right shows you the brush shape. Click OK to add the brush to the bottom row of the Brushes palette. Create a few more brushes; then choose File→New and practice painting using the new brushes. To delete a brush, select it and choose Delete Brush from the Brushes palette pop-up menu.

3 | Loading Brush Sets

You can add all your created brushes to the default Brushes palette, but often it's easier to group related brushes on their own palettes. To save the set containing your new brushes, choose Save Brushes from the Brushes palette pop-up menu. Name the set New Set and click Save. Photoshop also provides alternative brush sets in the Brushes and Patterns folder in the Goodies folder. To display one of these sets, choose Load Brushes from the Brushes palette pop-up menu, select a file, and click Open. To return to the default Brushes palette, choose Reset Brushes from the Brushes pop-up menu.

4 | Displaying Tool Icons

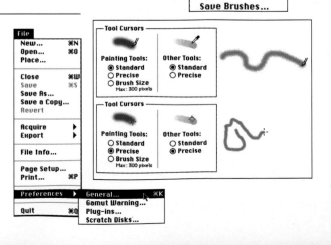

When you select a tool and move it onto the image, the tool becomes an icon of the selected tool. Each cursor has a different "hot spot," or point where the selection or painting begins. To apply paint with precision, you can change the cursor into a crosshair. To alternate quickly between the tool icon and a crosshair, press the Caps Lock key. To work with the precise cursors, choose File→Preferences→General and then click Precise under the Painting Tools and Other Tool options. To make the brush tool appear as the brush size in pixels, click Brush Size. To return to tool icons, choose Standard from the General Preferences dialog box.

Painting *Custom Brushes*

Mike Pantuso

Comments

In addition to the standard Brushes palette and the Assorted Brushes folder shipped with Photoshop, you can also create your own brushes using a shape, a pattern, or even part of an image.

Studio Usage

Many designers use small illustrations or text dingbats as brushes. Because an image is converted to grayscale as part of the customizing process, it's best to use high-contrast images to create the brush. To define brushes with soft edges, select shapes that have some gray values other than the extremes of black and white.

Related Techniques

The Marquee Tool   7

Using the Brushes Palette   15

Creating a Scale of Grays   78

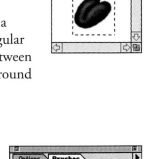

1 | Select the Shape

Draw a shape or choose File→Open (⌘-O) to select the element that you want to define as a brush. Double-click the Marquee tool. In the Marquee Tool Options palette, choose Rectangular from the Shape menu (you can also press Option as you click the Marquee tool to switch between the rectangular and elliptical shapes). Select the shape or image, leaving a little white space around the edges of the selection. The selection can be up to 1000 pixels by 1000 pixels in size.

2 | Define the Brush

Choose Window→Palettes→Show Brushes (or click the Brushes tab to bring the palette to the front of its group). Choose Define Brush from the Brushes palette pop-up menu. The brush shape appears in the Brushes palette. Double-click the brush to display the Brush Options dialog box. Enter a value in the Spacing text box that is a percentage of the brush diameter. This specifies the distance between the brush marks in a stroke. A higher value spaces the marks further apart. For small brushes, you can select Anti-Aliasing to make the brush paint with soft edges.

3 | Paint with the Brush

After the brush is added to the Brushes palette, it works just like any other brush. Select a tool (the Paint brush is used in this example) and stroke. You can use your custom brushes with any of the options in the Tool Options palette.

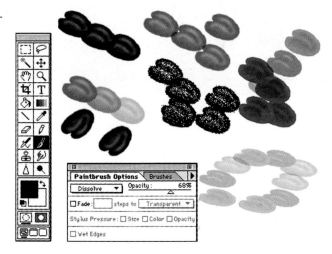

4 | Create a Custom Brushes Palette

You can group custom brushes on their own palettes. To create a brush set, add the brushes to an existing Brushes palette (use the Delete Brush command on the Brushes palette pop-up menu to eliminate brushes from the palette). Choose Save Brushes from the palette pop-up menu and save the set (to keep all your brush sets together, store them in the Brushes and Patterns folder in the Goodies folder that comes with Photoshop). To change to another brush set, choose Load Brushes from the pop-up menu. To return to the default palette, choose Reset Brushes from the pop-up menu.

Karin Schminke Unique Editions™

Comments

Most illustration and drawing applications allow you to display a grid to help structure and place art. Adobe Photoshop does not have a Grid command. You can simulate a grid by creating a template in an illustration program and then placing the grid in the Photoshop image. Although this example uses a grid of simple squares, this technique works with perspective grids, concentric circles, and so on.

Studio Usage

A grid is useful any time you need to step and repeat elements. Even art that appears to be randomly placed is often built on an imaginary grid—visualized by the artist. This technique uses Adobe Photoshop layers. For more information on layers, see section E, "Working with Layers."

Related Techniques

Textures on Layers   38

Defining Layers   50

1 | Design the Grid

Open your illustration or drawing program (Adobe Illustrator is the application used in this example) and create a grid of light blue lines. In the illustration program, choose File→Save and save the file in EPS format with the Preview option turned on. Name the file Grid Paper.

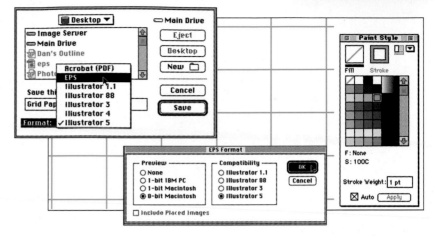

2 | Create a New Layer

In Photoshop, open the document you want to use. Choose Window→Palettes→Show Layers to display the Layers palette. The image has one layer named Background. Create a new layer by clicking the page icon at the bottom of the Layers palette. In the New Layer dialog box, name the layer *The Grid*, leave the opacity at 100%, and leave the mode at Normal. Click OK to create the layer. The new layer appears above the Background layer in the Layers palette.

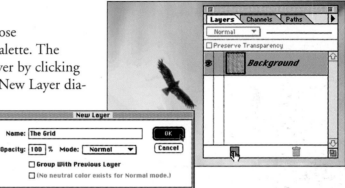

3 | Place the Grid

Click the eye icon next to the Background layer to turn off the Background. The image disappears, and you see a checkerboard pattern. You're looking at the Grid layer, the checkerboard indicating that the entire layer is transparent. (All layers are transparent until you put something on them). Choose File→Place. A rectangle, representing the size of the imported grid, appears in the Photoshop document. Click inside the rectangle to display the grid. The grid is now a floating selection, as you can see in the Layers palette. Choose Select→None to make the grid part of the new layer.

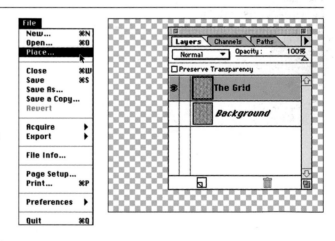

4 | Positioning the Grid

Click the far-left column (next to the Background layer) to make the layer visible again. The grid now appears over the image. Make sure that the Grid layer is the target layer (its name is highlighted in the Layers palette). If the Background is the current target layer, click The Grid layer name. Select the Move tool in the toolbox. Using this tool, drag the grid into position. Layers move independently of one another, so you can position the grid wherever you want without affecting the Background layer. When you want to view only the Background, click the eye icon next to the Grid layer to make the grid invisible.

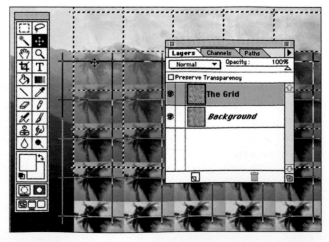

Painting *Sketching and Inking*

Anne S. Barrett

Comments

Although Photoshop is normally considered an image manipulation program, it can also be used to sketch and paint original art.

Studio Usage

A basic understanding of the Photoshop painting tools and their options is an essential skill, whether you're creating new artwork or modifying existing images. If you do a lot of painting, consider using a pressure-sensitive tablet (instead of a mouse) as your input device. These tablets provide a pen that's used to sketch directly onto the screen. Varying the pen pressure and the angle of the pen determines how the ink flows from the painting tool.

Related Techniques

Selecting Colors   14

Using the Brushes Palette   15

Defining Layers   50

1 | Create a Practice Layer

Choose File→Open to open a Photoshop document. Choose Window→Palettes→Show Layers to display the Layers palette. Although you can practice painting on the background layer, it's much easier to devote a separate layer to your painting practice. Choose New Layer from the Layers palette pop-up menu. In the New Layer dialog box, name the layer Paint Practice, leave the Opacity at 100%, and leave the mode set to Normal. Click OK to create the layer. Choose Edit→Fill. In the Fill dialog box, choose White from the Use pop-up menu and click OK.

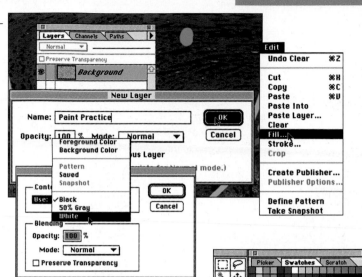

2 | Organize Your Palettes

Click the Swatches tab to bring the Swatches palette to the front of its palette group. Before you start sketching, separate the Brushes and the Tool Options palettes so that you can select both at the same time (this saves a click each time you want to change the brush shape or select a new tool option). To separate the palettes, click the Tool Options tab and drag the palette below the Brushes palette. As you drag, a dotted outline follows your movement. Release the mouse to display the palette in its new location. (To return a palette to a group, click the tab and drag it over the other palette.)

3 | Use the Paintbrush Tool

Select the Paintbrush tool, and then select a color and a small, hard-edged brush. In the Paintbrush Options palette, select the Fade option and type 64 in the steps box. Paint a stroke. The stroke begins with the foreground color and fades to transparenct (you can choose Background instead of Transparent to end the stroke in the background color). Change the step setting to 128 and stroke again. With more steps, it takes longer for the stroke to fade. Turn off the Fade option and paint to see full color throughout the stroke. Finally, select the Wet Edges option to paint with a watercolor effect.

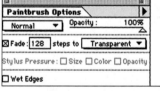
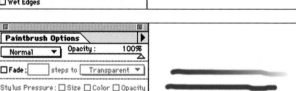

4 | Try Other Tools

Select the Airbrush tool and stroke. With a small, hard-edged brush, this tool's stroke looks very similar to the Paintbrush tool. Drag the slider in the Airbrush Options palette to vary the Pressure setting and paint a few more strokes. Select a large, soft-edged brush and stroke with the Airbrush tool. Apply multiple strokes over the same area and notice how the color builds.

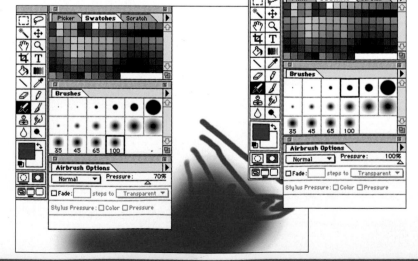

Painting *Using the Rubber Stamp Tool*

Robert Bowen, Photographer; Howard Berman, Client: Panasonic

Comments

The Rubber Stamp tool lets you paint with images. You can use it to duplicate portions of an image, revert to an earlier version of an image, paint with a pattern, or produce an image in the Impressionist style.

Studio Usage

There are several uses for the Rubber Stamp tool. First, it's an important creative tool, allowing you to duplicate elements within an image. Second, it allows you to restore parts of an image to the way they were when you last saved the file. When used this way, the Rubber Stamp tool becomes a powerful version of the Undo command because you can erase entire sets of editing corrections. Finally, it's probably the single most important tool in the retouching process.

Related Techniques

Custom Brushes   16

Scratches and Flaws   70

Using Filters to Clean Images   71

1 | Select the Rubber Stamp Tool

Choose File→Open to open the file that you want to use as the source image. You can choose to clone to the same file (on the same or a different layer), or you can choose File→New to copy an element to a new image. In this example, the sheep's head was cloned to a new document. Select the Rubber Stamp tool. In the Rubber Stamp Options palette, choose Clone (aligned) from the Option pop-up menu.

2 | To Use the Aligned Option

Locate the area you want to copy, press Option, and click to select a starting point (the nose is used in this example). Move the cursor below the starting point and drag to paint. A crosshair indicates the part of the image that you're cloning. As you paint, the crosshair moves in the same direction as the cursor. Release the mouse, move the tool to the right, and paint again. Notice that the distance between the crosshair and the point you're painting remains the same. When using the Aligned option, think of these two points as opposite ends of a straight line. The length and angle of the line stays the same until you Option-click to set a new starting point.

3 | To Use the Non-aligned Option

Choose Clone (non-aligned) from the Option pop-up menu in the Rubber Stamp Options palette. Option-click to define a starting point, move the cursor to a new location, and paint. Then move to another area and paint again. Notice that the starting point does not change. When you use the non-aligned option, the starting point remains the same, no matter where you paint on the image.

4 | Restore Part of an Image

Choose File→Save to save your source image. Select a portion of the image and then select a brush. Using one of the painting tools, intentionally mess up part of the source image. Select the Rubber Stamp tool and choose From Saved from the Option pop-up menu in the Rubber Stamp Options palette. Click anywhere in the image. A dialog box appears indicating that the last-saved version of the image is being loaded from the disk. Paint over the flaws you created. They are repaired using the stored version of the image. For an interesting effect, try varying the Opacity setting of the Rubber Stamp tool to restore original pixels over modified ones.

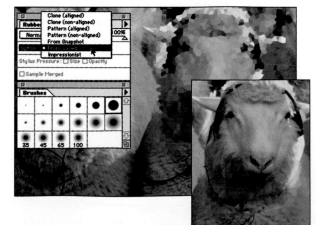

Painting *Twirl Filter*

Phil Howe

Comments

You can create almost any imaginable object using the painting tools. Some effects, however, are faster and easier to achieve using filters (small applications that expand Photoshop's basic functions). Adobe includes several filters with Photoshop. You can also buy plug-in filters from third-party vendors.

Studio Usage

This example uses the Twirl filter to create the smoke rings in the image. Because filters can produce varied effects, it's often tempting to overuse them. Resist the urge to "overfilter" an image—a more creative approach suggests a limited and aesthetic application of filters to emphasize or enhance intrinsic elements of the image.

Related Techniques

Shearing and Pinching   25

Wave and Zigzags   27

Pointillize and
Crystallize Filters   34

Facet Filter   35

1 | Create a Practice Layer

Practice using the filters on a separate layer. Choose File→Open to open a Photoshop document. Choose Window→Palettes→Show Layers to display the Layers palette. Create a new layer by clicking the page icon at the bottom of the Layers palette. In the New Layer dialog box, name the layer Filter Practice, leave the Opacity at 100%, and leave the Mode set to Normal. Click OK. Choose Edit→Fill. In the Fill dialog box, choose Black from the Use pop-up menu and click OK.

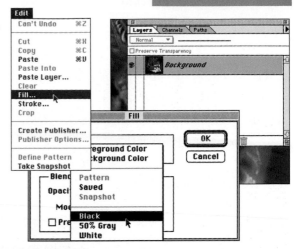

2 | Create a Test Object

Select a hard-edged brush and then select a color that contrasts with the black background. Select the Paintbrush tool and paint an angled line. Select a second color and draw an intersecting line. Select the Marquee tool and drag a Selection marquee around the section of the image that contains the X.

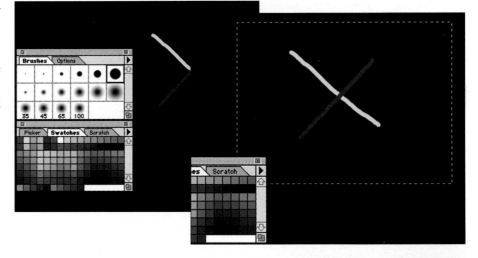

3 | Apply the Twirl Filter

Choose Filter→Distort→Twirl. In the Twirl dialog box, drag the Angle slider and watch the Preview box to see the different effects. When you find a look you like, click OK to apply the filter. Choose Edit→Undo Twirl to return to your original selection.

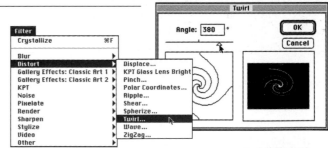

4 | Filter a Feathered Edge

You can modify the effect of a filter by feathering the edges of a selection before applying the filter. Feathering softens the transition between filtered and unfiltered areas. Choose Select→None and then use the Marquee tool to select a small section that includes the center of the X. Choose Select→Feather. In the Feather dialog box, enter a Feather value of about 8 pixels. Choose Filter→Twirl (notice that the last applied filter appears at the top of the Filter menu). Use the Zoom tool to magnify the area around the selection so that you can see the feathered edges.

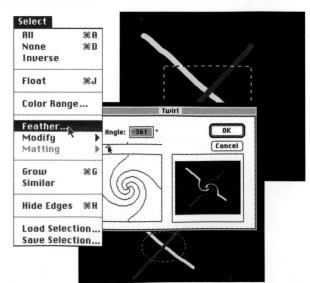

Painting *Applying the Spherize Filter*

Richard Smyth

Comments

The Spherize filter wraps a selection around a spherical shape. The image is distorted as it is stretched to fit the specified curve, giving the image a three-dimensional effect.

Studio Usage

Applying the Spherize filter is like photographing with a fish-eye lens. Unlike the camera, however, the Spherize filter not only gives the impression of stretching an image around a sphere, it also lets you wrap an image onto the inside or outside of a horizontal or vertical cylinder. By using the Spherize filter, you can accomplish the nearly-impossible feat of "bending light."

Related Techniques

Twirl Filter   20

Shearing and Pinching   25

Wave and Zigzags   27

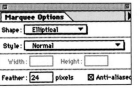

1 | Specify an Elliptical Marquee

The Spherize filter can be applied only to elliptical selections. If the selection isn't elliptical, Photoshop applies the filter to the largest ellipse that can fit within the selection. Because this filter produces abrupt transitions between filtered and unfiltered areas, apply a feathered edge when you select the area you want to distort. Double-click the Marquee tool to display the Marquee Options palette. Choose Elliptical from the Shape pop-up menu and enter a value in the Feather text box. (The higher the image resolution, the higher the feather value you need to achieve a soft edge.)

2 | Test the Selection

Drag the Marquee tool to select an oval area. To test the softness of the feathered edge, temporarily clear the selection by pressing the Delete key. Zoom in and examine the edges of the selection. To return to the original image, choose Edit→Undo Clear or press ⌘-Z.

3 | Apply the Filter

Choose Filter→Distort→Spherize. In the Spherize dialog box, leave the Mode set to Normal and drag the Amount slider to vary the amount of distortion. The Preview box shows the effects as you drag the slider. Dragging to the right results in positive values, pulling the image toward the viewer. Dragging to the left results in negative values, pushing the image away from the viewer.

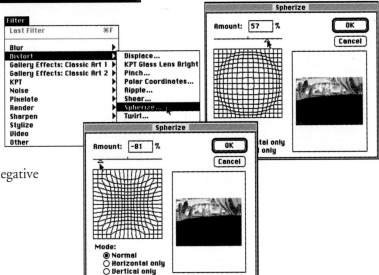

4 | Linear Distortion

The Normal Mode in the Spherize dialog box stretches the image over the surface of a sphere. Choosing the Horizontal or Vertical Mode stretches the image along a straight plane. These modes can have a dramatic effect on perspective. To see the effect of linear distortion, try using the Horizontal and Vertical options on images with strong horizontal or vertical lines.

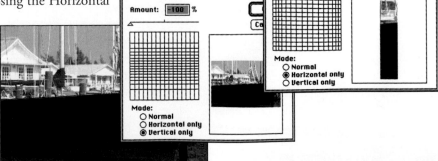

Painting *Creating Lighting Effects*

Sanjay Kothari

Comments

To convey an accurate sense of light, you need to model your image's created light on the rules of light in the world around you. It's especially important to notice how direction and distance affect the angle and intensity of light reflecting off objects. In this image, the artist uses his imagination, based on real-world reality, to produce an incredible example of hand-lighting.

Studio Usage

This technique offers a quick and easy way to create custom light sources in your images. By using a feathered selection and adjusting the light density, you can experiment with lighting effects until you achieve exactly the look you want. For more complicated lighting situations (such as lighting images composited from multiple images), see the Lighting Effects Filter (Part 1) and Lighting Effects Filter (Part 2).

Related Techniques

The Lasso Tool   5

Lighting Effects
Filter (1 and 2)   30, 31

Curves 1, 2   81, 82

1 | Define the Light Beam

Light beams are always triangular with the apex at the source of the light and the base defining the cast of the beam. Select the Lasso tool. Hold down the Option key and click to define the end points of the straight sides of the triangle. Release the Option key to trace the shape of the object to define the third side.

2 | Feather the Selection

Choose Select→Feather. Enter a value in the Feather Radius field. The brighter or closer the light is, the harder the edge of the beam (and, therefore, the smaller the Feather value). The dimmer or farther away the light is, the softer the beam (and the greater the Feather value). Higher resolution images need more feathering to produce a soft edge.

3 | Save the Selection in a Channel

It's a good idea to save a selection in a channel until you determine that it's the correct shape. Display the Channels palette and click the page icon at the bottom of the palette. In the Channel Options dialog box, name the channel and click OK. Set the background color to white and press the Delete key to clear the selection (you can't see the effect of feathering until you perform an action, such as filling or moving). In this case, you want to increase the feathering. Choose Select→Feather again and enter another value. Click the composite channel name (RGB or CMYK) to return to viewing the color channels.

4 | Adjust the Light Beam

Choose Select→Hide Edges or press ⌘-H to hide the selection border. To adjust the light intensity, choose Image→Adjust→ Brightness/Contrast. Drag the Brightness slider, or choose Image→Adjust→Curves, to manipulate the curve. If you use the Curves command, you can add color to the light or you can selectively emphasize its effect on shadow, midtone, or highlight areas. See the Curves 1 and Curves 2 techniques for more information regarding the use of this command.

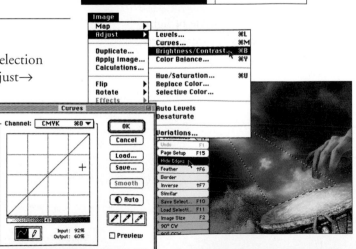

Peter Martin

Comments

In the world of authentic light and shadow, there are very few hard edges or solid colors. As our eyes perceive them, they are made up of blends and subtle shifts in color. The Gradient tool is used to reproduce the blends of colors in the natural environment.

Studio Usage

This example uses a rich gradient in the sky to demonstrate one of an almost unlimited array of gradients that you can create in Photoshop.

Related Techniques

The Magic Wand Tool   8

Managing Channels   59

1 | Create and Save the Selection

Unless you make a selection, the Gradient tool fills
the entire image. Select an area using one of the
selection tools. Display the Channels palette and
drag the selection icon (the dotted circle at the
bottom of the Channels palette) to the right
until it's *on top of* the page icon. This shortcut
automatically saves the current selection in a
new channel. In the Channel Options dialog box,
name the channel and click OK.

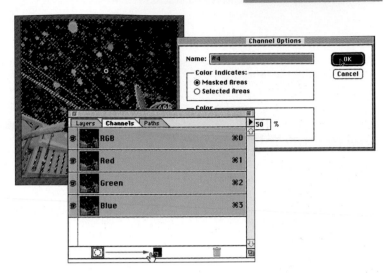

2 | Choose Gradient Tool Options

Double-click the Gradient tool. The Style pop-up menu
in the Gradient Tool Options palette allows you to
choose the beginning and ending colors for the gradient.
The last two options create a gradient that cycles
through all the colors that lie between the foreground
and background colors in the standard color wheel.
Clockwise Spectrum and Counterclockwise Spectrum
refer to the direction the cycle moves around the wheel.
Choose Counterclockwise Spectrum. Choose Linear from the Type pop-up
menu to create a gradient that fills from one point to another in a straight line.
(Radial fills from a center point outward.)

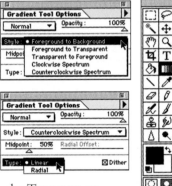
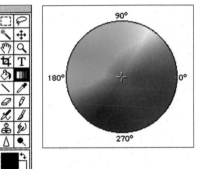

3 | Select the Foreground and Background Colors

Choose Window→Palettes→Show Scratch to display the Scratch palette
(or click the Scratch tab to bring the palette to the front of its group).
Select the Eyedropper tool in the toolbox and click the Scratch palette to
select a foreground color (the starting color for the gradient). Press Option
as you click to select a background color (the ending color for the gradient). The new colors appear in the color swatches in the toolbox.

4 | Drag to Create the Gradient

Click the point where you want the gradient to begin and drag to the point
where you want the gradient to end. You can experiment with various
Midpoint settings in the Gradient Tool Options palette to shift the point at
which the beginning color blends into the ending color. If the Midpoint
value is below 50%, most of the colors in the gradation occur near the beginning of the drag. If the value is above 50%, most of the colors occur toward
the end of the drag.

Painting *Gradient Masks*

Karin Schminke, Unique Editions™

Comments

With a little imagination, you can produce extraordinary effects by creating and applying geometric masks to images. By using the Lasso tool and the Gradient tool, this technique allows you to create a geometric gradient mask in a channel. You will also learn how to apply that mask to an image.

Studio Usage

Placing a gradient in a channel allows you to load the gradient as a selection and then apply a color that varies in opacity over the length of the selection. When color is applied to a gradient selection, the degree of transparency is determined by the amount of black, white, and gray levels in the gradient. Black in the gradient is completely opaque; white in the gradient is completely transparent; and gray levels represent varying levels of opacity in the gradient.

Related Techniques

The Lasso Tool   5

Managing Channels   59

Creating a Vignette Mask   62

1 | Create a Channel and the Geometric Selection

Open an image to which you want to apply a geometric mask. Choose Window→Show Rulers (⌘-R) to turn on the rulers in the document window. The rulers help you to create precise selections. From the Channels palette, choose New Channel from the palette's submenu. In the New Channel dialog box, name the channel Gradient Mask and then click OK; the channel appears in the document window and the Gradient Mask channel appears at the bottom of the Channels palette. To create the first part of the selection, select the Lasso tool from the toolbox; then Option-click the Lasso tool to create a triangular selection in a quadrant of the channel.

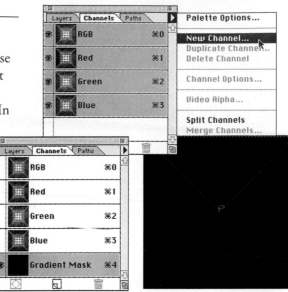

2 | Apply the Gradient

Double-click the Gradient tool to select the tool and to open the tool's Options palette. Set the Opacity to 100%; select Foreground to Background from the Style pop-up menu, set the Midpoint slider to 50%, and deselect the Dither option. In the toolbox, click the double-headed arrow in the upper-right corner of the swatches to swap the foreground and background colors. Hold down the Shift key (to constrain the blend to 90°) and drag from the bottom point of the triangle to the upper edge of the triangle. Choose Select→None (⌘-D) to deselect the selection.

3 | Complete the Geometric Pattern

Use the Option-Lasso selection method in Step 1 to complete the remaining quadrants in the Gradient Mask channel.

4 | Load the Selection

In the Channels palette, click the RGB channel to display the entire image. Choose Select→Load Selection. The Load Selection dialog box appears. Choose Gradient Mask from the Channel pop-up menu and click OK; the selection appears in the document window. To apply a color to the gradient mask, choose a foreground color and then choose Edit→Fill. Accept the default setting of Normal and set the Opacity to a value of approximately 70%. Click OK. The color is applied to the selection in varying degrees of opacity, depending on where the black, white, and shades of gray were placed in the gradient in the Gradient Mask channel.

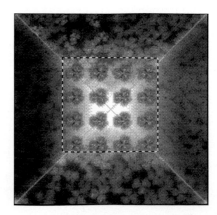

Painting *Shearing and Pinching*

Pamela Belding

Comments

The Shear and Pinch filters let you distort selections or entire images to create effects that mimic the distortion perceived in the natural environment by the eye. While a camera can "flatten" an image, the eye is subject to some measure of distortion.

Studio Usage

You can use the Shear and Pinch filters to create the illusion of reflection, smoke or haze, or other ethereal effects. For example, the Shear and Pinch filters are used for the artwork in this tip to create a ghost-like effect.

Related Techniques

Applying the Spherize Filter   21

Wave and Zigzags   27

Creating a Rainbow Effect   52

1 | Create a Selection

Using one or more of the selection tools, create a selection border to isolate the desired area. (If you are applying the filter to an entire image, you don't need to select the image.)

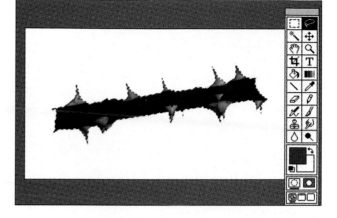

2 | To Apply the Shear Filter

Choose Filter→Distort→Shear. The Shear dialog box appears. In the top left corner of the dialog box, a grid containing a vertical line is displayed. The vertical line represents the plane of distortion. Drag the line to create a curve that represents how you want the selection or image distorted. Select the Wrap Around option to wrap the image to fill the undefined space left as a result of the direction that you drag. Select the Repeat edge pixels option to extend the color of the edge pixels, which is determined by the direction in which you drag, and then click OK.

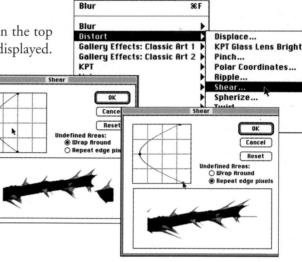

3 | To Shear an Image along the Horizontal Plane

The Shear filter enables you to shear only along a selection's vertical plane. If you want to shear an image along a horizontal plane, start by rotating the image 90° and then apply the Shear filter. To rotate an entire image, deselect if necessary (⌘-D), choose Image→Rotate, and then select the 90° CW or the 90° CCW option.

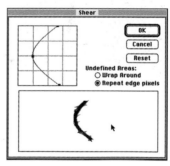

4 | To Apply the Pinch Filter

Choose Filter→Distort→Pinch. The Pinch dialog box appears. To pinch toward the center point of the image, enter a positive number in the Pinch dialog box; to pinch in an outward direction, enter a negative value in the Pinch dialog box. If the selection is an arbitrary shape, feather the selection before applying the Pinch filter to blend the edges of the selection into the background pixels.

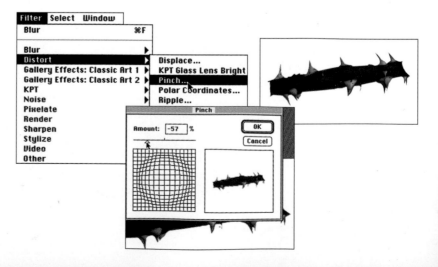

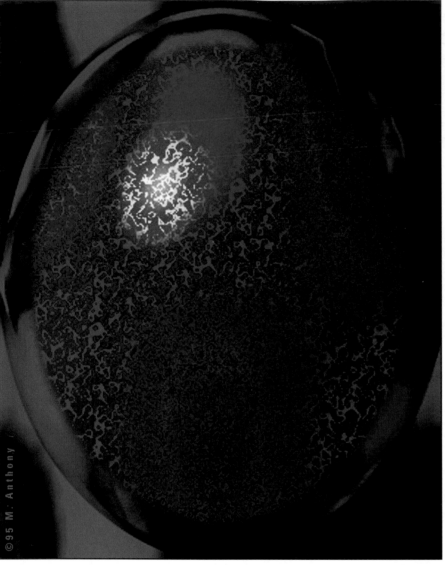

©95 M. Anthony

MADworks ®, *Mitchell Anthony*

Comments

Using a little ingenuity and some of Photoshop's many filters, you can create a library of textures for use as backgrounds, fills, or elements in composite images.

Studio Usage

You can create textures by scanning textured items on a flatbed scanner or by using Photoshop filters. A simple example of a texture is of a "rag" or fiber-filled paper. When you create textures for use as backgrounds, isolate the texture on a separate layer.

Related Techniques

Using a Grid
to Place Art   17

Defining Layers   50

Resolution and Image Size   65

1 | Create a New Document

Choose File→New ⌘-N to create a new document. Enter a document size and resolution; then click OK.

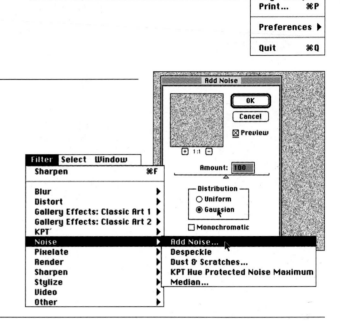

2 | Add Noise

Choose Filter→Noise→Add Noise. The Add Noise filter adds random pixels to a selection; enter the amount of pixels that you want generated in the document. Select the Gaussian option to view the difference between the Uniform option and the Gaussian option. Click OK to apply the noise settings.

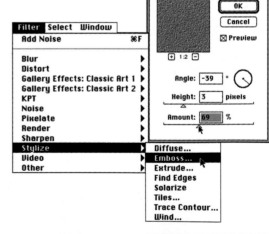

3 | To Add Dimension to the Texture

Choose Filter→Stylize→Emboss. The Emboss dialog box appears, containing three options: Angle (the direction that imaginary light is coming from); Height (how high the pixels are raised above the surface of the image; and Amount (the intensity of the contrast between the lightest and the darkest pixels). Experiment with the sliders until the desired effect is produced. The angle setting can be entered manually or can be generated by dragging the line inside the angle circle.

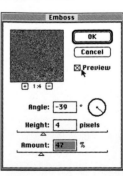

4 | Experiment

Create a new document and try adding brush strokes to the file before you generate noise. Try Filter→Blur→Blur or Filter→Blur→Blur More before applying the Emboss filter. Try feathering a selection and then adding noise and the emboss filter.

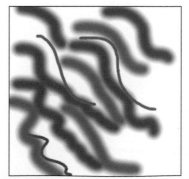

Painting *Wave and Zigzags*

THERE'S A NEW WAVE COMING

Richard Smyth

Comments

The Wave and Zigzag filters can create dramatic effects by allowing you to warp selections or entire images. For example, you can create a sense of movement or reflection by applying them to a selection or to an entire image.

Studio Usage

Smythe's "New Wave" almost makes you feel the room moving, and is a powerful example of mixing content with function—the wave concept with the ocean. Other uses for the distort filters include many levels of reflection—in particular, the appearance of objects seen mirrored in water or metal.

Related Techniques

Shearing and Pinching   25

1 | Create a Selection and Apply the Wave Filter

Create a selection and then choose Filter→Distort→ Wave. The Wave dialog box appears, containing several options that allow you to define and shape the waves. Select Sine, Triangle, or Square for the wave type. In the Wave Generators field, drag the slider or enter a value from 1 to 999 for the number of wave generators; the higher the number, the choppier the wave. To set the minimum and maximum values for the wave length, drag the Wavelength sliders or enter values in the Wavelength Min. and Max. fields. To set the wave height, drag the Amplitude sliders or enter values in the Amplitude Min. and Max. fields. To control the magnitude of the distortion in the horizontal and vertical dimensions of the wave, drag the sliders or enter values in the Scale Horiz. and Vert. fields.

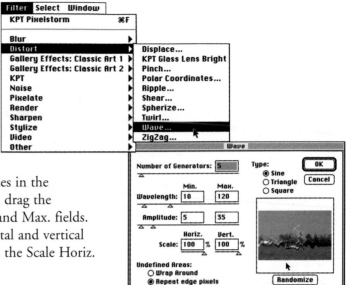

2 | To Slow the Roll

Set Number of Generators to 1; the Wavelength to Min: 1, Max: 433; and the Amplitude to Min: 5, Max: 59. This creates a slower, more natural wave. Seasick yet? Click OK to view the results and then choose Edit→Undo (⌘-Z) to undo the Wave filter.

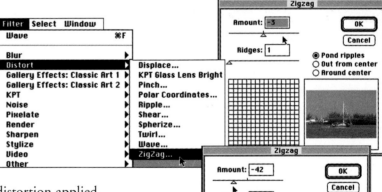

3 | To Create a Zigzag Effect

Choose Filter→Distort→Zigzag. The Zigzag dialog box appears. The Amount field represents the magnitude of distortion; enter a value between 0 and -3. The Ridges option defines the number of direction reversals of the zigzag, from the center of the selection to the edge of the selection; enter a value of 1. These settings represent "ground zero," with no distortion applied. Then begin moving the sliders. Drag the sliders to make adjustments; then click OK to apply the settings to the image.

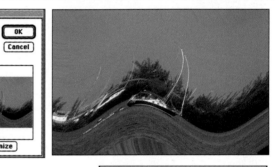

4 | A Stone's Throw

Choose the Zigzag filter again, enter a value of 40 in the Amount field, set the Ridges value to 5 or 6, and then click OK. The result is a realistic looking reflection being distorted by an object dropped into water.

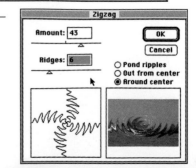

Javier Romero

Comments

Adobe Photoshop's painting capabilities let you achieve a level of subtlety that can't be approached by many drawing programs. Using the painting and selection functions to enhance your illustrations is a simple process.

Studio Usage

Starting with black and white line art, you can achieve many effects previously only possible when using an airbrush and a frisket (an adhesive-backed sheet of thin material placed over an illustration to mask certain areas during inking or painting). In this example, you use a painting mode to mask (protect) the black areas in the illustration.

Related Techniques

Selecting Colors   14

Custom Brushes   16

1 | Import the Artwork

In Photoshop choose File→Open, select your Adobe Illustrator line art file from the list, and click Open. The Rasterizer dialog box appears. Enter a resolution that suits the final output and choose CMYK Color from the Mode pop-up menu. In the imported artwork, only the black channel contains data since you're starting with black and white artwork.

2 | To Paint with a Color

Select the Swatches palette and click a color. Double-click the Paint Bucket tool to display the Paint Bucket Options palette. Set the Tolerance to 32 and select Anti-aliased, 100% Opacity, and Normal mode. Choose Foreground from the Contents pop-up menu. Click a white area within the artwork to fill it with color. Because the artwork is anti-aliased, the edges next to the black lines are bordered with gray, leaving small unfilled areas at the edges of the selection.

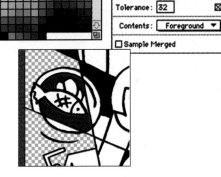

3 | To Clean Up Selection Edges

Double-click the Paintbrush tool, set the Opacity to 100%, and choose Darken from the Mode menu in the Paintbrush Options palette. The use of the Darken mode affects only pixels that are lighter than the color you're painting with and prevents the color from covering the existing black lines. Select a small brush, zoom in with the Zoom tool, and then paint the edges of the selection.

4 | To Fill a Selection with a Gradient

Select the Lasso tool, press Option, and click to select straight line segments. It's okay if you include part of the black lines in the selection—the paint will not cover the black lines because you're painting with the Darken mode. Set the foreground and background colors for the gradient, and then double-click the Gradient tool, making sure the

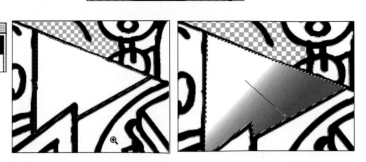

Darken mode is selected in the Gradient Tool Options palette. Drag the Gradient tool to create the gradient. Continue coloring the image using the Paint Bucket, Gradient, and Paintbrush tools.

Painting *Floating Selections*

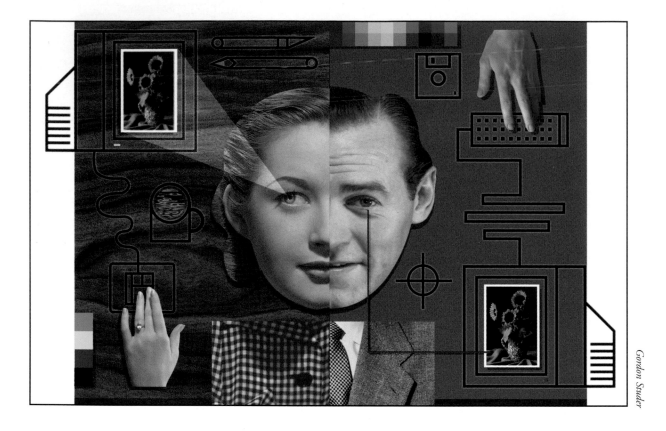

Gordon Studer

Comments

When you move a selection that is not located on a separate layer, the underlying (background) pixels are displayed. You can float a selection to make a copy of the area you want to move, which leaves underlying pixels intact. A floating selection can be modified, used to create new layers, or moved to another image.

Studio Usage

Floating selections are useful when you want to make a copy of a selection within the same document, create a new layer for a selection, or move a selection to another document. It can also be used to accomplish many special effects, such as transparency or diffusion.

Related Techniques

Selection Tools and Methods   5-13

Painting Modes   42-49

Defining Layers   50

1 | Create a Floating Selection

Open an image and select a portion of the image you want to float. Choose Select→Float (⌘-J) to create a copy of the selection directly on top of the selection.

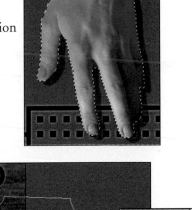

2 | To Move a Floating Selection

With a selection tool selected, move the cursor within the selection; the pointer becomes an arrow. Drag a small distance to move the selection and notice that the original selection area remains intact. Choose File→New to create a new document and arrange the two document windows side-by-side. Drag the floating selection from the original image onto the new document window and release the mouse button when a black border appears within the new document window. The selection is moved to the new document.

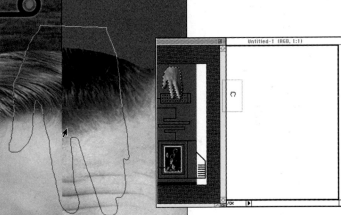

3 | To Modify Floating Selections

With the selection active, open the Layers palette. The name Floating Selection appears at the top of the Layers palette. Drag the Opacity slider to the left until the reading is 50%. The opacity of the floating selection is altered. Increase the opacity to 75% and select Dissolve from the pop-up menu in the Layers palette. A portion of the background shows through the floating selection.

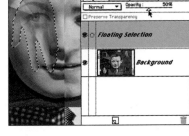

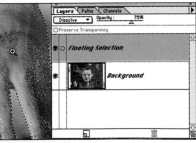

4 | To Create a New Layer for a Floating Selection

Drag the Floating Selection layer to the New Layer icon at the bottom of the Layers palette. The New Layer dialog box appears with the current layer settings. Enter a name for the floating selection and click OK to create a new layer.

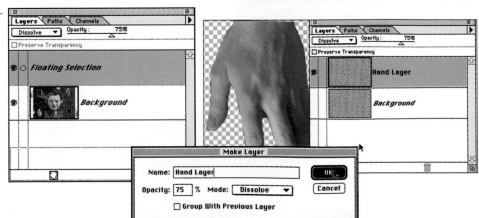

Painting *Lighting Effects Filter (Part 1)*

Lisa Rivard

Comments

Although Photoshop provides many techniques to produce lighting effects—such as the use of channels, brightness, and levels—few rival the capabilities of the Lighting Effects filter. This filter is similar to those found on high-end engineering and rendering systems.

Studio Usage

There are many instances when lighting can be a challenge. For example, combining elements from the same image or mixing images from different sources often requires that each component's lighting be adjusted in the final image. Fine-tuning the lighting solves the problem of differences in shadows and intensity carried over from the original images. The Lighting Effects filter can be used only on RGB images.

Related Techniques

Creating Lighting Effects 22

Creating Basic Textures 26

Lighting Effects Filter (Part 2) 31

1 | Choose the Lighting Effects Filter

Open the file containing the object you want to light. Choose Filter→Render→Lighting Effects. The left side of the Lighting Effects dialog box is a preview window with icons along the bottom for adding or deleting lights. Choose Spotlight from the Light Type pop-up menu. The spotlight casts an ellipse of light that is brightest at the source and gradually falls off. The handle at the lower-right indicates the light source, and the center circle indicates the focus point (where the light is pointing). The line connecting the light source and focus point defines the direction and angle of the light.

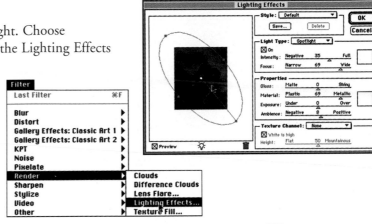

2 | To Change the Width and Location of the Beam

Three other handles surround the border of the oval. Drag one of these three handles to reduce the width of the beam. To move the light source, drag the focus point diagonally up and left until the light source sits directly on top of the object.

3 | To Change the Direction of the Light

To rotate the light, drag the light source. To change the light angle, drag the light source to shorten or lengthen the line (a shorter line produces a sharper angle). By adjusting the size, shape, and location of the light, you can achieve the exact effect you need. You can apply this filter to a selection after you have composed the images, or you can apply it to entire images after compositing.

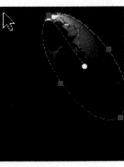

4 | To Change the Lighting Style

Choose Omni from the Light Type pop-up menu to create the effect of a light bulb held over the image. A circle surrounds the focus point. Drag a handle to adjust the light size. When the area is small, the light is close to the image and very bright. When the area is large, the light is farther away and dimmer. For an angled, unfocused light, such as the sun, choose Directional from the Light Type pop-up menu. To change the amount of background lighting, drag the Ambience slider. Drag toward Positive to tint the image with the color in the swatch or drag toward Negative to darken the effect.

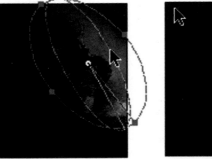

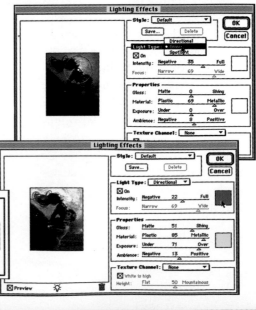

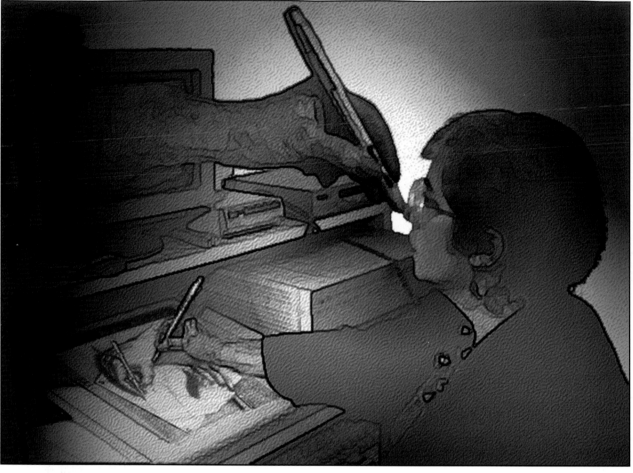

Rhoda Grossman

Comments

You can use the Lighting Effects filter to create a single light—as you did in Lighting Effects Filter (Part 1)—or you can add up to 15 additional lights. As a starting point, try using the pre-created lighting styles shipped with Adobe Photoshop. You can also modify these styles or create and save your own styles. This Lighting Effects filter enables you to create an embossed effect by shining lights through different grayscale textures. This filter requires considerable computing power to render.

Studio Usage

The use of this filter is an effective way to combine colored lights of varying intensities or to add interesting effects when creating composites, 3-D images, or any image requiring consistent and complex lighting. The Lighting Effects filter can only be used on RGB images.

Related Techniques

Selecting Colors   14

Creating Lighting Effects   22

Creating Basic Textures   26

Lighting Effects Filter (Part 1)   30

1 | Create a Texture Channel

Create a new channel by choosing New Channel from the Channels palette submenu or by clicking the page icon at the bottom of the Channels palette. Name the channel Texture Channel. Choose Filter→Noise→Add Noise and enter 70 in the Amount box in the Add Noise dialog box. Click OK to apply the filter. Choose Filter→Blur→Blur More to diffuse the texture.

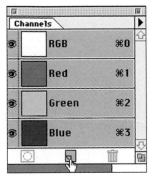

2 | Create a Multiple Light Source

Make sure that the RGB channel is selected and then choose Filters→Render→Lighting Effects. In the Lighting Effects dialog box, choose Triple Spotlight from the Style pop-up menu. Each circle in the preview indicates the focus point for a light (where the light is pointing). Click one of the circles. The line running from the focus point to the light source handle defines the direction and angle of the light. Adjust the positions of the lights. Drag the focus point to move the light. Drag the light source to change the light angle or direction. Use one of the other three handles around the ellipse to broaden or narrow the beam of the spotlight.

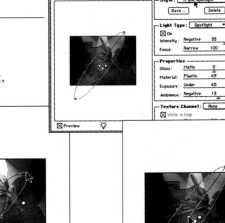

3 | To Change Lighting Properties

Each light can have its own color. Select a light and then select a color for that particular light by clicking the color swatch in the Light Type section of the Lighting Effects dialog box. Drag the sliders in the Properties section to adjust the gloss (reflective surface), material (plastic reflects the color of the light while metallic reflects the color of the object), exposure, and ambience (diffused light that hits all the surfaces with the same strength).

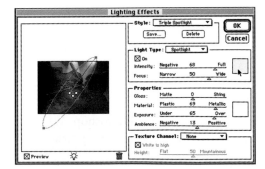

4 | To Add Textured Lights

Shining the lights through grayscale textures in the Texture channel allows you to control how light bounces off the image. The texture produces surfaces that appear to rise or descend—creating a 3-D effect. If you select White is high, white areas indicate peaks and black areas indicate valleys. Select one or more of the lights and choose the Texture Channel you created from the Texture Channel pop-up menu at the bottom of the dialog box.

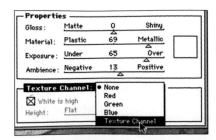

Painting *Simulating a Color Halftone*

Mike Pantuso

Comments

There may be times when you want to display or simulate the effect of four-color halftone screens in an image. This specialized Photoshop filter can achieve that effect without resorting to microphotography.

Studio Usage

When a design calls for a simulation of a halftone with big halftone dots—as a background, a mask, within a selection, or for the entire image—the Color Halftone filter is indispensable. This comic book look is particularly well-suited for cartoons and images relating to the graphic arts. For the artwork in this tip, the Color Halftone filter has been applied around the perimeter of the illustration.

Related Techniques

Defining Layers   50

Managing Channels   59

1 | Create a Channel for the Effect

Create a new channel by choosing New Channel from the Channels palette submenu or by clicking the page icon at the bottom of the Channels palette. Name the channel Mask Channel. Select the Marquee tool. (If necessary, Option-click the tool until you see the elliptical marquee shape.) Press Shift as you drag the elliptical marquee to draw a circle in the new channel. Press the Delete key to fill the circle with the background color (white). This makes the circle the unmasked (unprotected) area in the channel. Click the RGB channel (or press ⌘-0) to return to the RGB channel.

2 | Apply the Filter

Choose Filter→Pixelate→Color Halftone. In the Color Halftone dialog box, enter 20 in the Max. Radius box. Click OK. Large dots now obscure the detail in the image.

3 | Reduce the Dot Size

Choose Undo from the Edit menu to remove the filter's effect. The last filter you used always appears at the top of the Filter menu. If you simply choose the filter from this location, Adobe Photoshop applies the filter using the last settings entered in the filter's dialog box. Press Option as you choose Color Halftone from the top of the Filter menu. Pressing Option as you choose the last used filter enables you to adjust the settings before reapplying the filter. Change the Max. Radius setting to 4 pixels and click OK. With the lower setting, the dots are much smaller.

4 | To Vary the Filter's Effect

Press Option as you choose Filter→Color Halftone, enter a screen angle value of 45 for all four channels, and click OK. This lines up all four screens, allowing you to see only black dots. For a different effect, modify the selection mask by clicking the Mask Channel and choosing Select→Feather. Enter a value in the Pixels box (higher numbers produce more feathering). Press the Delete key one or more times to create a halo around the circle. Return to the RGB channel and Choose Filter→Pixelate→Color Halftone to apply the filter again. You can see that the soft mask blends the halftone screen effect into the continuous tone portion of the image.

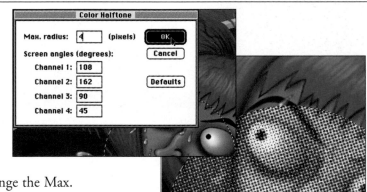

Painting *Ripples in the Water*

Jacqueline Comstock

Comments

Using a combination of Photoshop painting tools and filters, you can create the illusion of shimmering or moving water—even when you have no original artwork.

Studio Usage

This technique creates realistic water surfaces and works well for backgrounds, textures, and fills. As you experiment with various water effects, you may want to save the images to build a library of water effects.

Related Techniques

Creating Simple Gradients   23

Wave and Zigzags   27

Defining Layers   50

Resolution and Image Size   65

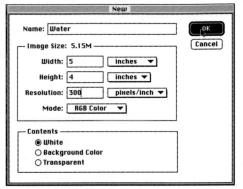

1 | Create a New Document

Choose File→New to create a new document. In the New dialog box, enter the dimensions and resolution that match your project requirements. To create a layer for the water effect, click the page icon at the bottom of the Layers palette, name the layer, and then click OK.

2 | Create a Gradient

Select a dark blue foreground color and set the background color to black. Select the Gradient tool and drag from the upper-left corner to the lower-right corner to create a gradient.

3 | Paint the Ripples

Set the foreground color to white. Using a medium-sized, slightly soft brush, paint a series of long lines in a single direction. Cross each of the lines with one or two roughly perpendicular lines. You can vary the brush sizes to produce several different weights of crossed lines.

4 | Apply the Ripple Filter

Choose Filter→Distort→Ripple. In the Ripple dialog box, enter approximately 870 in the Amount box and click the Large option. Experiment with different settings using the preview box to see the results. When you have the effect you want, click OK to apply the filter.

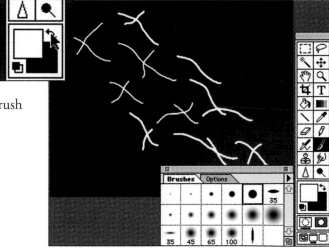

Painting *Pointillize and Crystalize Filters*

Victor Bruja

Comments

A wide range of filters are available for Photoshop—both from Adobe and from third-party developers. All of these filters can be used alone or in conjunction with other filters. Filters provide a quick and easy way to produce complex and unique effects that would be difficult—if not impossible—to achieve by using the painting tools.

Studio Usage

Filters work particularly well on soft-edged (or feathered) selections. In this example from educational publisher Frog Publications, the Crystallize filter is applied to a soft edge to create an interesting border effect.

Related Techniques

Shearing and Pinching   25

Managing Channels   59

1 | Create a Channel

When a grayscale image is created, it has only a single channel—the black channel. To create an additional channel, click the page icon at the bottom of the Channels palette. The new channel appears at the bottom of the Channels palette and in the document window.

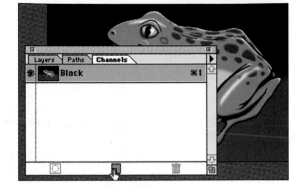

2 | Edit the Mask in the Channel

Double-click the Marquee tool. In the Marquee Options palette, choose Elliptical from the Shape menu and then enter a value in the Feather text box (the higher the number, the softer the mask). With the new channel selected, draw an oval. Press Delete to fill the selection with white. Next, select the black channel and choose Select→Inverse to reverse the selected area. Press Delete again. The result is a white oval around the image.

3 | Apply the Pointillize Filter

Choose Filter→Pixelate→Pointillize. In the Pointillize dialog box, drag the slider to the left. Smaller cell values produce a finer effect. The pre-view box in the dialog box shows the filter's effects as you change the settings.

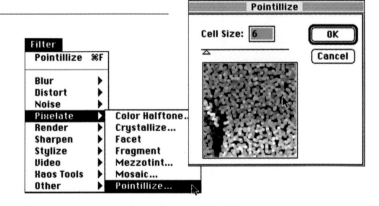

4 | Apply the Crystallize Filter

Choose Filter→Pixelate→Crystallize. In the Crystallize dialog box, drag the slider to adjust the size of the cells until the value is between 10 and 20. Click OK. Notice that the soft mask creates a gradual filtering effect between the frog and the edges of the image.

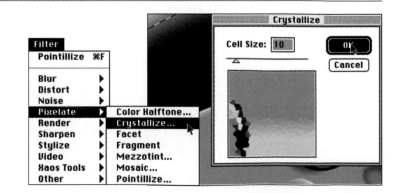

Painting *Facet Filter*

Rhoda Grossman

Comments

Most Photoshop editing works best when you use soft edges to make colors blend smoothly into each other. In certain traditional media, such as oil painting, this color-mixing effect doesn't occur. Instead, the areas where colors meet are stark and one color stops abruptly where the next begins. When you want this hard-edged effect in a Photoshop document, use the Facet filter.

Studio Usage

The Facet filter automatically analyzes an image, determines the major areas of solid or similar colors, and then clumps like-colored pixels to emphasize those areas. There are no options for this filter; Photoshop does the work for you. The Facet filter produces an abstract look that effectively simulates painting with oils. Try experimenting with the filter by applying it two or more times, blurring some areas between applications.

Related Techniques

Selecting Colors   14

Pointillize and
Crystallize Filters   34

Anti-Aliasing   107

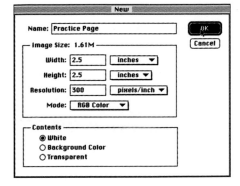

1 | Create a New Document

Choose File→New to create a new document. In the New dialog box, enter 2.5 inches for the width and the height, and a resolution of 300 ppi. Choose RGB Color from the Mode menu, select White from the Contents section, and then click OK.

2 | Draw a Crosshatch

Select a soft, medium-sized, round brush. Select the Paintbrush tool and create a series of interlocking lines using primary colors—reds, greens, blues, and blacks. Select the Zoom tool and drag a marquee around a section of the image where the colors intersect.

3 | Apply the Facet Filter

Choose Filter→Pixelate→Facet. Look at the edges of the brush strokes. If necessary, use the Hand tool to scroll the image. The softness is gone, almost looking as if you had used a hard-edged brush. There is a difference, though—new colors appear at the junction of strokes (a result of the clumping effect). Choose Facet from the top of the Filter menu to reapply the filter. The effect is more subtle after the first application.

4 | Apply the Facet Filter to a Document

Open a document and select a feathered area; then apply the Facet filter. The image here is an excellent example of using digital tools to simulate oil painting and hand-inking.

Painting *Mezzotints*

Gary Poyssick

Comments

Mezzotints, dating back to the middle ages, represent the earliest attempt to create screened images. In Photoshop, you can achieve this effect automatically using the Mezzotint filter. You can also produce this effect manually by screening through original patterns.

Studio Usage

The Mezzotint filter is one way to simulate the graininess of a true mezzotint. Mezzotints are particularly useful for adding interest to simple black-and-white images. While mezzotints print best at high resolutions, they also produce very acceptable output on laser printers and standard office copiers.

Related Techniques

Creating Basic Textures   26

Pointillize and
Crystallize Filters   34

Facet Filter   35

1 | Apply the Mezzotint Filter

Open an image and choose Filter→Pixelate→ Mezzotint. The Type pop-up menu in the Mezzotint dialog box provides a choice of 10 patterns. Select each pattern and preview the effects in the Mezzotint dialog box. Try applying some of the patterns to portions of the image and then choose Edit→Undo→Mezzotint to return to the original image. You can also experiment with printing the results to see how this filter produces excellent output even at 300 dpi. In the example artwork, the patterns were produced using the Fine dots, Grainy dots, and Short strokes options.

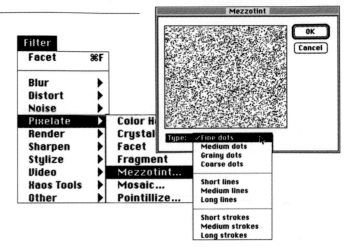

2 | Create Your Own Pattern

Open an image you want to alter; then choose File→New to create a document of the same size for the pattern file. Enter a Resolution of 300, choose Grayscale, and click OK. Choose Filter→Noise→Add Noise. In the Add Noise dialog box, enter 500 for the Amount, select Gaussian and Monochromatic, and then click OK. Choose Filter→Blur→Blur More twice to diffuse the pattern.

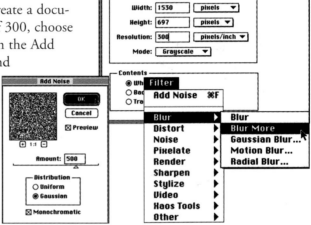

3 | Convert the Noisy Image to a Pattern

In order to use the grayscale document as a pattern, you must convert it to a bitmap image. Choose Mode→Bitmap. In the Bitmap dialog box, select Diffusion Dither and click OK. Choose Select→ All or press ⌘-A to select the entire image; then choose Edit→Define Pattern.

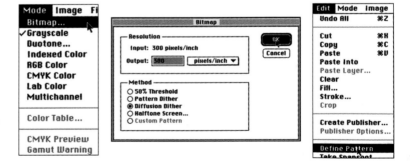

4 | Use the Pattern to Screen the Image

Return to the image that you want to screen. Convert the image by choosing Mode→Bitmap. (If the document is in color, you need to choose Mode→Grayscale first and then convert the grayscale image to a bitmap). In the Bitmap dialog box, select Custom Pattern. The pattern you defined in Step 3 is used to map the tonal values of the original image—producing a mezzotint effect. The pattern is heavier in the darker areas of the image and lighter in the brighter portions.

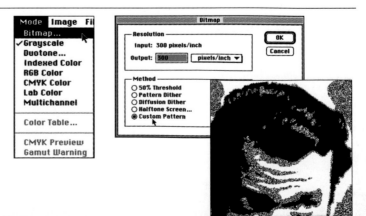

Painting *Clouds Filters*

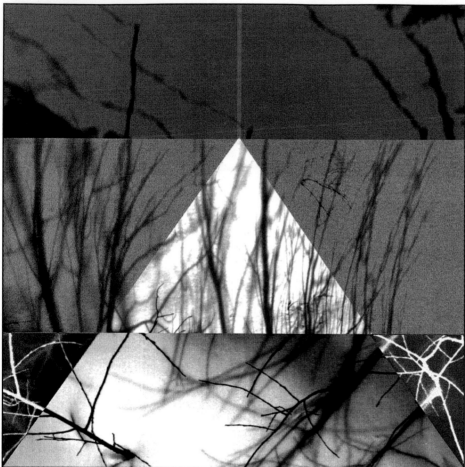

Karin Schminke Unique Editions ™

Comments

Photoshop allows you to simulate certain types of cloud effects, even when you don't have original artwork. The Clouds and Difference Clouds filters can produce a wide variety of effects.

Studio Usage

The Clouds and Difference Clouds filters don't produce the kind of billowy cumulus clouds often found in stock art. Instead, the clouds appear in an abstract or hazy pattern. These filters work well for creating surrealistic backgrounds. The clouds appear thicker and change colors as you repeatedly apply the filters. Choosing Difference Clouds several times creates ribs and veins that resemble a marble texture. You can also create burnt and distressed metals, sandstorms, and many other textures.

Related Techniques

Creating Basic Textures   26

Wave and Zigzags   27

Ripples in the Water   33

Defining Layers   50

1 Create a New Document

Choose File→New to create a new document. Enter 2.5 inches for the Width and the Height, and 300 for the Resolution. Choose RGB from the Mode menu, select White for the background Contents, and then click OK.

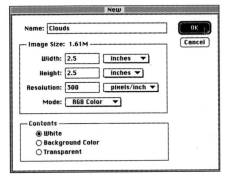

2 Apply the Clouds Filter

The Clouds filter uses random values between the foreground and background colors to generate the clouds. To simulate a sky, select a blue for the foreground color and white for the background color; then choose Filter→Render→Clouds. The entire image is filled with a soft, random cloud pattern. Pressing Shift as you select Filter→Render→Clouds produces a starker clouds pattern (this works for Difference Clouds, too). Try experimenting using different color combinations and applying noise, blurs, zigzags, ripples, and other filters to a cloud background.

3 Use Difference Clouds to Create Textures

Difference Clouds calculates the difference between the foreground and background colors and blends the values with the existing pixels. Choose File→New to create a document. Click the foreground color selection box in the toolbox to display the Color Picker. Enter these values in the text boxes: C 0%, M 60%, Y 13%, and K 0%. Click OK to create the foreground color. Click the background color selection box in the toolbox and enter these values in the Color Picker: C 0%, M 9%, Y 50%, and K 0%. Click OK to create the background color. Choose Filter→ Render→Difference Clouds.

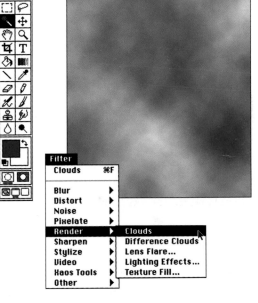

Painting *Textures on Layers*

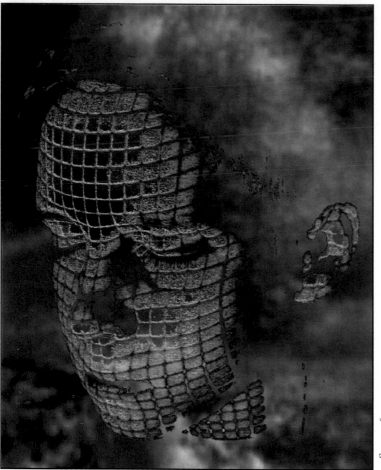

Michael J. Partington

Comments

As you create an image, you often make changes and modifications as your concept develops. Designing textures can be a particularly challenging task—often you'll want to try out many ideas before applying the texture and making the changes permanent. Putting textures on separate layers provides an unlimited number of "undos," allowing you the freedom to change your mind until you get the exact effect you want.

Studio Usage

Using layers lets you combine different filters and techniques without affecting the original image. When you're done making changes to a specific texture, you can merge the layers to save disk space and decrease the file size. Be sure you save the final version of the image before you flatten all the layers.

Related Techniques

Defining Layers 50

Global Color Adjustments 55

Grouping, Merging, and
Flattening Layers 57

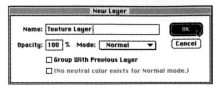

1 | Create and Name the Layers

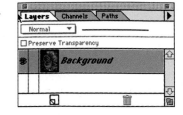

Open an image that has only a Background layer. If necessary, save the document in Photoshop 3.0 format, so that you can work with layers. Because you want to place the texture layer behind (under) the Background layer, you must first convert the Background layer to a standard layer. (Layers named Background are always the bottom layer.) To convert the Background layer, double-click the Background layer in the Layers palette, enter a new layer name, and click OK. Then click the page icon at the bottom of the Layers palette to create a new layer and name it Texture Layer.

2 | Create the Texture

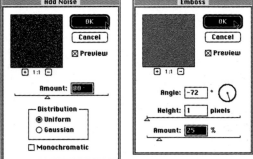

With the Texture Layer selected, choose Edit→Fill. In the Fill dialog box, choose Black from the Use menu and enter 80% for the Opacity. Make sure that the mode is set to Normal and that Preserve Transparency is not selected. Click OK to fill the layer. To add texture, choose Filter→Noise→Add Noise. In the Add Noise dialog box, enter 80 for the Amount, check that Uniform is seleced, and then click OK. To enhance the texture, choose Filter→Stylize→Emboss. Select the Preview box. Try out various settings in the Emboss dialog box until you've created a texture you like. Click OK.

3 | Applying the Texture to the Overlying Image

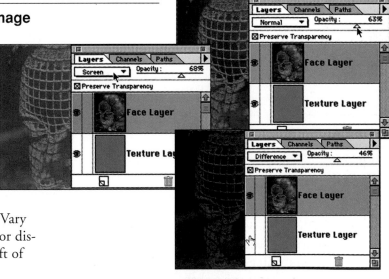

Drag the Texture Layer down in the Layers palette until it's below the image layer. Click the Face layer (the top layer) and adjust the Opacity to allow the texture to show through. Now experiment by selecting different layer modes. Keep the top layer selected and choose Multiply from the Mode menu. Multiply combines the pixels in the two layers to make a darker image. Choose Screen from the Mode pop-up menu. Screen lightens the image and produces a washed-out effect. Vary the modes and opacities for both layers. To hide or display individual layers, click the eye icon to the left of the layer name.

4 | Clearing Portions of the Original Image

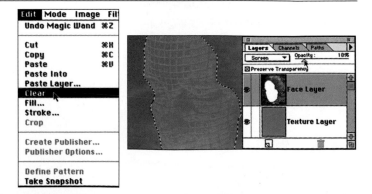

To allow the texture to show through parts of the image, select the image layer in the Layers palette, select the desired areas, and then choose Edit→Clear. Unlike pressing the Delete key (which fills a selection with the background color) or pressing Option-Delete (which fills a selection with the foreground color), the Clear command deletes the selected pixels in the target layer. This allows the pixels in the underlying Texture Layer to show through completely.

Painting *Replacing Colors*

Mike Pantuso

Comments

The Replace Colors command lets you make a color selection by color and then adjust the hue and saturation of the selected color without leaving the dialog box. By combining selections with color adjustment, this command does the work of the Color Range and the Hue/Saturation/Brightness commands in one easy step.

Studio Usage

Adjusting colors with the Replace Colors command works very well where colors are clearly recognizable—like spot colors in illustrations, cartoons, and graphics.

Related Techniques

The Magic Wand Tool   8

The Color Range Command   9

Selecting Colors   14

Hue and Saturation   86

1 | Choose the Replace Color Command

Open the image in which you want to adjust the color. Choose Image→Adjust→Replace Color. In the Replace Color dialog box, drag the Fuzziness slider to 0. (The Fuzziness slider works like the Tolerance setting for the Magic Wand tool—it increases or decreases the number of selected pixels based on their color similarity to the pixel you click.) If necessary, click the Selection option under the preview window. As you add to or subtract from the selection, this preview displays the current selection. Select the Preview checkbox (above the eyedroppers) to see the effect in the image as you make adjustments.

2 | Select the Colors You Want to Change

Click the left eyedropper in the Replace Color dialog box and then click in the image to select a color. The preview box shows the areas that contain the selected color. Drag the Fuzziness slider to the right to increase the selection. You can also use the plus and minus eyedroppers to add to or subtract from the selection. (Note that this is only a temporary selection for changing colors—after you click OK there is no selection in the image itself.) To reset the options while in the Replace Color dialog box, hold down the Option key and press Cancel.

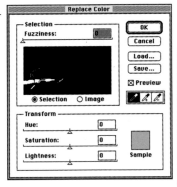

3 | Adjust the Color

To change the hue in an image—for example, yellow to blue, or green to red—drag the Hue slider in the Replace Color dialog box. To change the saturation or lightness of the color, drag the corresponding slider. If you click the Image option, you'll see the image in the preview box. (Use the Image option when the part of the image you want to select is hidden by the dialog box.) Click OK to apply the changes.

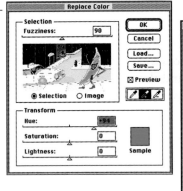

Painting *Posterize*

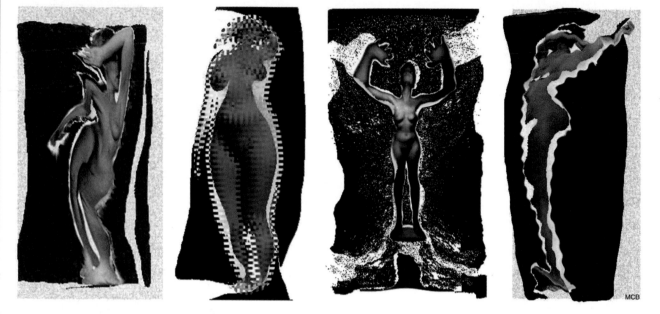

Melissa C. Beckman

© MELISSA C. BECKMAN 1991

Comments

Posterizing refers to a reduction in the number of brightness (or gray) values in an image. When a channel contains the full complement of 256 levels of gray, it gives the impression of a continuous tone image. The reduction of the gray levels removes shading and produces flat areas of color, resulting in a screen-printed effect.

Studio Usage

Posterizing can be used in a wide variety of creative ways, such as giving a hand-painted look to a halftone image or creating posters with a limited number of colors. Posterization permanently removes color information from an image—so be sure to preview the effect before you apply the Posterize command.

Related Techniques

Selecting Colors   14

Creating Simple Gradients   23

Facet Filter   35

1 | Create a New Document

Choose File→New and create a document that's 5 inches square with a resolution of 72 ppi. Choose RGB Color from the Mode menu and leave the background Contents set to White. Name the image Posterization and click OK.

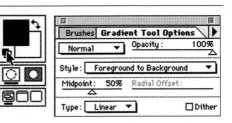

2 | Create a Gradient

Click the default colors icon in the toolbox to return to the default black foreground and white background colors. Double-click the Gradient tool to display the Gradient Tool Options palette. Set the Mode to Normal, the Opacity to 100%, and choose Foreground to Background from the Style pop-up menu. Drag the Midpoint slider to 50%, choose Linear from the Type pop-up menu, and deselect the Dither option. Drag a horizontal gradient across the image. The gradient, which contains all the gray values from 0 (black) to 255 (white), appears very smooth.

3 | Posterize the Image

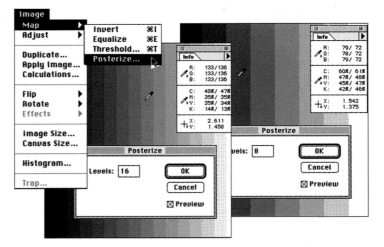

Select the Eyedropper tool and choose Window→Palettes→Show Info. You can use the Eyedropper tool to measure pixel values and check the readouts in the Info palette. Choose Image→ Map→Posterize. In the Posterize dialog box, select Preview and enter 16 in the Levels dialog box. The image is divided into 16 bands of brightness. Move the Eyedropper across the image and watch the Info palette. The numbers on the left show the current pixel values (256 levels of gray), and the numbers on the right show what the values will be after applying the command (16 levels of gray). Without clicking OK, enter 8 in the Levels dialog box to see the effect of further posterization.

4 | Experiment with Other Images

Choose File→Open and open an image. Practice posterizing using different Level settings. You can also try adjusting the sharpening and contrast settings prior to applying the Posterize command.

Painting *Using Quick-Edit*

Bob Hamor

Comments

Depending on the size and resolution of your image, scanned files are often quite large. When the file size exceeds the amount of RAM available for Photoshop, the program relies on virtual memory to store portions of the active image on disk—even while you're working on it. When you're using virtual memory (called a scratch disk in Photoshop), the program frequently reads and writes data to the disk, dramatically slowing down all operations.

Studio Usage

Adobe Systems recommends that you have 3 to 5 times the file size available in RAM. This means that a 15 megabyte image can require a memory allocation of 45 to 75 megabytes—more than many systems can support. To avoid working with very large files, Photoshop includes a module called Quick Edit. Quick Edit allows you to open and work on a small portion of a large file. This can speed editing if you're experimenting with complex painting techniques or special effects. The Quick Edit module opens Photoshop 2, Scitex CT, and *uncompressed* TIFF files.

Related Techniques

Resolution and Image Size   65

Canvas Size   66

Resolution and Screen
Frequency Requirements   68

1 | Open a Large Image

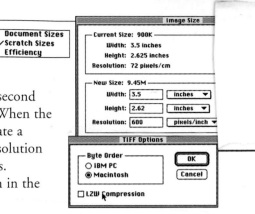

To check your RAM, click the triangle in the bottom border of the document window and select Scratch Sizes. The first figure shows the memory being used for all open images; the second number shows the total amount of RAM available to Photoshop. When the first number exceeds the second, you're using virtual memory. Create a large document by opening an existing image and increasing its resolution until the file size exceeds the available RAM. Choose File→Save As. Choose TIFF from the Format menu. Deselect LZW Compression in the TIFF Options dialog box and click OK.

2 | Acquiring Portions of a Large Image

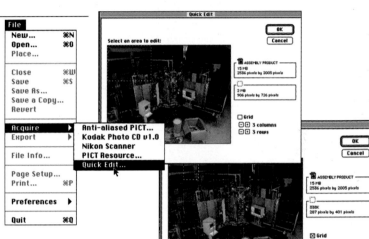

Choose File→Acquire→Quick Edit. Select a file name from the file list and click Open. The Quick Edit dialog box provides two ways to select part of the image: you can draw a marquee around the area you want to work on, or you can use the Grid option. Select Grid to divide the image into tiles. Click the +/- buttons to increase or decrease the number of tiles. Click a tile to make it the current selection. Two information boxes appear at the right side of the dialog box. The top box tells you the file size and dimension of the total file. The bottom box tells you the file size and dimensions of the current selection. Click OK to open part of the file.

3 | Making Changes to the Opened Portion

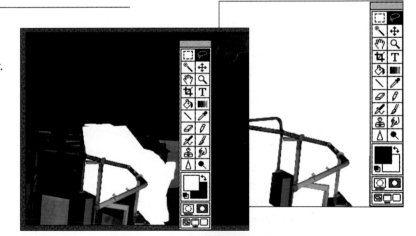

The selected portion appears in a new window. Make the desired changes. As you work, you'll notice that the file is edited quickly because you're working in a small file.

4 | Saving the Changed Portion

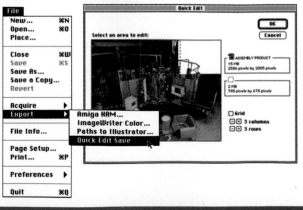

When you're finished editing, choose File→Export→Quick Edit Save. The portion of the document is written back to the original file. Open the file using Quick Edit again. The preview in the Quick Edit dialog box shows the modifications you've made to the original file. Select another section and repeat the process until all edits are complete.

Painting Modes *Normal*

Michael J. Partington

Comments

The Adobe Photoshop painting modes allow you to create a variety of effects by painting only those pixels that meet a certain condition. When you use a painting tool and select a painting mode, the current foreground color and opacity setting is applied to or mixed with the underlying image pixels to create the resulting effect. For example, painting in Normal mode paints the underlying image pixels with the current foreground color and the current opacity setting, while painting in Lighten mode paints only those underlying image pixels that are darker than the current foreground color.

Studio Usage

The next several tips describe how you can use painting modes to color grayscale images, to blend the edges of objects you've copied into a file, or even to affect individual layers within a document. The painting modes can be set for use with any painting tool. You can select a painting mode for an entire layer or when using the Fill or Stroke commands from the Edit menu.

Related Techniques

Selecting Colors   14

Painting Modes   42-49

Defining Layers   50

Managing Channels   59

Removing Casts   87

1 | Open an Image and Select a Foreground Color

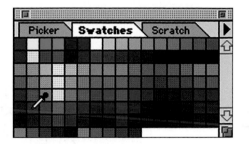

The easiest way to see the effect of a painting mode is to experiment with an RGB grayscale image. If you don't have a grayscale image, open a color image, convert it to grayscale, and then choose Mode→RGB to create an RGB grayscale image. Choose a foreground color using one of the color selection methods (Picker, Swatches, or Scratch pallettes).

2 | Select a Painting Tool

Double-click a painting tool in the toolbox to select the tool and its corresponding Options palette. Make sure that Normal is selected from the Mode pop-up menu and that the Opacity slider is set to 100 percent.

3 | Paint in Normal Mode

Paint directly on the grayscale image with the selected painting tool. Because the foreground color is applied at 100% opacity, none of the underlying image pixels show through. Next, change the Opacity slider to 50 percent and paint on the grayscale image again. Notice that the color is now partially transparent, allowing some visibility of the underlying image pixels.

Michael J. Partington

Comments

You may have seen the use of the Dissolve mode in presentation programs, when one slide or scene slowly breaks up into pixels to reveal the next slide or scene. The Dissolve mode creates random pixelization over the surface of a selection or an entire image.

Studio Usage

There are many tasks that demand that one image shows through another, such as the creation of a composite image.

Related Techniques

Selecting Colors   14

Painting Modes   42-49

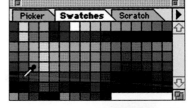

1 | Open an Image and Select a Foreground Color

The easiest way to see the effect of a painting mode is to experiment with an RGB grayscale image. If you don't have a grayscale image, open a color image, convert it to grayscale, and then choose Mode→RGB to create an RGB grayscale image.

2 | Select a Painting Tool

Double-click a painting tool in the toolbox to select the tool and its corresponding options palette. (The Dissolve mode works best with the Airbrush tool or a large, soft-edged brush.) Choose Dissolve from the Mode pop-up menu and make sure that the Opacity or Pressure slider (depending on the tool) is set to 100 percent.

3 | Paint in Dissolve Mode

Using the selected painting tool, paint on the grayscale image. The foreground color is dissolved at 100 percent opacity. If you are using the Airbrush tool, you can adjust the Pressure slider to vary the rate at which the paint is applied. If you hold down the Airbrush tool in the same area indefinitely, the paint eventually becomes completely opaque. When applying the Dissolve mode to a selected area using the Edit→Fill command, the opacity level you define also determines how much of the selection area is affected. For example, if you choose a 50 percent opacity level and paint into a circle, the Dissolve mode affects only 50 percent of the surface area.

Painting Modes *Multiply*

Michael J. Partington

Comments

The Multiply mode multiplies the color value of the pixels in each channel by the foreground color, which always results in a darker color. Successive overlapping strokes create a progressively darker color. Multiplying any color with black produces black, and multiplying any color with white produces white. The Multiply mode can be used with any painting tool or can be set for an entire layer.

Studio Usage

One of the best uses for the Multiply mode is the creation of detail or overlapping colors in transparent selections. Glass, smoke effects, and other similar see-through properties are good candidates for the Multiply mode.

Related Techniques

Selecting Colors 14

Painting Modes 42-49

1 | Open an Image and Select a Foreground Color

The easiest way to see the immediate effect of a painting mode is to experiment with an RGB grayscale image. If you don't have a grayscale image, open a color image, convert it to grayscale, and then choose Mode→RGB to create an RGB grayscale image.

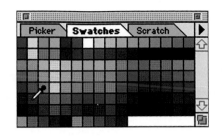

2 | Float a Selection

With a selection tool, choose an area you want to darken. By floating a selection, the underlying pixels won't be affected when you move the selection. Choose Select→Float (⌘-J) to float a copy of the image on top of the selection.

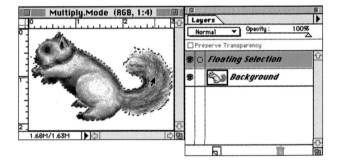

3 | Move the Selection and Choose Multiply

Open the Layers palette. A temporary layer named Floating Selection appears at the top of the Layers palette. Drag the Floating Selection to the new layer icon (the page icon) at the bottom of the Layers palette. The New Layer dialog box appears. Choose Multiply from the Mode pop-up menu in the dialog box and then click OK. The selection is moved onto a new, transparent layer with the pixels in the same position as those on the original image. The selection is darkened because the Multiply mode has been applied to the entire layer.

Painting Modes *Screen*

Michael J. Partington

Comments

The Screen mode multiplies the inverse color of the image pixels with foreground color, always resulting in a lighter color. The Screen mode can be likened to applying bleach to a selection or document.

Studio Usage

The Screen mode is helpful when you want to lighten specific areas of an image or an entire image.

Related Techniques

Selecting Colors   14

Painting Modes   42-49

Hue and Saturation   86

1 | Open an Image and Select a Foreground Color

The easiest way to see the immediate effect of the Screen mode painting mode is to experiment with an RGB image. Make sure that RGB is selected in the Mode menu; then select a foreground color from the Picker palette or the Swatches palette, or create a new color using the Scratch palette.

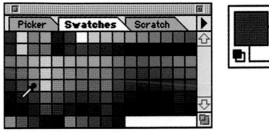

2 | Select a Painting Tool

Double-click a painting tool in the toolbox to select the tool and its corresponding options palette. Make sure that Screen is selected from the Mode pop-up menu and that the Opacity slider is set to 100%. If you use the Brush tool, select the Wet Edges option to cast a watercolor effect on the brush strokes.

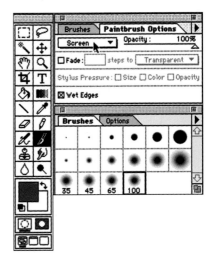

3 | Paint Using Screen Mode

Begin painting on the RGB image. The areas you paint are lightened. Each time you paint over the same area, the area becomes progressively lighter.

Painting Modes *Overlay*

Michael J. Partington

Comments

The Overlay mode darkens (multiplies) or lightens (screens) the pixels in the underlying image, depending on the color of the underlying pixels and the foreground color. The highlights and shadows of the underlying image are maintained by blending the pixels from the underlying image with the foreground color. Where the image is transparent, no foreground color is applied.

Studio Usage

You can use the Overlay mode for many purposes, but the most obvious example is for borders, or for using one image or shape to determine the shape of another.

Related Techniques

Selecting Colors   14

Painting Modes   42-49

Global Color Adjustments   55

1 | Open an Image and Select a Foreground Color

Open an RGB image or a grayscale image that has been saved in RGB Mode. If you don't have a grayscale image, open a color image, convert it to grayscale, and then choose Mode→RGB to create an RGB grayscale image. Choose a foreground color from the Picker palette or the Swatches palette, or create a new color using the Scratch palette. If you use the Picker palette to select a color, make sure that the foreground swatch is selected before you choose a color.

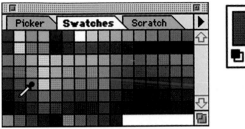

2 | Select a Painting Tool

Double-click a painting tool in the toolbox to select the tool and its corresponding Options palette. Choose Overlay from the tools Options palette and set the Opacity slider to 100%.

3 | Paint in Overlay Mode

Paint on the image using a painting tool. If the object is positioned on a white background, you don't need to select the object because the white pixels won't be affected. You can also isolate an overlay color by placing it on its own layer. Create a new layer, choose Overlay from the New Layer mode dialog box, and then choose Edit→Fill to fill the layer with the current foreground color. If you don't like the results, simply select and delete the color and then choose another.

Painting Modes *Soft and Hard Light*

Soft Light

Hard Light

Michael J. Partington

Comments

Soft and Hard Light modes work in the same manner as a gelatin filter by tinting the existing tones in a selection or over an entire image.

Studio Usage

Although removing casts is important, there are times when you might want to tint an image, background, or art element toward a specific color range. The Soft Light mode can also be used to enrich dominant colors in an image without changing the saturation.

Related Techniques

Creating Lighting Effects   22

Floating Selections   29

Defining Layers   50

1 | Select the Area

Open an image and select the area to which you want to apply either of the light filters. Soft and Hard light can be applied to an entire image, resulting in a visible cast, or used to affect a specific area.

2 | Float the Selection and Create a New Layer

If you've selected a specific area, make sure that the selection is active and choose Select→Float (⌘-J). In the Layers palette, a temporary selection, named Floating Selection, appears at the top of the palette. Drag the Floating Selection onto the New Layer icon at the bottom of the layers palette. The New Layer dialog box appears. Choose Soft Light from the Mode pop-up menu and click OK to create the new layer.

3 | To See the Effect of the Light Modes

Turn off the Background layer, either by clicking the eye icon next to the layer or by Option-clicking the eye icon next to Layer 1 (to turn off all layers but the selected one.) Choose a bright pink or orange hue for the foreground color; then press Option-Delete to fill the selection area on the Layer. Turn on the Background layer by clicking the leftmost column next to the layer and note the tinted effect on the selected region. With both layers visible, make sure that Layer 1 is selected and then select Hard Light from the pop-up Mode menu. The lighting effect is intensified. This mode simulates bright light being shone through the "gelatin" of the screen. Move the Opacity slider to about 50 percent to lessen the harshness of the light effect.

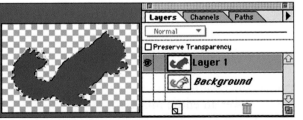

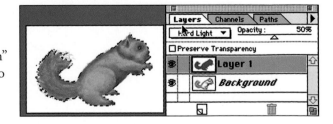

RGB Grayscale—Normal

RGB Grayscale—Darken 75%

RGB Grayscale—Lighten 75%

Michael J. Partington

Comments

The Darken and Lighten modes compare the paint (foreground) color to the color values in each channel of an image. These two modes can then paint those pixels that fall within a certain criteria. The Darken mode paints only those pixels that are lighter than the foreground color, and the Lighten mode paints only those pixels that are darker than the foreground color.

Studio Usage

One of the best uses of the Darken and Lighten painting modes is for coloring RGB grayscale images. In this example, the same foreground color is used to show how the Darken and Lighten modes differ when applied to the same RGB grayscale image.

Related Techniques

Selecting Colors   14

Painting Modes   42-49

File Formats   121-126

1 | Open a Grayscale Image

Open a grayscale image to which you want to apply color. Make sure that RGB is selected under the Mode menu, so that you can paint with color on the grayscale image. Choose a color from the Swatches palette or the Picker palette, or create your own color using the Scratch palette.

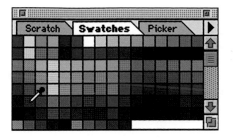

2 | Paint Using Darken Mode

Double-click a painting tool to select the tool and its corresponding options palette. Choose Darken from the pop-up menu in the options palette. If desired, select an Opacity setting using the slider in the painting tool's options palette. Select the object that you want to color and then paint on the object. Only the pixels that are lighter than the selected foreground color are affected.

3 | Paint in Lighten Mode

Choose Lighten from the painting tool's Options palette and paint on the desired area of the image. If the object you're painting is positioned on a white background, you don't need to select the object because the white pixels won't be affected. Only the pixels that are darker than the foreground color are affected.

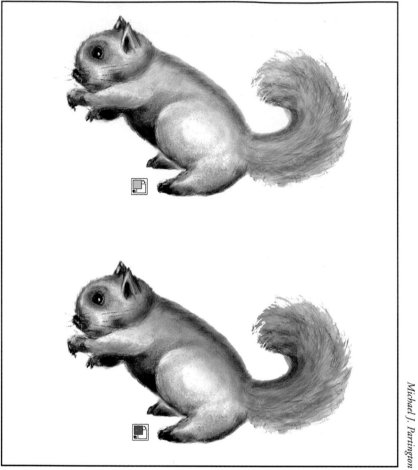

Michael J. Partington

Comments

The Difference mode compares the color and brightness of the pixels in each channel of the image to the color and brightness of the foreground painting color. If the foreground color has a higher brightness value than the image pixels, it is added to the color value of the image pixels to create a new color. If the foreground color has a lower brightness value than the image pixels, it is subtracted from the color value of the image pixels to create a new color.

Studio Usage

The Difference mode produces a variety of results depending on the color and brightness of the image pixels (as compared to the color and brightness of the foreground pixels). You can experiment with the Difference mode to alter parts of an image or to change the hue of an entire image.

Related Techniques

Selecting Colors   14

Painting Modes   42-49

1 | Open an Image and Select a Paint Color

Open a color or grayscale image and choose a foreground color using the Swatches palette or the Picker palette, or create your own color using the Scratch palette.

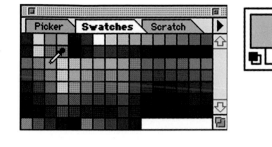

2 | Select a Painting Tool

Double-click a painting tool to select the tool and its corresponding options palette. Choose Difference from the pop-up menu in the options palette. If desired, select an Opacity setting using the slider in the painting tool's options palette.

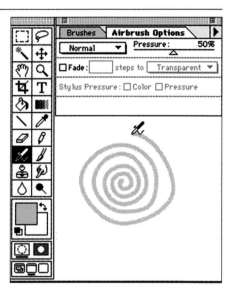

3 | Paint in Difference Mode

To apply the Difference mode to an object, select the object using any of the selection tools. To apply the Difference mode to an entire image, choose Edit→Fill and then choose Difference from the pop-up menu. Click OK to apply the mode to the entire image. The results are surprising. For example, in this sample a pink tone was used to paint the initial shape, and the green foreground color applied using the Difference mode produced a magenta effect.

Mike Pantuso

Comments

The ability to create layers for separate elements of a document is one of the most powerful features in Adobe Photoshop. Layers allow you to isolate and move individual parts of an image without disturbing underlying pixels. You can think of layers as individual pieces of acetate—each layer can be manipulated separately, but is part of a larger, complete image when combined.

Studio Usage

You can use layers whenever you need to isolate and edit individual areas of a document. For example, before layers, type was difficult to manipulate; now you can isolate and edit type elements without disturbing underlying pixels.

Related Techniques

Creating a Rainbow Effect   52

Type on Layers   53

Global Color Adjustments   55

Managing Channels   59

1 | Create a New Layer

New documents are composed of a single layer, called the Background layer. To create additional layers, choose New Layer from the Layers palette submenu, or click the page icon at the lower-left corner of the Layers palette. The New Layer dialog box appears. Enter a name for the new layer and then click OK. The new layer appears at the top of the Layers palette, and it is the frontmost object in the painting order.

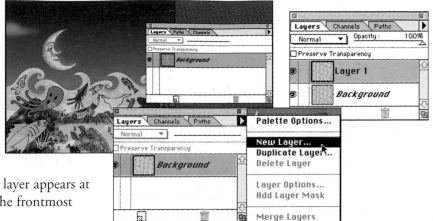

2 | Add Artwork to the New Layer

To draw, paint, or move objects to a layer, the layer must be selected in the Layers palette. Make sure that the new layer is selected, and then choose a painting tool and draw on the new layer. In the column to the left of the layer name, an eye icon indicates that the layer is visible. Click the eye icon to hide the layer; the painting on that layer disappears. Click in the column again to display the layer.

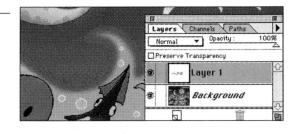

3 | Move the Artwork on the New Layer

Select the Move tool from the toolbox and drag to move the object on the new layer. Notice that none of the pixels on the background layer is affected.

4 | Change the Opacity of the Layer

To change the opacity of a single layer, make sure that the layer is selected and then drag the Opacity slider. If you change the brush opacity and the layer opacity, the brush opacity percentage is multiplied by the layer opacity percentage to create a new opacity level. For example, if the brush opacity is set to 80% and the layer opacity is set to 15%, any objects that you create will be at 12% opaque.

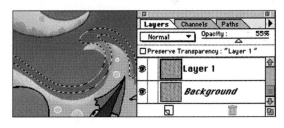

5 | Change the Layer Order

You can change the order of layers to change the viewing order; however, you cannot change the position of the Background layer (unless you rename the Background layer by double-clicking the layer and entering a new layer name). Create a second layer, enter a name for the layer, and then click OK. Use a painting tool to draw on the new layer and then drag the new layer downward until a thick black line appears at the bottom of the first layer. Release the mouse button; the first layer you created moves into the topmost position (as indicated in the Layers palette), and the artwork on the second layer is displayed behind the first layer.

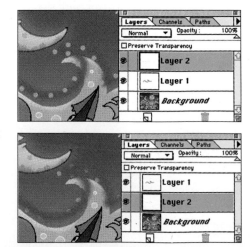

Jacqueline Comstock

Comments

You can use layers to create drop shadows behind type or objects. Drop shadows can be filled with a single color, a gradient, or with levels of gray.

Studio Usage

Drop shadows created on individual layers can be edited independently of the primary object. After you have created a drop shadow on a layer, you can use the Multiply mode to ensure that the shadow blends with the background image instead of knocking out the background image.

Related Techniques

Creating a Rainbow Effect   52

Type on Layers   53

Global Color Adjustments   55

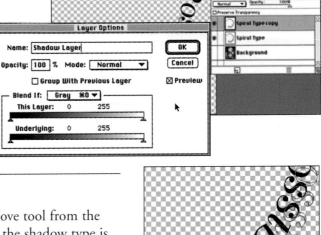

1 | Copy the Primary Layer

The type in the example artwork has been placed on a layer. To create a layer for the drop shadow, drag the primary layer to the page icon at the bottom of the Layers palette. A copy of the primary layer is created and displayed at the top of the Layers palette. Click the Preserve Transparency option at the top of the Layers palette. This option preserves all the transparent areas around the type, making it possible to fill the type with a new color without having to first select it. To rename the shadow layer, double-click the layer to select the Layer Options dialog box and then enter a name for the new layer. At this point, the Shadow layer is the frontmost layer in the painting order.

2 | Reposition the Shadow Type

Make sure that the shadow layer is selected; then select the Move tool from the toolbox and drag to reposition the shadow type. As you drag, the shadow type is displayed as an outline, making it easier to see and to reposition.

3 | Blur the Edges of the Drop Shadow

Select a color for the drop shadow type; then choose Edit→Fill to fill the type with the new color. The Preserve Transparency option enables you to fill the type without first selecting it. (All the areas around the type have been preserved as transparent areas.) To soften the edges of the shadow type, deselect the Preserve Transparency option so that the edges (transparent areas) can be affected by the blurring filter. Deselect the Preserve Transparency option; then choose Filter→Blur→Gaussian Blur and enter a value for the percentage of blurring desired. Click OK. The higher the value, the more blurred the edges of the shadow type will be.

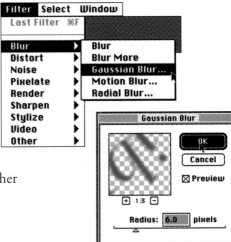

4 | Reposition the Shadow Layer

In the Layers palette, drag the shadow layer downward until a thick black line appears below the type layer and then release the mouse button. The shadow is positioned behind the primary layer. To mix the shadow color with the background color, make sure that the shadow layer is selected. Choose Multiply from the Style pop-up menu in the Layers palette. The Multiply option blends the shadow and background colors by multiplying the background color by the shadow color—resulting in a darker color.

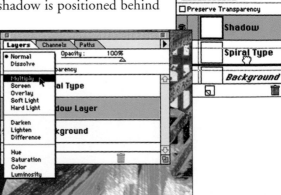

Gary Poyssick

Comments

This tip shows you how to use layers and Photoshop's Shear filter to create one of nature's most colorful phenomena—the rainbow.

Studio Usage

This tip highlights the flexibility of using layers to create realistic effects in Photoshop.

Related Techniques

Shearing and Pinching 25

Defining Layers 50

Global Color Adjustments 55

Creating a Lens Flare Effect 56

1 | Create a New Layer

Create a new layer by choosing New Layer from the Layers palette submenu or by clicking the page icon at the bottom of the palette. The New Layer dialog box appears. Choose Screen from the Mode pop-up menu and click OK. The Screen option multiplies the inverse colors of the selection by the inverse colors of the underlying background pixels, which lightens the rainbow and makes it look more realistic.

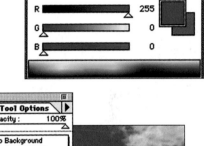

2 | Create the Rainbow Attributes

Using the rectangular Marquee tool, draw a rectangle of the approximate length and height of the rainbow you want to create. Using the Swatch palette or the Picker palette, set the Foreground color to a bright red and set the Background color to a bright magenta.

3 | Apply the Rainbow

Double-click the Gradient tool in the tools palette to select the tool and to open the Gradient Tool Options palette. Choose Counterclockwise Spectrum from the Style pop-up menu and drag to 60% on the Midpoint slider. The midpoint is the point at which the foreground color begins to blend with the background color. Setting the midpoint to 60% creates a greater amount of red in the gradient—just as in nature. Drag the Gradient tool from the top of the rectangular selection to the bottom of the rectangular selection.

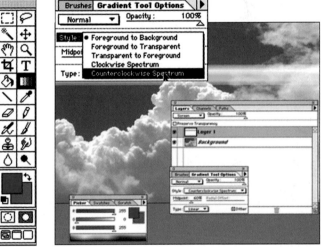

4 | Create the Rainbow Shape

With the selection still active, choose Image→Rotate→90° CW (clockwise). Choose Filter→Distort→Shear. The Shear dialog box appears. Drag the handles to bow the selection, creating the curve of the rainbow. Click OK; then choose Image→Rotate→Free and drag a corner of the selection to reposition the rainbow. When the rainbow is positioned as desired, position the pointer within the selection area and click to apply the new rotation.

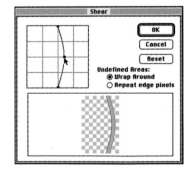

5 | Soften the Rainbow

Choose Filter→Blur→Gaussian. The Gaussian dialog box appears. Make sure that Preview is selected; then drag within the Preview box to bring the rainbow into view if it isn't visible. Click OK to apply the blur to the rainbow. If desired, use a painting tool at a low opacity or the Smudge tool to further edit the ends of the rainbow.

The wind stirs the flying waterfall and
sends in refreshing music,
The moon is risen over the opposite peak
and the bamboo shadows are cast over
my paper window.
As I grow older, the mountain retreat
appeals all the more strongly to my
feeling,
Even when I am buried, after death,
underneath the rock, my bones will be
as transparent as ever.
— Jakushitsu

Anonymous

Comments

The ability to isolate type elements on layers is a powerful enhancement to Adobe Photoshop 3.0. By placing type elements on individual layers, type can be manipulated without affecting underlying pixels.

Studio Usage

Although the Type tool in Photoshop is useful for creating simple type, it is not a substitute for creating type in professional drawing programs, which provide comprehensive type controls. When working with type that requires precise adjustment, create the type in a drawing program and then import and place the type onto an individual layer in Photoshop.

Related Techniques

Defining Layers 50

Global Color Adjustments 55

Managing Channels 59

Importing and
Exporting Paths 115

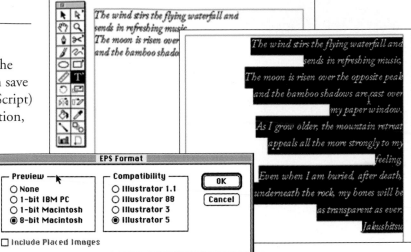

1 | Create the Type

Using a drawing program, create and refine the type you want to use in Photoshop, and then save the document as an EPS (Encapsulated PostScript) file. Make sure that you choose a Preview option, which enables you to view the type in Adobe Photoshop. If you do not choose a Preview option, the type will print to an output device, but you will not be able to view it onscreen.

2 | Create a Layer for the Type

Create and name a new layer in Adobe Photoshop by choosing New Layer from the Layers palette submenu or by clicking the page icon at the bottom of the Layers palette.

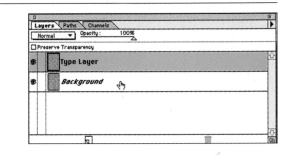

3 | Place the Type

With the type layer active, choose File→Place. Locate the file containing the type and click Open to place the type in the Photoshop document. The type appears selected within a rectangle. If desired, scale the type by dragging the handles at the corners of the rectangle. To place the type, position the pointer inside the rectangle and click to place the type. To deselect the type, choose Select→None (⌘-D).

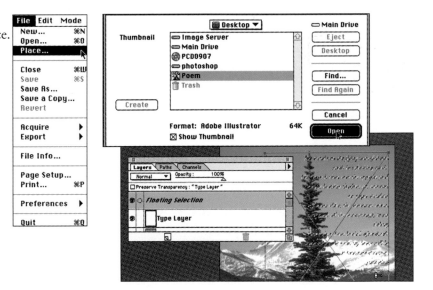

4 | Edit the Type

When the type has been scaled, you can manipulate it without affecting any underlying pixels. If you don't like the results of your editing, delete the type and reimport it from the original application. If your type requires extensive editing, return to the drawing program, edit the type, and then place it again in Photoshop.

Working with Layers *Adjusting the Color of Placed Images*

Bill Morse

Comments

Placing imported artwork on individual layers enables you to manipulate the artwork on each layer without globally affecting the document. For example, you can correct or adjust the color of artwork on a single layer without affecting the color of artwork on other layers.

Studio Usage

When creating composite images, it is helpful to place various elements of the artwork on individual layers so that adjustments can be made to individual pieces of artwork. In this example, artwork created in other programs is imported onto individual layers, and then the color is adjusted on each layer. This technique enables you to experiment with several options prior to finalizing an illustration.

Related Techniques

Defining Layers   50

EPS   122

1 **Create a New Layer**

Create and name a new layer by choosing New Layer from the Layers palette submenu or by clicking the page icon at the bottom of the Layers palette.

2 **Place the Image**

Choose File→Place, locate and select the EPS file you want to import, and then click Open to place the EPS file in the Photoshop document. The artwork is placed onto the selected layer. Position the artwork on the layer by dragging the rectangular box surrounding the artwork. Click in the center of the rectangle to "drop" the artwork on the layer. The rectangle disappears, but the artwork remains selected. Deselect the artwork by choosing Select→None (⌘-D).

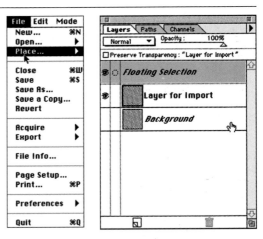

3 **Adjust the Color of the Artwork**

Choose Image→Adjust→Hue/Saturation. Drag the sliders to adjust the hue, saturation, and lightness of the artwork. (The Hue and Saturation sliders do not affect black or white artwork. If you want to change the hue of black or white artwork, either apply a color to the artwork before importing it, or select the area within Photoshop and choose a color from the Paint swatches.)

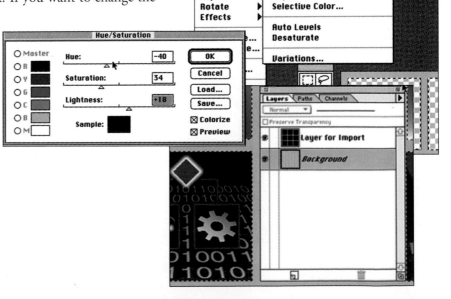

Oko & Mano, Inc.

Comments

If you work with documents containing several layers, you've probably noticed that any changes you make to color values affect only the active layer. This tip shows you how to make global adjustments to layered documents.

Studio Usage

If you've created a document using multiple layers and the document requires a global adjustment, this technique allows you to save time by simultaneously affecting all the layers.

Related Techniques

Defining Layers   50

Type on Layers   53

Curves 1, 2   81, 82

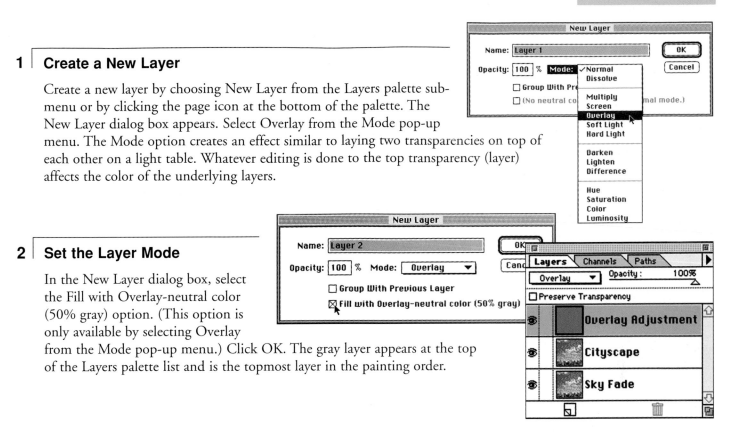

1 | Create a New Layer

Create a new layer by choosing New Layer from the Layers palette sub-menu or by clicking the page icon at the bottom of the palette. The New Layer dialog box appears. Select Overlay from the Mode pop-up menu. The Mode option creates an effect similar to laying two transparencies on top of each other on a light table. Whatever editing is done to the top transparency (layer) affects the color of the underlying layers.

2 | Set the Layer Mode

In the New Layer dialog box, select the Fill with Overlay-neutral color (50% gray) option. (This option is only available by selecting Overlay from the Mode pop-up menu.) Click OK. The gray layer appears at the top of the Layers palette list and is the topmost layer in the painting order.

3 | Make Color Adjustments

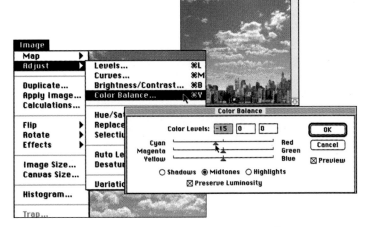

With the neutral gray layer selected, choose Image→Adjust→Color Balance. The Color Balance dialog box appears. Drag the sliders to adjust the overlay color, which affects the various colors on all the underlying layers. To better understand how the overlay effect works, turn off the overlay layer by clicking the eye icon in the left column next to the layer—the color adjustment vanishes on all the under-lying layers. Click the eye icon again to display the overlay layer, which reapplies the color adjustment to the underlying layers. Currently, this is the only way to adjust all the layers in a single image without merg-ing or flattening the document.

4 | Editing Overlay Adjustments

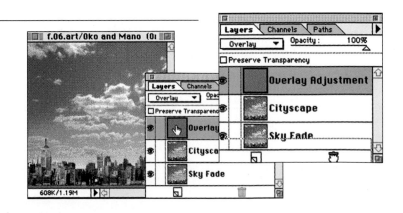

While the Color Balance dialog box is open, hold down the Option key and click Reset to return to the original neutral-gray settings. If you have exit-ed the dialog box and aren't satisfied with the results, delete the Overlay layer by dragging the layer to the Trash icon at the bottom of the Layers process and then start again.

Scott Kelly, Mac Today Magazine

Comments

Photoshop provides a Lens Flare filter that simulates the effect of shining a bright light into a camera lens. The Lens Flare filter is one of the Rendering filters, which you can learn more about in the Painting Tips section of this book.

Studio Usage

There are numerous ways to generate soft, round, glowing effects using the lighting effects in Adobe Photoshop. This technique creates a lighting effect on a separate layer so that it can be edited independently of the artwork on other layers.

Note: *Lens Flare only works in RGB mode.*

Related Techniques

Creating Lighting Effects   22

Defining Layers   50

Creating Drop Shadows   51

Brightness and Contrast   80

1 | Create a Layer for the Lens Flare

Create a new layer by choosing New Layer from the Layers palette sub-menu or by clicking the page icon at the bottom of the Layers palette.

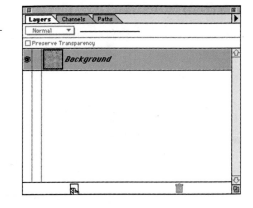

2 | Set the Layer Mode

Enter a name for the layer; then choose Screen from the Mode pop-up menu. Select the Fill with Screen-neutral color (black) option, which is available only by choosing Screen from the Mode menu. Click OK.

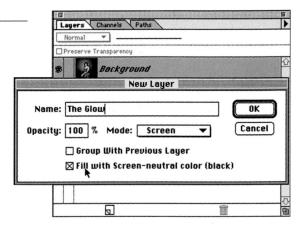

3 | Apply the Lens Flare

Choose Filter→Render→Lens Flare. The Lens Flare dialog box appears. Choose a lens type and then drag within the black preview area to position the center point of the flare. If desired, adjust the brightness of the flare; then click OK to apply the flare to the layer. You can move the flare by selecting the Move tool from the toolbox and dragging on the layer.

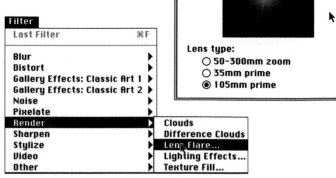

Working with Layers *Grouping, Merging, and Flattening Layers*

Karin Schminke, Unique Editions™

Comments

The more you learn about how layers work, the more effectively you can use them in creating effects for your artwork. One of the most important aspects of working with layered documents is the ability to group, merge, and flatten layers to organize the artwork and to reduce the file size of the final document.

Studio Usage

Documents composed of layers are saved in Photoshop 3.0 format. You can group the layers you want to manipulate as a single layer. If you want to use your Photoshop artwork in other programs, you must first *flatten*, or combine, all the layers. In addition, each layer in a document increases the file size by 100 percent, so you will want to flatten the layers in a document to reduce the final file size when the artwork has been completed.

Related Techniques

Defining Layers   50

Creating a Rainbow Effect   52

Global Color Adjustments   55

1 | Open a Layered Document

Open an image that contains multiple layers. If you don't have an image that contains more than two layers, open an existing document and create two new layers with which to work.

Tip: *To bypass the New Layer dialog box when creating a new layer, hold down the Option key and click the page icon at the bottom of the Layers palette.*

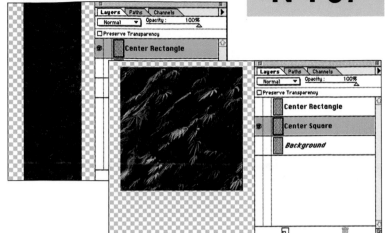

2 | To Group Layers

When you want to manipulate several layers as a single layer, Adobe Photoshop gives you the ability to group them. For example, after several layers are grouped, you can use the Move tool to simultaneously move an object on all the grouped layers. To create a group of layers, select one layer and then click the column to the right of the eye icon next to all the layers that you want to include in the group. After you group layers, a four-pointed arrow icon appears in the column next to each layer included in the group.

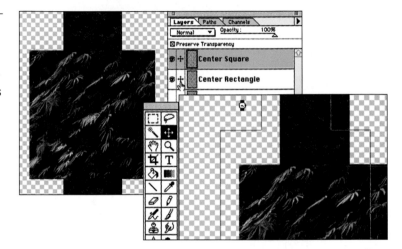

3 | To Merge Layers

Create a group of two or more layers and then choose Merge Layers from the Layers palette submenu. The grouped layers are now merged into a single layer.

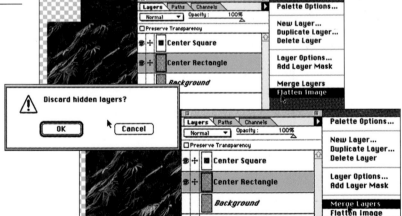

4 | To Flatten an Image

After you have completed an image and no longer need to adjust individual elements within the artwork, choose Flatten Image from the Layers palette submenu. Flattening images compresses all the layers into a single layer, thus reducing the file size. If your artwork may need future adjustment, save a copy of the file with the layers intact on an external device.

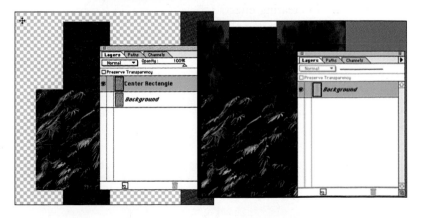

Rich Lovato

Comments

You can save selections so that you don't have to reselect an area every time you want to work with it. When you save a selection, it is automatically stored in a channel. (Think of a channel as a holding area for the selection.) Channels are also used to store color information about images. For example, in an RGB image, each color (red, green, and blue) is stored in a separate channel.

Studio Usage

The ability to create and save intricate selections is an extremely important skill to develop when working with Photoshop. You will save a tremendous amount of time by saving selections. Each document can contain up to 24 channels.

Related Techniques

Channel Selection Method   60

Creating a Vignette Mask   62

Importing Custom Masks   63

1 | Create a Selection

Click a selection tool in the toolbox; then create a selection marquee using the selection tools.

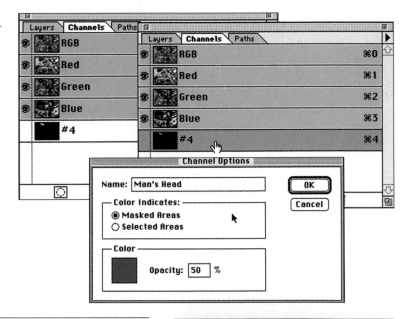

2 | To Save the Selection

With the selection still active, choose Select→Save Selection. The Save Selection dialog box appears. Click OK. The selection is saved in a channel, which can be thought of as a storage area.

Tip: Because saving selections is one of the most common tasks in Photoshop, you may want to place the Save Selection command in your Commands Palette.

3 | To View and Name a Channel

Select the Channels palette tab and scroll to the bottom of the palette. A new channel, labeled #4, has been added to the palette. A thumbnail preview displays how your selection looks in the channel. Each time you create a new channel, a number is assigned to it. As you add channels, the numbers are assigned in ascending order. To name a channel, double-click the numbered channel to select the Channel Options dialog box. Enter a name for the channel and then click OK.

4 | To Load a Selection

Click the #0 channel at the top of the Channels palette to display the entire image. This channel, called the *composite channel*, displays all the color channels simultaneously. Choose Load Selection from the Select menu. The Load Selection dialog box appears. The Channel pop-up menu contains a list of all the channels in the document. Choose the desired channel from the pop-up menu and then click OK. The selection you created and saved appears in the document. Each time you edit a selection in the document, be sure to choose Select→Save Selection to save the most recent version of the selection.

Karin Schminke, Unique Editions™

Comments

In addition to using channels to save selections, there are many other ways to use channels to create various effects in your documents. However, because each channel you add to a document increases the file size, it's important to know how to manage channels for the best results.

Studio Usage

You can use channels to create drop shadows, glowing effects, and fade outs. When working with very large documents, you will want to delete unused channels after you've used them in order to reduce the overall file size. For example, if you have used a channel to create a drop shadow, you can delete the channel after you have applied the drop shadow to the image.

Related Techniques

Saving Selections   58

Channel Selection
    Method   60

1 | To Create a New Channel

Choose New Channel from the Channels palette submenu or click the page icon at the bottom of the Channels palette. The Channel Options dialog box appears. Enter a name for the channel and then enter a color, if desired. Click OK. The new channel appears in the Channels palette and in the document window. Channels are always displayed in black and white in the Channels palette and when displayed individually.

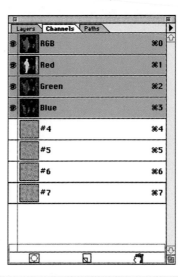

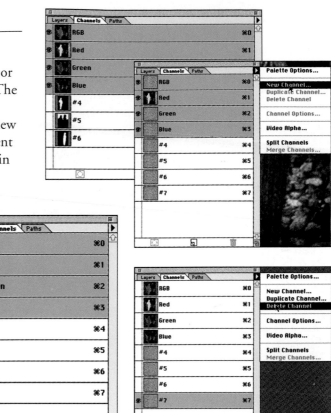

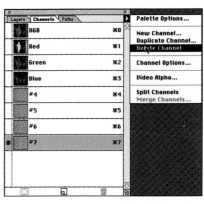

2 | To Delete a Channel

Drag the newly created channel to the trash icon found on the lower right side of the Channels palette. It disappears from the list. You can also choose to delete it from the pop-up menu the same way you add a new channel. Be sure, however, that the correct channel is selected at the time you choose this deletion menu option.

3 | To Copy a Channel

You can drag an individual channel to the new channel icon (the one with the folded corner) to make a copy of an individual channel. You can also drag channels around so that they are layered exactly as you want them to be.

4 | To Load a Selection

Because selection areas are created to either protect or isolate individual portions of an image, you often have to load a specific channel (selection). Click on the first channel (or press ⌘-0). Drag the desired channel to the dotted circle icon (the first in the bottom row of icons on the Channels palette). The selection automatically loads into the current window.

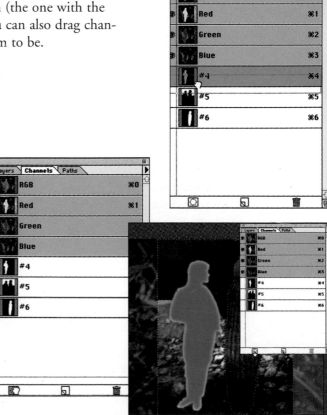

Bonny Lhotka

Comments

You can use a channel to isolate and select complex areas of an image. By selecting the channel containing the most contrast, you can then turn the contents of the channel into a selection.

Studio Usage

Some images are extremely difficult to select due to their complexity or to their proximity to other objects. This technique can often be used to isolate objects that are difficult to select—for example, hair or bubbles.

Related Techniques

The Magic Wand Tool   8

The Color Range Command   9

Managing Channels   59

1 | Select the Channel with the Most Contrast

Open an image that contains a complex area that you want to select. Click the Channels tab to select the Channels palette; then click the channel that displays the highest contrast of the object that you want to select. (In this example, the red channel contains the most contrast.)

2 | Copy the Channel

Copy the selected channel, either by choosing New Channel from the Channels palette or by dragging the selected channel to the page icon at the bottom of the Channels palette. The New Channel dialog box appears. Name the channel *Selection* and then click OK. The Selection channel appears in the document window and at the bottom of the Channels palette.

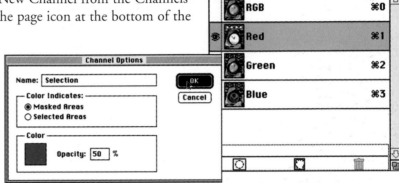

3 | Adjust the Channel

Choose Image→Adjust→Levels (⌘-L) to open the Levels dialog box. Drag the sliders to the right to compress the tones and to darken the image. Watch the image and click OK when you have the best isolation of the desired object.

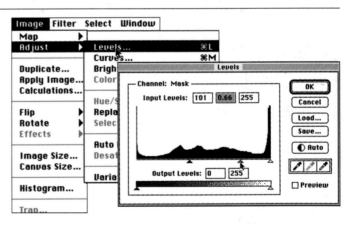

4 | Touch Up and Load the Selection

Using the Brush tool and black as the foreground color, paint over any areas that you want to eliminate from the selection. (Black makes an area completely opaque, eliminating it from the selection area.) Click the RGB channel to display the entire image and then drag the Selection channel onto the dotted circle icon at the bottom of the Channels palette. The desired selection appears in the document window, which then can be edited like any selection.

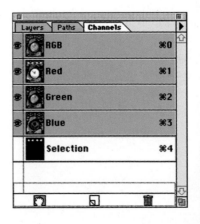

Working with Channels *Creating a Fade Effect*

Gary Popysick

Comments

To create an image that gradually fades over the length of the selection, you can create a gradient in a channel. You can then apply the selection from the channel to the image. This technique can be used with entire images or with selected objects in an image.

Studio Usage

This technique works well anywhere you want to create a shadow or fading effect over the length of the selection. The artwork in this example uses the technique to create the look of a soft reflection.

Related Techniques

Saving Selections   10

Creating Simple Gradients   23

Canvas Size   66

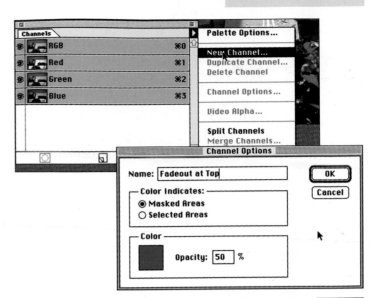

1 | Create a New Channel

Create a new channel by choosing New Channel from the Channels palette submenu or by clicking the page icon at the bottom of the Channels palette. The Channel Options dialog box appears. Enter a name for the channel and click OK. The solid black channel appears in the Channels palette.

2 | Create the Fade Effect

Black in a channel indicates an opacity level of 100%; white indicates complete transparency; and shades of gray indicate a percentage of opacity. To create a fading effect, use the Gradient tool to create a gradual transition from black to white (completely opaque to completely transparent). Select the Gradient tool and drag from the bottom to the top of the channel window. The channel is filled with a black-to-white gradient.

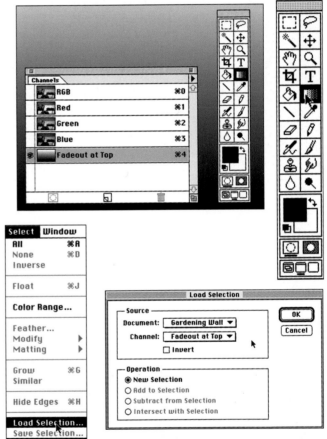

3 | Load the Selection

In order to apply the fading effect to the image, you must load the gradient selection from the channel into the document. Click the RGB channel (⌘-0 [zero]) to display the entire image, called the *composite image*. Choose Select→Load Selection. Select the channel name from the Channel pop-up menu. Click OK to load the selection.

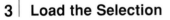

4 | Apply the Fade

Make sure that the Background color is set to white in the tools palette and then press the Delete key. Where the gradient in the channel was previously black, the white background color is applied at 100% opacity. Where the gradient was white, the area is now completely transparent or filled with 0% of the white background color. Where the gradient changed to various gray levels, the white background color is applied at various percentages of opacity. You can add color, depth, and contrast to an image by choosing a color other than white as the background color and then pressing the Delete key.

Sanjay Kothari

Comments

In traditional graphic arts, an illustration that gradually fades until it blends into the unprinted paper is called a *vignette*. When working with digital images, the same technique is called feathering, which is accomplished creating a selection and defining the amount of feathering (softness) you want applied around the selection.

Studio Usage

Before computers provided a way to soften the edges around images, a soft vignette was created using an airbrush. You can use Photoshop's feathering function for any number of effects: the glow of a lamp, the edge of a shadow, the clouds in the sky, and so on.

Related Techniques

Creating Lighting Effects   22

Defining Layers   50

Using Channels to
Create Shadows   64

1 | Create a New Channel

Open a document for which you want to create a vignette. Create a new channel by clicking the New Channel icon at the bottom of the Channels palette. Enter the name Vignette (or another desired name) in the Channel Options dialog box and click OK. The new channel is displayed in the document window and also appears at the bottom of the Channels palette.

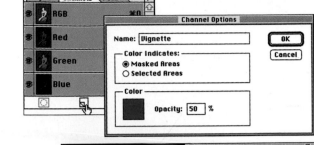
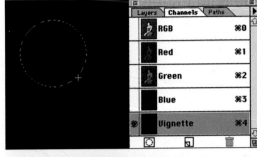

2 | Create a Selection

Select the Elliptical marquee tool from the toolbox; then hold down the Shift key and drag to create a circular selection in the new channel. (Holding down the Shift key constrains the selection marquee to a circle.)

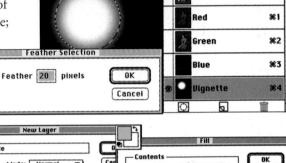

3 | Feather the Selection

With the selection still active, choose Select→Feather, enter a value of 20 pixels in the Feather Radius field, and then click OK. Press Delete; 10 pixels on either side of the selection marquee are softened. Deselect by choosing Select→None (⌘-D) and then click the composite channel in the Channels palette to display the entire image.

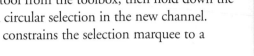

4 | Create a Layer and Load the Selection

After you've created the vignette in the channel, it's a good idea to create a new layer for the vignette so that it can be edited independently of the other parts of the image. Choose Window→Palettes→Show Layers and click the new layer icon at the bottom of the palette. Enter a name for the layer and then click OK. The new layer appears at the top of the layers palette. With the layer selected, choose Select→Load Select→Vignette (or other name you defined) and click OK. The selection marquee appears in the document window. Now you must apply a color to the vignette selection to make it visible. Choose a foreground color; then choose

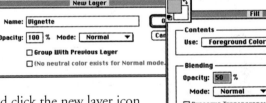
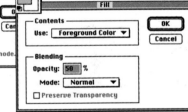

5 | Rearrange the Vignette Layer

At this point, the vignette appears on top of the image because it is positioned on the frontmost layer at the top of the layers palette. Drag the vignette layer downward in the layers palette to reposition it. If desired, select the Move tool and drag to move the vignette.

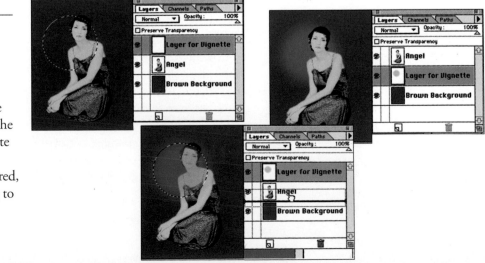

Jacqueline Comstock

Comments

Although Photoshop provides many tools to assist in developing masks, there are times when it is easier to create the basis or outline of the mask in a drawing program and then import the outline for the mask into a channel.

Studio Usage

Text shapes are an example of mask shapes that you might want to create in a dedicated illustration program. Any shape that contains complex elements can be created in an illustration program and then imported into a channel. After the illustration has been placed in a channel, it can be loaded like any other selection and then edited with the Photoshop tools.

Related Techniques

Painting Modes   42-49

Managing Channels   59

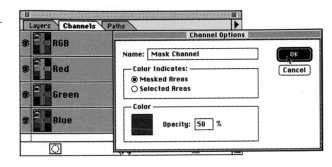

1 │ Create a Channel for the Mask

Choose Window→Palettes→Show Channels and click the new channel icon at the bottom of the palette to create a new channel. In the Channel Options dialog box, enter a name for the channel and then click OK. You'll import the artwork into this channel, which can then be loaded as a selection in the document. (If you created, or plan to create, the mask artwork in black, choose the Selected Areas option from the Color Indicates area of the Channel Options dialog box.)

2 │ Create the EPS Artwork

Create the artwork for the mask in a drawing program. (You can use any drawing program that allows you to save artwork in EPS format.) The artwork in this example was created in Adobe Illustrator. Save the document in EPS file format.

3 │ Import the Artwork

Select the channel you created for the mask by clicking it in the Channels palette. Choose File→Place, locate the EPS file from the file list, and then click OK. The imported image appears within a rectangular boundary in the channel. Click within the border of the rectangle to place the artwork in the channel; the rectangular border disappears, but the artwork remains selected. If desired, choose a Selection tool and drag to reposition the artwork; then choose Select→None to deselect all the artwork. Depending on the colors you used to create the artwork, it appears in the channel as black, white, or in shades of gray.

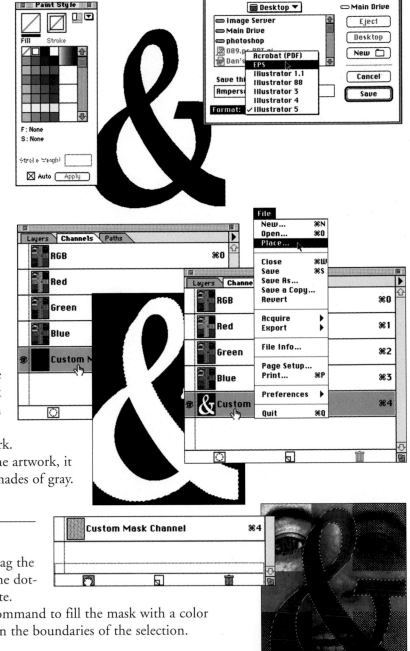

4 │ Load the Mask as a Selection

To load the selection mask onto the image, drag the mask channel onto the rectangle containing the dotted circle at the bottom of the Channels palette.
After the mask is loaded, use the Edit→Fill command to fill the mask with a color or use any of the painting tools to paint within the boundaries of the selection.

Denise Salles

Comments

You can use channels to create soft, realistic shadows for objects. In this example, the artwork was created in Adobe Illustrator and placed in Photoshop.

Studio Usage

This technique can be used to create a shadow for any selected area. The steps are simple: create and save the selection, reposition the selection where you want the shadow to appear, apply feathering to the selection, create a separate layer for the selection, load and fill the selection, and finally, reposition the layer to position the shadow behind the object.

Related Techniques

Defining Layers   50

Managing Channels   59

Creating a Vignette Mask   62

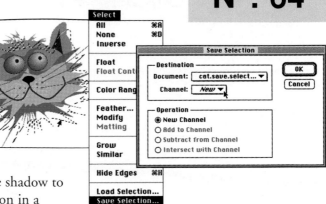

1 | Create the Shadow Selection

Start with an image in RGB mode; then select the desired area or object using a selection tool. (Make sure that any open areas, for example, the middle portion of the letter A, are included in the selection.) With the selection tool still active, hold down the Command and Option keys and drag to reposition the selection marquee where you want the shadow to be applied. Choose Select→Save Selection to save the selection in a channel. (In an RGB image, the default channel name in which the selection is saved is named #4.)

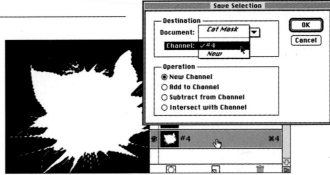

2 | Feather the Selection

With the selection still active, open the Channels palette. The new channel appears at the bottom of the Channels palette. Click the channel in the Channels palette to display the channel in the document window. Choose Select→Feather, enter a value in the dialog box, and then click OK. The higher the value you enter in the Feather dialog box, the softer the shadow around the selection area will be. Choose Select→Save Selection, choose #4 (the default channel name) from the Channel pop-up menu, and click OK. The feathering is applied to the selection in the channel. Click the RGB channel to return to the composite image and choose Select→None (⌘-D) to deselect everything.

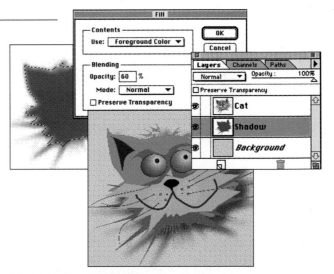

3 | Create a Layer for the Shadow

Open the Layers palette and click the new layer icon at the bottom of the palette. When the New Layer dialog box appears, enter a name for the layer and click OK. With the new layer active in the Layers palette, choose Select→Load Selection. Select the #4 channel (the default channel name) from the Channel pop-up menu; click OK. Choose Edit→Fill, enter the desired percentage of the fill color, and then click OK to apply the color to the shadow selection.

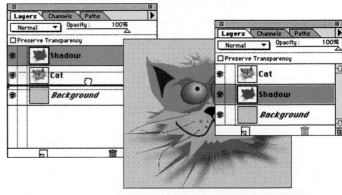

4 | Reposition the Shadow Layer

To position the shadow behind the object, drag the shadow layer below the object layer in the Layers palette. When a black line appears below the object layer, release the mouse button to position the shadow layer behind the object.

Mitchell Anthony, MADworks®

Comments

File size is proportional to image size and resolution. For example, the file size for a 4×5 image with a resolution of 200 ppi is the same as the file size for an 8×10 image with a resolution of 100 ppi. The file size for a 4×5 image with a resolution of 200 ppi is four times the file size of a 4×5 image with a resolution of 100 ppi. Your goal is to create the smallest possible file that has the dimensions and resolution you need. (Bigger files require more RAM and disk space, and they take longer to process and print.)

Studio Usage

Resizing an image changes the dimensions and can affect the image resolution and file size. When you reduce an image, you either keep the same resolution and reduce the file size, or you keep the same file size and increase the resolution. The image quality is not changed and may even be slightly improved. When you enlarge an image, you either keep the same resolution and increase the file size, or you keep the same file size and reduce the resolution. Enlarging an image often degrades the image quality. If you need to enlarge an image more than 150%, rescan instead of resizing.

Related Techniques

Canvas Size   66

Resolution and Screen
Frequency Requirements   68

Sharpen Filters   73

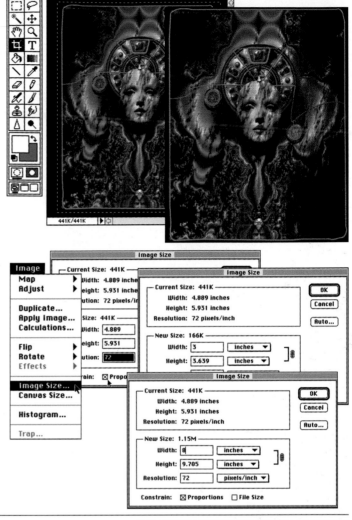

1 | Crop the Image

Choose File→Open to open an image. Check the file size in the box at the lower-left of the document window (this file is 441K). When you crop an image, some pixels are eliminated. In most cases, you don't change the resolution (although the Cropping Tool Options palette does enable you to crop to a specific size and resolution). Select the Cropping tool and drag a marquee around the area you want to keep. Move inside the selected area until you see the scissors icon and then click. Notice that the file size is reduced to 375 K. Choose Edit→Undo Crop or press [⌘-Z] to return to the original image size.

2 | Resize without Changing the Resolution

Choose Image→Image Size. In the Image Size dialog box, make sure that the Proportions option is selected and enter 3 in the Width box. The Height automatically changes to 3.639 and the Resolution stays at 72 ppi. The file size is reduced to 166 K (Photoshop eliminates some pixels). Enter 8 in the Width box. The Height changes to 9.705 and the Resolution stays at 72 ppi. The file size increases to 1.15 MB (Photoshop manufactures some pixels). Reducing an image doesn't usually affect the image quality; enlarging an image can make it appear out of focus.

3 | Resize Changing the Proportions

Deselect the Proportions option. When this option is off, the height, width, and resolution settings are independent of one another. Enter a different value in the Width or Height box and leave the resolution at 72. You can see that the other dimension does not change and the file size increases. There are a few instances when you might want to distort an image as you resize. This can be useful for special effects or for generating film for flexographic package or label printing, which require slightly distorted images to reproduce correctly.

4 | Resize Changing the Resolution

Select Proportions again and then select the File Size option. This option keeps the file size constant when you change the dimensions (the file always contains the same number of pixels). Enter 3 in the Width box. The height changes and the resolution jumps to 117.333 ppi. Photoshop packs the pixels closer together to fit them in the smaller space—this increases the resolution. Enter 8 in the Width box. The height changes and the resolution drops to 44 ppi. Photoshop spreads out the pixels to fit the larger space—this decreases the resolution. For the best image quality, avoid increasing the resolution in Photoshop.

Resolution *Canvas Size*

Sanjay Kothari

Comments

Each Photoshop document sits on an imaginary canvas. In most cases, the canvas is the same size as the image and you don't see it. The Canvas Size command lets you scale this imaginary canvas independently of the image.

Studio Usage

When you increase the canvas, Photoshop surrounds the image with the canvas, which appears in the current background color. If you reduce the canvas, you crop the image. You might need to increase the canvas to enlarge the working space when you're creating composite images or when you want text to stand out on a different color or texture.

Related Techniques

Resolution
and Image Size   65

Resolution and Screen
Frequency Requirements   68

1 | Specify the Final Image Resolution

Choose File→Open and open the image you want to combine with other elements. Select Image→Image Size and enter the resolution you need for the *final* image. Click OK. The image size remains the same, but the resolution and file size decreases.

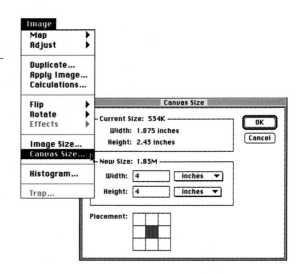

2 | Increase the Canvas Size

Choose Image→Canvas Size. In the Canvas Size dialog box, enter the dimensions of the final image.

3 | Determine the Placement of the Existing Image

By default, the image is centered in the new canvas. The Placement option in the Canvas Size dialog box lets you determine where the canvas should be added. In this instance, you want the canvas to appear below and to the right of the image. Click the upper-left box in the Placement grid. The gray box indicates where the image will appear in relation to the new canvas. Alternately, you can add the canvas while leaving the image in the center and then use the Move tool to drag the image to its new location.

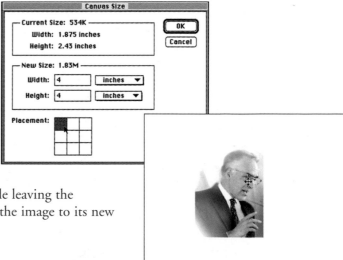

Resolution *JPEG*

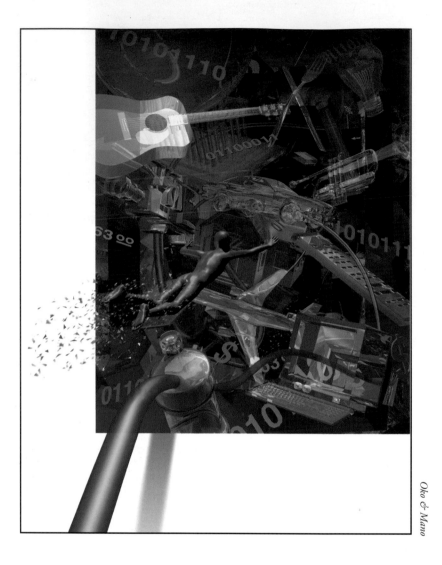

Oko & Mano

Comments

JPEG is a compression standard developed by the Joint Photographic Electronic Group. Increasingly, JPEG is becoming more accepted as a standard format for high-quality color output. As one of Photoshop's file formats, JPEG could have been included in the "File Formats" section of this book. Since JPEG compression can have a dramatic impact on image quality; however, it is included in this resolution section instead.

Studio Usage

When you save using JPEG, you can choose from four quality settings. The lower the quality, the less space the file occupies. JPEG is "lossy" compression, which means that after an image is compressed, it is not identical to the original image when decompressed (some data is lost). In most cases, if you use the Maximum quality option, the difference between the original and decompressed image is indistinguishable.

Because JPEG compression can cause a slight sharpening of some pixels, save your file in JPEG format before you perform final retouching.

Related Techniques

Resolution and Screen Frequency Requirements 68

Photoshop 3.0 File Format 121

EPS 122

DCS (Desktop Color Separations) 123

1 | Open a Large File

Choose File→Open and open a large file, saved in some format other than JPEG. This example is a 22 MB, TIFF file. Choose Image→Image Size. Compare the Current Size value in the Image Size dialog box with the file size in the Finder. You can see that the "virtual" file size (the amount of RAM occupied by the file when it's opened) is the same as the disk space required to store an uncompressed version of the file.

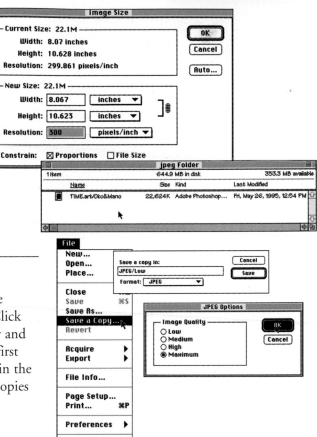

2 | Save a Copy in JPEG Format

Choose File→Save a Copy. In the Save dialog box, name the file JPEG/Low and choose JPEG from the Format pop-up menu. Click Save. In the JPEG Options dialog box, select Low image quality and then click OK. Close the file. Save two more copies of the file, first selecting Medium quality and then selecting Maximum quality in the JPEG Options dialog box. When you're done, you'll have four copies of the file—the original and the three compressed files.

3 | Crop the Original Image

Choose File→Open and open the original file one more time. Select the Cropping tool. Drag a marquee around a small, but identifiable, section of the original image and crop it at full resolution. Displaying a cropped portion of the original file will reduce the memory requirements on your system as you compare the original to the compressed images.

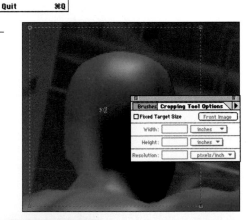

4 | Compare the Image Quality

Return to the Finder and compare the file sizes. In this case, the file size reduction ranges from around 40 times smaller (at the Low and Medium settings) to 10 times smaller at the Maximum setting. Choose File→Open and select the JPEG/Low file. Zoom in on both files. Arrange the windows so that you can compare the two images. The Low option file shows a noticeable loss of quality and a recognizable pattern created by the compression. Open and compare the Medium version and the Maximum version to the cropped image. The Maximum quality file looks identical to the original image.

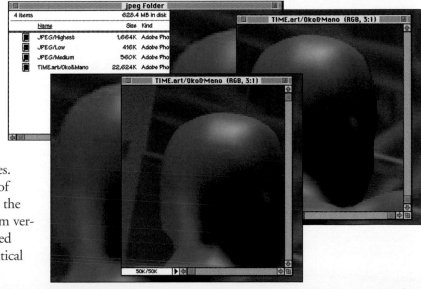

Resolution *Resolution and Screen Frequency Requirements*

DICKSON

Ellie Dickson

Comments

The image resolution you need is determined by how you're going to use the image. If the image will be displayed on a monitor (for example, as part of a multimedia CD-ROM or on the World Wide Web), then a resolution of 72 ppi is adequate. Most monitors can't display at resolutions higher than 72 ppi (pixels per inch), so higher resolution files don't improve image quality; they only needlessly increase file size. The situation is different when you're going to print the image using a halftone screen. Then you need higher resolutions to accommodate the screen frequency of the halftone screen used to print the image.

Studio Usage

Most printing professionals suggest that you provide between 1.5 to 2 times the number of pixels per inch for every dot on the halftone screen. This means that if you're printing with a screen frequency of 100 lpi (lines per inch), you need an image resolution of 150 to 200 ppi. You should avoid enlarging an image or increasing its resolution in Photoshop. Enlarging an image (and simultaneously reducing the resolution or forcing Photoshop to add pixels to maintain the same resolution) always results in a loss of quality. Increasing resolution also requires Photoshop to create pixels and deteriorates the image.

Related Techniques

Resolution and Image Size   65

Canvas Size   66

1 | Check the Image Size

Choose File→Open to open an image. Choose Image→Image Size. The Image Size dialog box tells you the current file size, height, width, and resolution of the image. The file size is proportional to the image resolution. For example, the file size of a 4-by-5 image with a resolution of 200 ppi is four times the size of a 4-by-5 image with a resolution of 100 ppi. In this example, the image is approximately 31 inches by 20 inches with a resolution of 72 ppi. The file size is 9.7 megabytes.

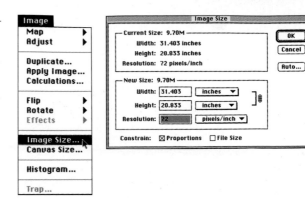

2 | Determine the Resolution Automatically

Click the Auto button in the dialog box. The Auto Resolution dialog box appears, containing the line screen value for the current size and resolution settings. In the Auto Resolution dialog box, enter 150 in the Screen text box and click the Good option. A quality setting of Good calculates the needed resolution by multiplying 1.5 times the screen frequency (1.5 times 150), resulting in an image resolution of 225 ppi. With an image this large, a resolution of 225 ppi results in a file size of almost 95 megabytes! Do not click OK to change the image size.

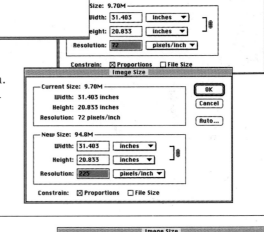

3 | Reduce the Image Size

Most page layouts do not require an image this large. Resize the image by entering 6 in the Width text box (make sure the Proportions option is selected to maintain the image ratio and the File Size option is deselected to maintain the current resolution). Reducing the image size while keeping the resolution at 225 reduces the file size to a manageable 3.46 megabytes. Press Option and click the Cancel button (which now reads Reset) to return to the original image dimensions.

4 | Determine the Correct Scan Size

You can use the Image Size dialog box as a calculator to determine which scan size you need to get the desired resolution. Deselect the Proportions option at the bottom of the dialog box. Suppose that you want to print using a 150 lpi halftone screen, but you also want to produce top-quality output. To accomplish this, use a screen frequency ratio of 2:1 to determine the image resolution. (When you choose Best Quality in the Auto Resolution dialog box, Photoshop automatically uses a 2:1 ratio.) Two times 150 equals a resolution of 300 ppi. Enter 300 in the Resolution text box and select Proportions again. Photoshop calculates that the scan size should be 7.537 by 5 to produce a 300 ppi image.

Victor Bruha, Frog Publications

Comments

The Macintosh Operating System uses small digital images for system icons. You can use any digital image to create your own disk, folder, application, or document icon.

Studio Usage

Many designers use this technique to create unique icons for distribution of sample or demo disks, digital résumés, and other items. You can also customize icons on your own desktop, making it easier (and more fun) to identify important projects and documents.

Related Techniques

Resolution and Image Size   65

Canvas Size   66

1 | Size the Canvas

Open the image you want to use for the icon. Choose Image→Canvas Size. If necessary, adjust the canvas size until the image is square. Allow some extra room around the edge of the image.

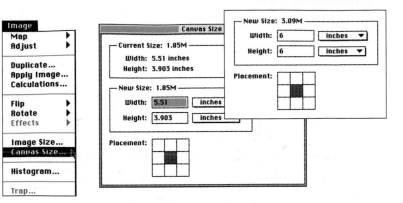

2 | Crop the Image

Double-click the Cropping tool. In the Cropping Tool Options palette, select Fixed Target Size. Set the target to a width and height of 32 pixels and a resolution of 72 ppi. Crop the image. If necessary, choose Image→Adjust→Brightness and Contrast or press ⌘-B to adjust the image's tonal range and density. Zoom in to check the results. Choose Select→Select All or press ⌘-A to select the entire image. Choose File→Copy or press ⌘-C to copy the image to the Clipboard.

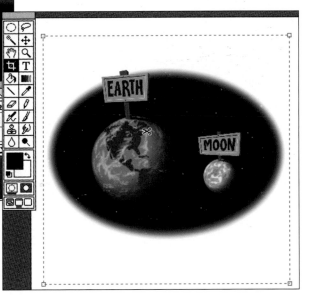

3 | Assign the Icon to an Object

Return to the Finder and select the object whose icon you want to replace. This example replaces the icon for the Client Folder. Choose File→Get Info or press ⌘-I. Press the Tab key to select the icon in the small box in the upper-left corner of the Info dialog box. Choose Edit→Paste or press ⌘-V to paste the icon into position. Close the Info dialog box. If necessary, choose View→By Icon. The new icon appears in the Finder.

Richard Hommell

Comments

Scratches and flaws often come from damaged film or prints that have been processed or stored improperly. Flaws can also be part of the original subject, as is the case of the old sailboat used in this technique. The boat in this image was retouched and then filtered by using the Facet filter to achieve an oil-painting look.

Studio Usage

There are several ways to clean up an image, and you'll often need to use a variety of techniques to correct a single image. The use of Photoshop's tools enables you to remove flaws, scratches, logos, unwanted objects—even people. In fact, you'll be amazed at the tricks you can play by substituting one reality for another.

Related Techniques

Custom Brushes   16

Curves 1, 2   81, 82

1 | Adjust the Image Before Retouching

Open the image that you want to retouch. Choose Image→Adjust→Levels. The Levels command lets you adjust the brightness and contrast in an image. In this case, the black Input Levels triangle in the Levels dialog box was dragged to the right, increasing the shadows in the image (more pixels were mapped to a black value). You should always make tonal adjustments before you retouch an image. Making tonal adjustments after retouching sometimes makes a retouched area appear more obvious.

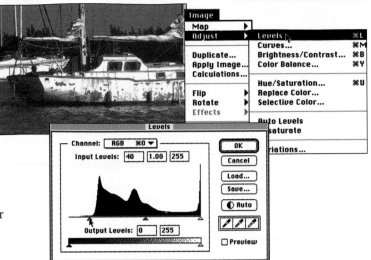

2 | Select the Area to Retouch

Using the selection tools, select the area or areas that you want to retouch. If the selections are difficult or complex, choose Select→Save Selection to store the selections in channels, so that you can reuse them if necessary.

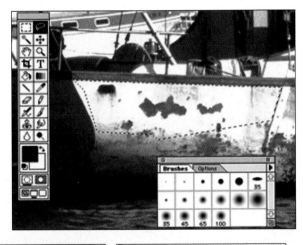

3 | Clone Small Areas

Double-click the Rubber Stamp tool and choose Clone (aligned) from the Option pop-up menu in the Rubber Stamp Options palette. Option-click to sample a point that's as similar as possible to the tonal value that you want to reproduce. Move the cursor along the edge of the flawed area and begin painting. Watch the crosshair that indicates your sampling point. Resample as necessary and paint in from several directions. Be careful of repetitive motion, which can cause unnatural repeating patterns of pixels or tones. Work in small areas and use short strokes, so that you can undo your last stroke easily.

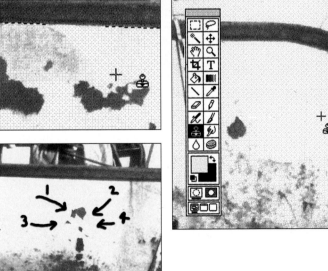

4 | Copy and Paste Large Areas

If you need to retouch a large area and have a clean, similar area to copy from, use the Marquee tool to make a rectangular or elliptical selection. Press Option and drag the selection over the damaged area. Pressing Option duplicates, rather than moves, the selection. Alternate between the Rubber Stamp tool and this copy-paste technique until you've removed all the flaws in the image.

Skip Gandy

Comments

The process of "cleaning" original or first-time scans is an extremely important retouching effort, and it can be quite time-consuming. The use of specialized filters often eliminates the need to use Photoshop's cloning and painting capabilities.

Studio Usage

Many images contain dust, scratches, or flaws introduced during scanning. When you have scans that need to be retouched, try using filters to make large-scale corrections before you concentrate on fine-tuning the small areas using Photoshop's tools.

Related Techniques

Scratches and Flaws 70

Unsharp Masking 74

The Dodge, Burn, and
Sponge Tools 75

Creating a Scale of Grays 78

1 | Make Tonal Adjustments

Open the image and choose Image→Adjust→Levels or Image→Adjust→Curves to adjust the tonal range of the image. Always make brightness and contrast corrections before retouching with painting tools or applying filters to an image.

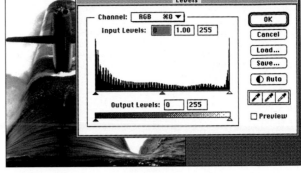

2 | Despeckle the Image

Choose Filter→Noise→Despeckle. The Despeckle filter finds the edges in an image (areas where significant color changes occur) and blurs all the selection except those edges. In effect, this removes noise while preserving detail. Blurring with the Despeckle command can help remove the lumps and speckles that low-end scanners often introduce during the scanning process

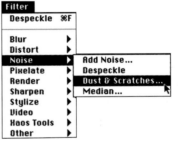

3 | Remove Dust and Scratches

Choose Filter→Noise→Dust & Scratches. In the Dust & Scratches dialog box, adjust the preview box zoom ratio and move around in the image until you can see the area that you want to correct. Drag the Threshold slider to 0 so that you can examine all the pixels in the image or selection. (The Threshold option determines the range of tones that will be blurred.) Drag the Radius slider to the right or left until the defects disappear. Stop when you have the smallest radius that eliminates the defects. Increase the threshold gradually until it's as high as possible without displaying the flaws.

4 | Finishing Touches

Zoom in and examine the image. Use the Rubber Stamp tool and an appropriate brush shape to fix any flaws or scratches that the filters missed. Wide, flat brushes (angled, vertical, or horizontal) work well for retouching.

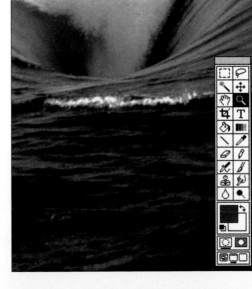

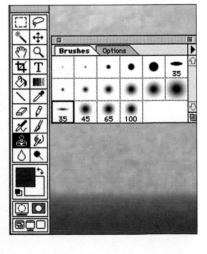

Retouching Images *Blur Filters*

Anne Farrell

Comments

Photoshop offers several filters and tools that let you blur all or part of an image. Often, a blurry image is associated with being out of focus, but blurring can add an artistic effect as well as effectively camouflaging imperfections in an image.

Studio Usage

In many cases, blurring actually improves an image by creating a subtle mix of pixels. Blurring can be useful, for example, to soften areas with too much contrast or to blend edge areas where pixels of two contrasting colors don't line up evenly.

Related Techniques

Custom Brushes   16

Embossed Type   106

1 | Apply the Blur Filter

Select the Zoom tool and drag a marquee around a small portion of the image. Choose Filter→Blur→Blur. The Blur filter eliminates noise in contrasting areas of the image and smoothes transitions between defined lines and shaded areas. This filter has a very slight effect, so you may not see any difference. Choose Edit→Undo Blur and Edit→Redo Blur to switch between the before and after versions of the selection. End by undoing the Blur filter, so that you're back at the original image. (If you accidentally apply the filter, choose File→Revert to get back to the unfil-

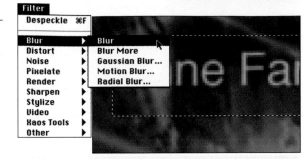
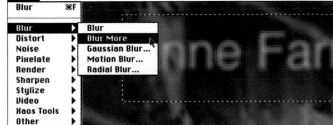

2 | Apply the Blur More Filter

Choose Filter→Blur→Blur More. The Blur More filter produces an effect that's about three to four times stronger than the Blur filter. Use the Undo command to move between the before and after versions. With this more intense blurring, you can see that the pixels are mixed at the edges of areas with sharp contrast or color change. The Blur filters can be used effectively with selections to smooth visible edges. Choose Edit→Undo Blur More to return to the original image.

3 | Try the Other Blur Filters

Choose Filter→Blur→Gaussian Blur to blur the pixels using a bell-shaped curve. This produces a soft, random blur. In the Gaussian Blur dialog box, adjust the Radius to see different effects. Click Cancel to close the box without applying the filter. Choose

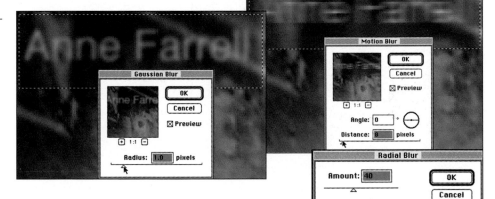

Filter→Blur→Motion Blur to blur the selection in a particular direction. In the Motion Blur dialog box, experiment with the Angle and Distance options. Click Cancel. Choose Filter→Blur→Radial Blur. In the Radial Blur dialog box, select Spin to blur along circular lines or Zoom to blur along radial lines. Vary the Amount setting. Click Cancel again.

4 | Using the Blur Tool

Double-click the Blur tool. If the tool does not look like a drop of water, choose Blur from the Tool pop-up menu in the Focus Tools Options palette. (When the tool looks like a triangle, it sharpens instead of blurs.) Select a brush and paint over a portion of your image. The Blur tool works well to soften overly-sharp edges and reduce detail within complex selections.

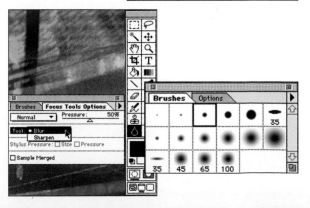

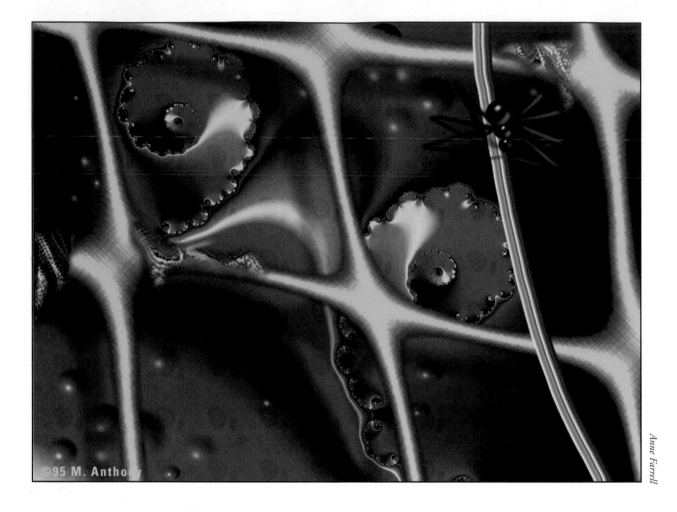

©95 M. Anthony

Anne Farrell

Comments

When you sharpen an image, the pixel values are intensified—often resulting in increased visibility of specific details and an emphasis on edges. However, sharpening can emphasize flaws or discontinuities in an image, so it must be used carefully.

Studio Usage

Sometimes an entire image needs to be sharpened, and in other cases only specific areas need increased focus or detail. Use the Sharpen filters with caution; if you shift the pixel values too much you may end up with unwanted contrast in certain areas.

Related Techniques

Using Filters to
Clean Images 71

Blur Filters 72

Unsharp Masking 74

1   Apply the Sharpen Filter

Select the Zoom tool and drag a marquee around a small portion of the image. Choose Filter→Sharpen→Sharpen. Like all the Sharpen filters, this filter intensifies the contrast between adjacent pixels. Look closely at an edge area to see the effect. If you can't see the change, choose Edit→Undo Sharpen and Edit→Redo Sharpen several times. This switches you between the sharpened and unsharpened versions of the selection. Finish by undoing the Sharpen filter so that you're looking at the unfiltered image. (If you accidentally apply the filter, choose File→Revert to get back to the original image.)

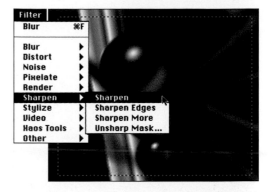

2   Apply the Sharpen More Filter

Choose Filter→Sharpen→Sharpen More. The Sharpen More filter produces an effect that's equivalent to multiple applications of the Sharpen filter. Use the Undo command to move between the before and after versions. The filter's effect produces a more visible shift in the darker pixels of the selection. Choose Edit→Undo Sharpen More to return to the original image.

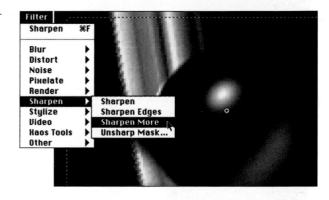

3   Apply the Sharpen Edges Filter

Choose Filter→Sharpen→Sharpen Edges. The Sharpen Edges filter preserves the overall smoothness of the image and changes only the areas with a wide jump in tonal values—the pixels that define edges. Zoom in on several edge areas and choose Edit→Undo Sharpen Edges and Edit→Redo Sharpen Edges to see the dramatic effect of this filter. Finish by choosing Edit→Undo Sharpen Edges to return to the original image.

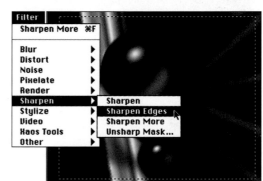

4   The Sharpen Tool

Double-click the Sharpen tool. If the tool does not resemble a triangle, choose Sharpen from the Tool pop-up menu in the Focus Tools Options palette. (When the tool looks like a drop of water, it blurs rather than sharpens.) Select a low pressure, select a brush, and begin painting. Increase the pressure until you get the effect you want. The Sharpen tool works well to sharpen soft edges and increase clarity and focus. It can also bring out hidden details in an image.

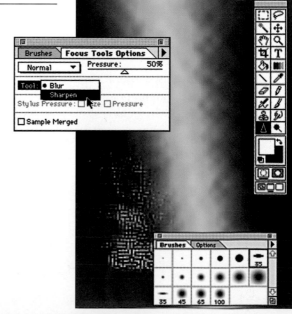

Richard Hommell

Comments

Unsharp masking is an unusual term for a sharpening technique, but that's exactly what this filter does. The name reflects the conventional method used to sharpen images on film—a blurred positive film (hence, the name unsharp) is sandwiched with a sharp negative film and the result is shot on high-contrast photographic paper. The resulting lighter and darker line on each side of an edge gives the edge added emphasis.

Studio Usage

When you purchase a scan produced on a high-end scanner, unsharp masking is often part of the scanning process. Make sure that you ask your vendor if the image has undergone unsharp masking. When you produce your own scans on a desktop scanner, you should run this filter on *all* your images. Since the Unsharp Mask filter includes all the capabilities of the Sharpen, Sharpen More, and Sharpen Edges filters, many professionals use this filter exclusively for all their sharpening needs.

Related Techniques

Scratches and Flaws 70

Blur Filters 72

Sharpen Filters 73

1 | Choose the Unsharp Mask Filter

Choose Filter→Sharpen→Unsharp Mask. Drag the Unsharp Mask dialog box to a location where you can see the part of the image you want to work on or watch the filter's effect in the dialog box preview window. As with all filters, you can save a lot of time by trying out a filter on a small representative section of the image—for example, areas with skin tones—before applying it to a larger area or the entire image.

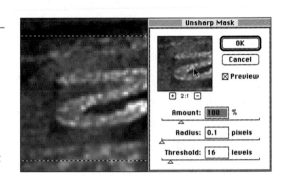

2 | Adjust the Amount Setting

Drag the Amount slider to several different settings in 50% increments and watch the changes. A setting of 100% produces twice the effect of 50%; a setting of 200% produces four times the effect of 50%, and so on. Look at the edges of an area and you'll see a halo effect. These are the lines that accentuate the edges. Too much sharpening distorts the image. You might find it useful to over-sharpen first and then gradually reduce the Amount setting until you get a realistic effect. Do not apply the filter yet.

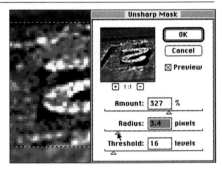

3 | Adjust the Radius Setting

Drag the Radius slider to enter several values. This setting controls the number of pixels that are sharpened, depending on how far they are from the edge. Low values sharpen only the edge pixels, resulting in crisper images. Higher values sharpen more pixels surrounding the edge, producing softer, higher-contrast images. In general, use a higher Radius setting for high-resolution images. A Radius value of 1.0 to 1.5 is usually acceptable for 8×10 images with a resolution of 300 dpi to 350 dpi. Setting the Radius too high can cause a keyline effect when you apply the filter.

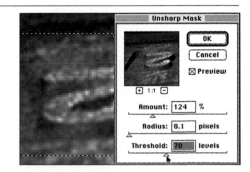

4 | Adjust the Threshold Setting

Drag the Threshold slider to enter several settings. This setting specifies a tolerance range (the numerical difference necessary between two adjacent pixels for sharpening to occur). The Threshold setting lets you prevent overall sharpening that can introduce noise into the image. A low value sharpens more pixels (a value of zero sharpens all the pixels in the image). A high value excludes more pixels (a value of 255 doesn't sharpen any pixels). Begin experimenting with a value of about 16 to 32. This threshold usually produces smooth transitions with well-defined edges.

Mary Silhman

Comments

Dodging and burning are photographic terms used to describe common manipulations made to prints in the darkroom. Dodging refers to holding back light from an area to produce a lighter tone. Burning refers to letting more light through to an area to produce a darker tone. Traditionally, photographers use pieces of cardboard taped to a coat hanger to dodge areas and focus light with their fingers and hands to burn in areas. (This is the origin of the icons used to indicate the Dodge and Burn tools in Photoshop).

Studio Usage

Whenever you have small areas that need minor lightening or darkening, these two tools provide just the right amount of control. They are two of the most frequently used retouching tools.

Related Techniques

Scratches and Flaws   70

Curves 1, 2   81, 82

Adjusting Shadows, Midtones, Highlights   83, 84, 85

1 | Use the Dodge Tool

Select a brush and double-click the Dodge tool. In the Toning Tools Options palette, choose Dodge from the Tool pop-up menu, Midtones from the Mode pop-up menu, and set the Exposure to 50%. Locate an area with middle tones and paint a stroke. Only the middle tones are lightened. Choose Highlights from the Mode menu and stroke a different area. Only the lighter pixels are lightened. Choose Shadows from the Mode menu and stroke a third area. Only the darkest pixels are lightened. Multiple strokes over the same area eventually lighten the area totally, removing all detail.

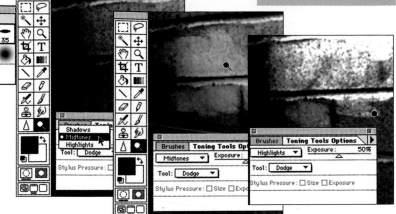

2 | Use the Burn Tool

Choose Burn from the Tool pop-up menu in the Toning Tools Options palette (or press Option as you click the tool in the toolbox to cycle through the tools). Locate a light area in the image and stroke. The area darkens. Choose Edit→Undo Burn Tool and set a different exposure and then stroke again. The Burn tool is particularly effective for dodging specular highlights or darkening overexposed areas in the original photograph that were not corrected in the scanning process.

3 | Use the Sponge Tool

Choose Sponge from the pop-up menu in the Toning Tools Options palette (or press Option as you click the tool in the toolbox to cycle through the tools) and choose Desaturate from the Mode pop-up menu. Paint a stroke and notice how the color becomes more diluted. Choose Saturate from the Mode pop-up menu and stroke a different area. The color becomes more dense. The Sponge tool is useful for subtly isolating areas in an image or bringing small areas of out-of-gamut colors into gamut.

4 | Dodging or Burning a Path

You can also use the Dodge and Burn tools to stroke a path. Choose Window→Show Palettes→Paths Palette. Click the Pen tool and draw a path. Select a brush from the Brushes palette and double-click the Dodge or Burn tool. Set the options you want in the Toning Tools Options palette. Click the stroke path icon (the second icon from the left at the bottom of the Paths palette). The outline of the path is lightened (if you choose the Dodge tool) or darkened (if you choose the Burn tool). This technique works well to create glows or to isolate important areas in an object.

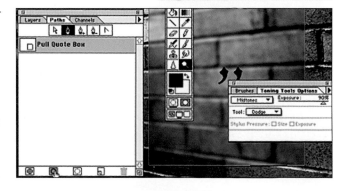

Retouching Images *Descreening*

Judith Moncrieff

Comments

There are times when the only available copy of an image is one that's already been printed. You can't simply scan and use printed images from magazines, brochures, or other existing sources because the halftone screens used in printing cause patterns that make the scans unusable.

There are several steps that can improve the scan quality of printed materials, but such scans can never equal the quality of original scans from transparencies or prints.

Studio Usage

Copyright law restricts you from using existing materials (unless you created them in the first place and still retain all rights). Sometimes, however, you may need to use an existing image as a placeholder during the design process, in anticipation of creating original photography for the final image. At other times you may be forced to use screened images because that's all the client has to work with. This can happen, for example, when you're repurposing existing materials for a multimedia project.

Related Techniques

Resolution and Image Size   65

Blur Filters   72

Sharpen Filters   73

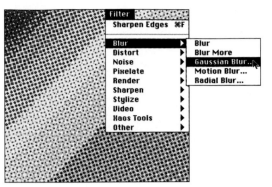

1 | Scan the Image at a High Resolution

Scan the printed image at the highest possible resolution; the more pixel information you have to work with, the more manipulations you can perform to improve the image. The patterns of the halftone dots will be clearly visible in the new scan. Choose File→Open and select the image. Choose Filter→Blur→Gaussian Blur.

2 | Apply the Gaussian Blur Filter

In the Gaussian Blur dialog box, use the plus (+) or minus (-) buttons under the Preview window to zoom in until you can see the halftone dots. Adjust the Radius slider in small stages, moving about a half a pixel at a time. Stop when you've lost the dot pattern but can still see the important detail in the image. Click OK to apply the filter.

3 | Sharpen the Results

Choose Filter→Sharpen→Sharpen. Apply the filter and use the Zoom tool to zoom in to check the results. Try sharpening the image once more; if the second application introduces noise or distorts the image, choose Edit→Undo Sharpen.

4 | Resize the Image

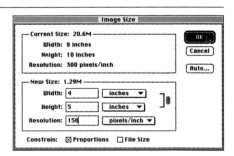

If the image is too large, choose Image→Image Size and enter the correct dimensions in the Image Size dialog box. Select the Proportions option if you want to keep the same height-width ratio. Deselect File Size to keep the same or reduce the resolution. Reducing the size of a scanned halftone image also helps reduce and disguise the halftone screen dots. If you select the File Size option, Photoshop automatically increases the resolution when you decrease the dimensions. The resulting blurring might make the dots less noticeable, but it often makes the image appear out-of-focus.

Judith Moncrieff

Comments

When an image is output to a press, it is converted from continuous tones (pixels) to a series of halftone dots. Presses are incapable of reproducing continuous tones and use a series of colored halftone dots printed at different angles to simulate the continuous tones as closely as possible. The amount of ink that is applied to a halftone dot determines where the image is light and where the image is dark.

Studio Usage

This section shows you how to work with RGB files before converting the images to CMYK files for printing. Although this may conflict with what you've heard, you may be able to achieve better results making corrections *before* converting images to CMYK.

Related Techniques

Creating a Scale of Grays 78

RGB versus CMYK 79

Curves 1, 2 81, 82

Adjusting Shadows, Midtones, Highlights 83, 84, 85

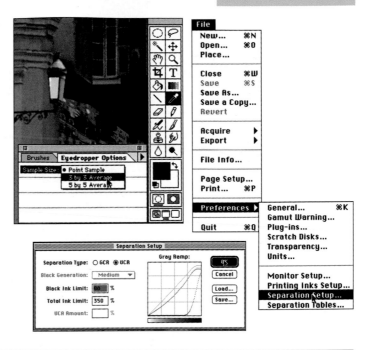

1 | Preparing an Image

Double-click the Eyedropper tool to select the tool and the Eyedropper Options palette. From the Sample Size pop-up menu in the Options palette, select 3 by 3 Average. Choose File→Preferences→Separation Setup. Select UCR as the Separation Type. Enter 80 as the Black Ink Limit and 350 as the Total Ink Limit. These settings provide sufficient image data to work on just about any press you may find. Fine tuning these values can be done after you've run work on a specific press. The rest of this section assumes you've made these adjustments.

2 | Select the Highlights

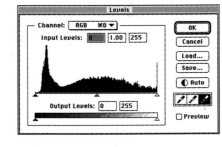

Open an RGB Image. Choose Image→Adjust→Levels (⌘-L) and look at the distribution of pixel values shown in the histogram. The triangle at the left side of the graph represents the bright pixels, and the triangle at the right side of the graph represents the dark pixels. In the lower right section of the dialog box, there are three eyedroppers. Select the hollow eyedropper (the one located on the right) and click a region of the image that represents the whitest (brightest) portion of the image. (Do not select bright areas based on washed-out areas or areas of reflection.)

3 | Select the Shadows

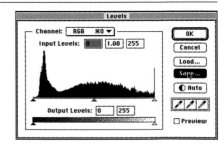

Select the black-filled eyedropper and click the blackest (darkest) portion of the image. This determines which regions of the image receive the most ink. Click OK when you've selected both the lightest and darkest areas of the image and then save the image.

4 | Saving Levels Adjustments

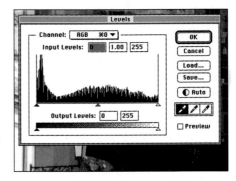

Setting the highlight and shadow of an image can often compensate for over- or under-exposure that occurs during the photographic session. If you have several images that contain the same basic faults, you can save level settings and then apply them to each image.

Computer Artist: Robert Bowen Photographer: Ryszard Horowitz Client: Unisys

Comments

When you make color and tonal corrections to an image, all the color and grayscale values change. For example, what starts as 20% gray may change to 14% gray or 2% gray—leaving no reference to the original color or grayscale value. In order to have an unchanging visual reference of the actual percentages of grays in an image, you create a scale of grays in a drawing program and then import it onto its own layer in the Photoshop image.

Studio Usage

If you want to reestablish the high-lights, midtones, and shadows in an image you've edited, you can use the scale of grays as a point of reference. You can also use the Eyedropper tool and select grays from the scale to reestablish highlights, midtones, and shadows. In this example, the gray scale was created in Adobe Illustrator.

Related Techniques

Adjusting Tonal Ranges 77

Brightness and Contrast 80

Curves 1, 2 81, 82

Adjusting Shadows,
Midtones, Highlights 83,
84, 85

1 | Create the Scale

Open Adobe Illustrator or another drawing program and create a rectangle about 1.5 inches tall and about 3/4 inches wide. Copy the rectangle and then paste it 13 times to create a total of 14 rectangles. Align the rectangles horizontally.

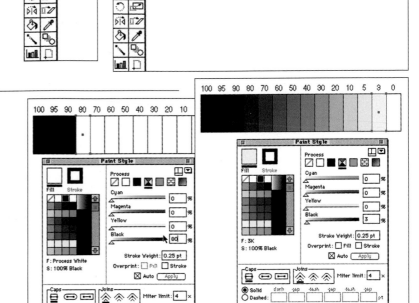

2 | Label and Assign Scale Values

Starting at the top of the leftmost rectangle, type a label for the percentage of gray over all the boxes, starting at 100 and ending with 0. Be sure to fill the 0% box with white—if it is left blank, it will be read as transparent in Photoshop and won't be useful.

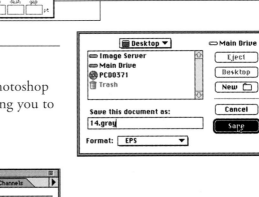

3 | Save the Scale as an EPS File

Save the file as an EPS image so that it can be placed directly into a Photoshop document. Be sure to turn on the Preview option before saving, allowing you to see the placed image in the Photoshop document.

4 | Open the Scale and Create a New Layer

In Photoshop, open the document you want to adjust and then open the Layers palette. Create a new layer by clicking the page icon at the bottom of the Layers palette and then name the layer. With the new layer still active, choose File→Place and select the Scale you created in the drawing program. When you begin making adjustments, the scale will remain unaffected because it has been isolated on a layer. Select the Background layer (or another layer you're working with) and begin making adjustments. The gray scale remains untouched as you make adjustments to the image—serving as an excellent tool to use as a yardstick of gray values. You can also select the highlight and shadow values directly from the ramp if there are no easily discernible regions in your image.

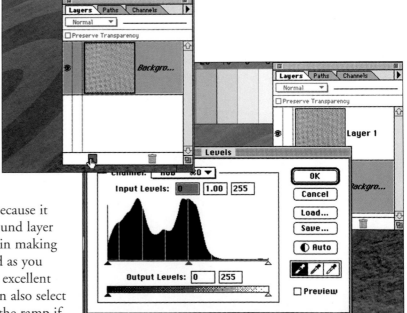

Mitchell Anthony, MADworks®

Comments

The destination of your image determines the mode in which the image must be saved. For example, if you are outputting an image to press, the image must be saved in CMYK mode; if you're outputting to a CD-ROM or to screen, the images should be saved in RGB mode. However, even when you are outputting images to press, work in RGB mode until the file is finalized and then change the file to CMYK mode. RGB files are much smaller than CMYK files, allowing you to work more quickly and efficiently while editing.

Studio Usage

Each time you change from RGB to CMYK mode and then back to RGB, some degradation occurs. To avoid this degradation, you can turn on the CMYK Preview option, which allows you to simulate the CMYK environment while working in RGB mode.

Related Techniques

File Formats   121-126

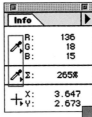

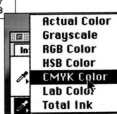

1 | Open the Info Palette

The Info palette displays information about RGB and CMYK color values. Choose Window→Palettes→Show Info to open the Info palette. The Info palette displays two eyedroppers with small arrowheads adjacent to them. Hold down the mouse button on the small arrow next to the eyedropper at the top of the palette and choose RGB color from the pop-up menu. Set the bottom eyedropper to display CMYK values.

Note: If the second palette option is set for Actual Color or RGB, then only one eyedropper shows in the Info palette.

2 | Turn on CMYK Preview

Choose Mode→CMYK Preview. This option simulates CMYK color values while you're working in RGB mode. (The only time you need to use this option is if you are outputting to press.)

3 | Set Options

The options are Amount and Distribution. The Amount of noise you may add ranges from 1 to 999. This specifies the number of shades of each channel color, more or less, that Photoshop can generate. If you set this much higher than 255 you may get colors on the opposite end of the color model. Set this at 10. The Distribution was set at Uniform for a smoother effect. Try to preview the image using the Gaussian setting—just for comparison.

4 | Convert the Image

Before you convert an image from RGB to CMYK, archive a copy of the image in RGB mode in case you need to return to the original file to make additional adjustments. When you've saved a copy, choose Mode→CMYK Color to convert the image from RGB to CMYK. You may notice a slight change in color because the RGB color gamut can produce a much larger range of color than the CMYK (printed inks) gamut.

Greg Vander Houwen

Comments

Brightness refers to the lightness values for each pixel in an image. Contrast refers to the tonal range between the lightest and darkest pixels in an image.

Studio Usage

The Brightness and Contrast command is the easiest way to make generalized tonal adjustments to an image. However, because adjusting the brightness and contrast of an image compresses the values captured in the original scan, use the command judiciously.

Related Techniques

Adjusting Tonal Ranges   77

Creating a Scale of Grays   78

Curves 1, 2   81, 82

Adjusting Shadows, Midtones, Highlights   83, 84, 85

1 | Check the Levels of the Image

Open an image you want to adjust and choose Image→Adjust→Levels (⌘-L). The Levels dialog box appears. The histogram represents the distribution of pixels in the image, from white to black. In a well-balanced image, there should be a smooth and fairly even distribution of pixels from white to black.

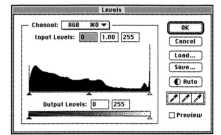

2 | To Adjust Brightness

Choose Image→Adjust→Brightness/Contrast (⌘-B). Increase the Brightness by moving the Brightness slider to +20 and then click OK. Choose Image→Adjust→Levels (⌘-L) to display the histogram again. The black point (the triangle at the lower-left side of the graph) has moved. The range of pixels is still present, but has increased in brightness (decreased in blackness). This adjustment may diminish or "wash out" the highlighted areas of an image.

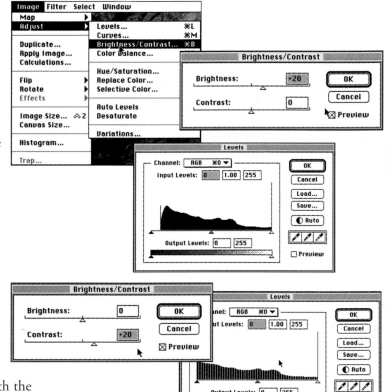

3 | To Adjust Contrast

Choose File→Revert to restore the pixel values from the original file. Choose Image→Adjust→ Brightness/Contrast (⌘-B). Increase the contrast to +20 and again check the Levels in the image with the Image→Adjust→Levels command. They appear somewhat flattened but contain ridges across the entire histogram. These ridges represent jumps in contrast in each of the tonal ranges. Slight contrast adjustments can often improve the overall look of an image that is improperly lit or exposed.

4 | Applying Brightness and Contrast to Partial Areas

Create a rectangular Marquee selection. Choose Image→Adjust→ Brightness/Contrast (⌘-B). Increase the brightness until the selected area is light enough to allow a placed object to be easily displayed; then position the object in the brightened area.

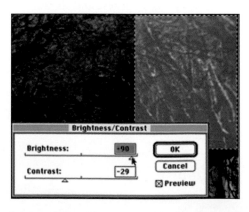

Sanjay Kothari

Comments

The Curves command, like the Levels command, allows you to make tonal adjustments to images.

Studio Usage

The Curves dialog box allows you to affect the range of tonal values in an image with great precision. When you open the Curves dialog box, a diagonal line appears within a grid. The diagonal line represents the full range of tonal values in an image: shadows, midtones, and shadows. You can drag the diagonal line to affect different areas of an image, and you can click on the line to add points for greater adjustments to specific areas. At the bottom of the grid, the Input label displays the original tonal values of the image, and the Output label displays the adjusted tonal values of the image.

Related Techniques

Adjusting Tonal Ranges 77

Creating a Scale of Grays 78

Adjusting Shadows, Midtones, Highlights 83, 84, 85

Removing Casts 87

1 | Open an Image

Open an image containing a good range of tonal values and choose
Image→Adjust→Curves (⌘-M). The Curves dialog box appears.

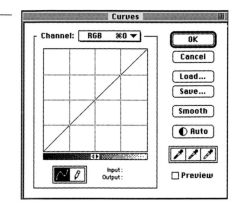

2 | Measure Tonal Values

Position the cursor over the
image; the pointer becomes the
eyedropper tool. Drag over various areas of the image—as you
drag, a range indicator moves
along the diagonal line to indicate where the pixels fall within
the tonal range of the image. For example, dragging
in a light area of an image moves the range indicator
toward the top of the diagonal line, representing the highlight
area of the tonal range. Dragging in a dark area moves the range
indicator toward the bottom of the diagonal line, representing
the shadow area of the tonal range.

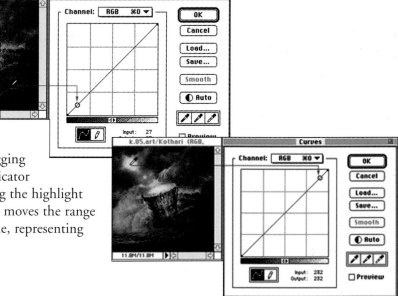

3 | Adjust the Midtones

To adjust the tonal range of an image, drag the
diagonal line in the Curves dialog box. Where you
position the pointer on the diagonal line determines
the tonal range you want to adjust. Make sure that
the Preview option is selected and then position the
pointer at the middle of the diagonal line where it
intersects with the grid. This point represents the
midtone values in the image. (In an RGB image,
the Input and Output values are 128 at the midpoint.) Drag downward from the midpoint to
slightly darken the midtone values of the image. To
delete a point (and the adjustment), drag the point to the edge of the grid
and release the mouse button; the point disappears. In the next tip, you'll
learn about making more precise adjustments to tonal areas of an image.

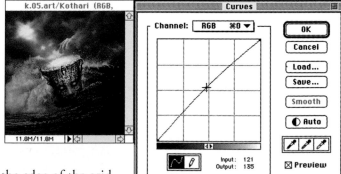

Lisa Rivard

Comments

Images are composed of three tonal elements: highlights, which represent the brightest parts of the image; midtones, which define the midrange tonal values in an image; and shadows, which represent the darkest parts of the image. The Curves command allows you to adjust the specific tonal ranges of an image with great precision. You can add an additional 14 points to the diagonal line in the curves dialog box to affect the overall tonal range of the image.

Studio Usage

Using curves to add or subtract tonal value within specific ranges can increase the detail in shadow and highlight areas of an image, balance the midtones, or tone down over-exposed regions of an image. This process isn't something you learn immediately—it requires practice and a structured approach. Before you use the Curves command to alter specific tonal ranges, set the black and white points in the image.

Related Techniques

Sharpen Filters 73

Adjusting Tonal Ranges 77

Adjusting Shadows, Midtones, Highlights 83, 84, 85

1 | Analyze the Curves Dialog Box

Open an image containing a good range of tonal values and choose Image→Adjust→Curves (⌘-M). The Curves dialog box appears. To affect specific areas of the document with additional precision, add three points to the diagonal line by clicking where the grid lines intersect on the line. These points represent quarter tones: the highest point on the diagonal line controls highlight values, from the brightest to 25% darker; the second and third points represent the midtone range; and the fourth point represents the shadowed area, from the darkest to 25% lighter.

2 | To Increase Image Sharpness

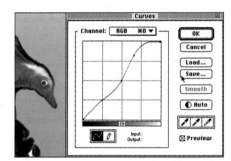

Look for a bright area of the image containing some detail. Increase the tonal value of the highlights by dragging point 1 (the highlight point) upwards. Notice the loss of detail in the region. Then decrease the tonal values in the highlight area by lowering the point; notice the increase in contrast and detail. This type of adjustment is much more accurate and discriminating than that achieved using a sharpen filter.

3 | To Adjust Overall Balance

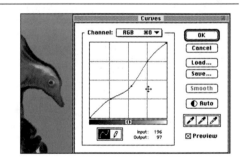

Make sure that the points you set along the diagonal line in the Curves dialog box are in their original positions; then click OK. Next, zoom in on an area of the image that contains midtones and press Option-⌘-M. Using the Option-⌘-M key sequence opens the Curves dialog box with the last set of points you created. Drag point 2 (the midtone point) downward and to the right to increase the midtone values. This step appears to darken the image overall; however, when you increase or decrease midtones in an image, the highlight and shadows areas are unaffected.

4 | To Bring Out Detail in Shadowed Areas

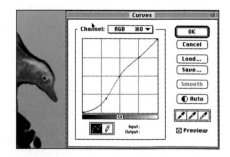

Shadow areas often contain details that cannot be seen in the original scan. Move the points on the graph back to their original positions and click OK. Zoom in on an area of the image containing shadows and then drag point 3 upwards to expose details in the shadow areas.

Sanjay Kothari

Comments

The shadows, or darkest areas in an image, often contain the most detail. There are several methods by which you can enhance the shadowed areas of images. You can lighten the shadows in an image by adding light, or you can increase the depth of shadowed areas by replacing some of the darker areas with a color.

Studio Usage

You can adjust the highlight, midtone, and shadow areas of an image separately, allowing you to fine tune and add depth to the image. This tip shows you how to use the Color Replace command to adjust and replace *specific* colors in the shadowed areas of an image, and how to use the Curves commands to adjust *all* the colors in the shadow regions of an image.

Related Techniques

Curves 1, 2   81, 82

Adjusting Single
         Ink Sets   89

UCR and GCR   119

1 | Measure a Shadow Area

Open a predominantly dark RGB image; then choose Window→
Palettes→Info to display the Info palette. At the top of the Info palette,
the image's color mode is displayed. When any tool is moved over the
image area, the color mode values are displayed in the Info palette.
Adjacent to each eyedropper, a pop-up menu allows you to choose a
different color mode. For example, if you choose grayscale, the eyedropper label is K (for black) and the image color values are displayed only
in percentages of black. Select grayscale from the first eyedropper
pop-up and then choose the color mode of your image from the second eyedropper pop-up.
Move any tool over a region of the image that contains detail in the shadows and
write down the values in the Info palette for later comparison.

2 | Adjusting Shadows Using Color Range

To easily add or subtract tonal values from
shadowed areas, you can use the Color Range
command in conjunction with the Curves dialog box. Choose Select→Color Range. Choose
Shadows from the pop-up menu and click
OK. The shadowed areas of the image are
selected. To preview the results of the adjustments you make in the Curves dialog box,
choose Select→Hide Edges (⌘-H). Choose
Image→ Adjust→Curves (⌘-M) to open the
Curves dialog box; then darken the shadowed
values by dragging downward in the shadow
area of the Curves dialog box. Move a tool
over the same area you measured in Step #1 and
compare the results in the Info palette; then click Cancel to exit
the dialog box without making the adjustment.

3 | Adjusting Specific Colors to Shadowed Areas

Choose Image→Adjust→Selective Color
and then choose Blacks from the pop-up
menu at the top of the dialog box. Add a
small percentage (5 to 10 percent) of cyan to
the blacks; then measure the area and compare the results in the Info palette from Step
#1. Adding a small percentage of cyan to the
blacks in an image can bring out detail in
dark areas, and adding a large percentage
(20% or more) can eliminate them.

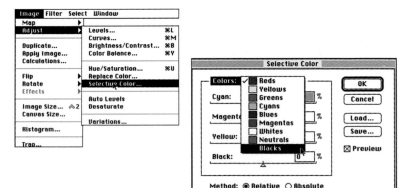

Pamela Belding

Comments

Most images contain the breadth of visual information in their midtones. Midtones are tones that fall midway between the lightest and darkest areas of the image.

Studio Usage

Improperly adjusted midtones make an image appear flat and washed-out. After adjusting the overall tonal range of an image, adjust the midtones to ensure depth and high-quality reproduction.

Related Techniques

Adjusting Tonal Ranges   77

Curves 1, 2   81, 82

Adjusting Shadows   83

1 | Identify the Midtones

Choose Select→Color Range and then choose Midtones from the pop-up menu. All the areas except the midtone areas are masked in white. Click OK or click Cancel to exit the dialog box without making a selection.

Tip: To see an image preview of only the midtones while still in the Color Range dialog box, choose White Matte from the Selection Preview pop-up menu.

2 | Adding and Subtracting Values in Midtone Areas

You can increase or decrease the midtone values in an image using the Curves dialog box. Choose Image→Adjust→ Curves (⌘-M) to open the Curves dialog box. On the diagonal line, drag from the center point upward and to the left to lighten the midtones, or drag downward and to the right to darken the midtones.

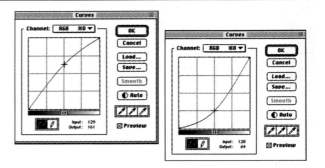

3 | Selecting Neutral Tones

You can also adjust midtones by selecting and modifying neutral areas of an image. Neutral areas are areas of the image that fall within a 10- to 12-percent range of each other. Choose Image→Adjust→Selective Color and then choose Neutrals from the pop-up menu. Click the Preview option and drag the color sliders to add or subtract from individual colors in the neutral areas of the image. You can also add or subtract color in two ways by selecting a Method option. The Absolute option adds or subtracts the percentage of the color adjustment to the value of the existing color, and the Relative option multiplies the increase or decrease in color by the original value and then adds or subtracts the product from the original value.

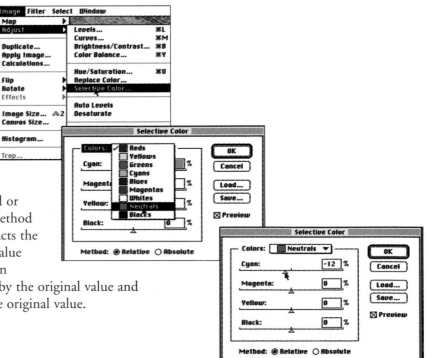

Marylu Miller

Marylu Miller

Comments

The lightest areas of an image are called the highlight areas. Highlight areas are composed of the lightest color values in each channel of the image.

Studio Usage

Be careful when selecting and adjusting highlight areas—making them too bright eliminates detail in the highlight areas. The darker the image, the more important the highlights are to the image because the difference between highlights and shadows determines the overall contrast of the image. Too little contrast results in a flat appearance and insufficient detail in the midtone areas of the image.

Related Techniques

Adjusting Tonal Ranges   77

Curves 1, 2   81, 82

Using Variations   88

1 | Identify the Highlights

Open a document, choose Select→Color Range, and then choose Highlights from the pop-up menu.

Tip: *To see an image preview of only the highlights while still in the Color Range dialog box, choose White Matte from the Selection Preview pop-up menu. All the areas except the highlight areas are masked in white.*

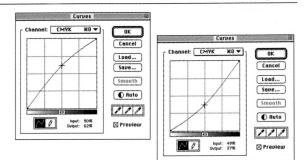

2 | Adjusting Curves

Choose Image→Adjust→Curves (⌘-M) to open the Curves dialog box. To lighten the highlights, position the pointer on the diagonal line near the top of the line (the highlight area) and drag downward and to the right. To darken the highlights, drag upward and to the left. The Input value displays the original lightness value, and the Output value displays the new lightness value.

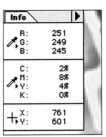

3 | What is White?

Images that contain a lot of white; for example, a shirt, an interior shot, or a snowy landscape, often suffer from a tint or cast in the white areas. If you're not working on a 24-bit color monitor, you can't see the color casts that may exist. With the Info palette open on your screen, select the Eyedropper tool and measure an area that appears to be white. In white highlights, there should be no less than a 3% difference between cyan, magenta, and yellow tones, and no more than 6% or 7% cyan. Cyan highlights actually *increase* the perception of white, but create a blue cast if the cyan percentage is too high (over 7%).

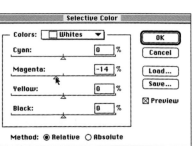

4 | Neutralizing White Highlights

Select Image→Adjust→Selective Color and then choose Whites from the pop-up menu. Add or subtract sufficient magenta and yellow until the white areas are in an appropriate neutral range. An example of an appropriate white highlight is 5% cyan, 3% magenta, and 3% yellow.

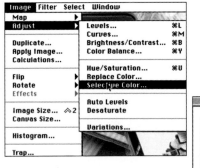

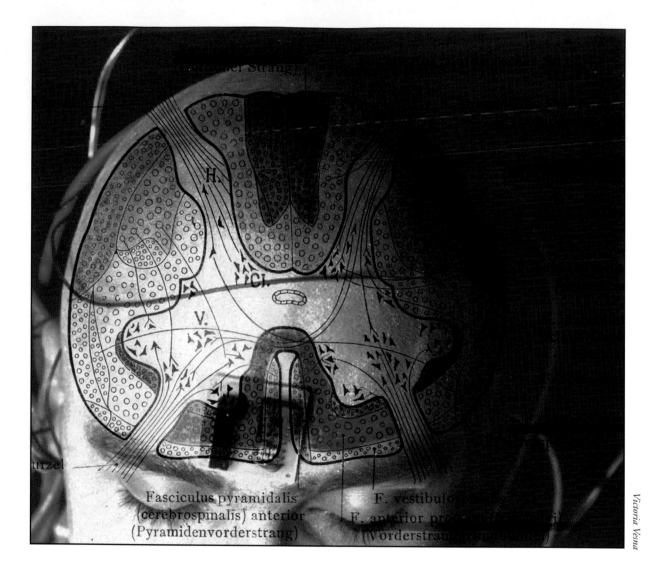

Victoria Vesna

Comments

Hue, saturation, and brightness are the three components of color. Hue represents the position of the color on the color spectrum (color wheel), saturation represents the depth (or tint) of the color, and brightness represents the darkness or lightness of the color.

Studio Usage

You use the hue and saturation controls for numerous reasons—to shift all the colors in an image or a selection, to change a specific color in an image or selection, or to add to or change the color of artwork imported from other programs.

Related Techniques

Painting Modes   42-49

Removing Casts   87

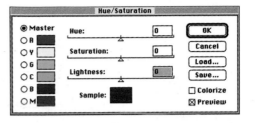

1 | Open a Document

Open a document or create a selection within a document you want to adjust; then choose Image→Adjust→Hue/Saturation (⌘-U) to display the Hue/Saturation dialog box.

Tip: If you are working with a selection, turn off the selection's edges (⌘-H) before opening the Hue/Saturation dialog box; it's easier to see the preview adjustments.

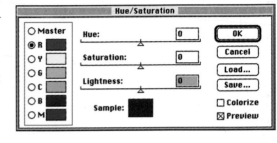

2 | Choose an Adjustment Option

Along the left side of the Hue/Saturation dialog box, color selection options are displayed. To select a specific color within the document for adjustment, click the desired color; to adjust all the colors in the document, click Master.

3 | Adjust the Hue and Saturation

After selecting a color option, drag the Hue slider to change the hue of the entire image or of the selected area. The starting number in the Hue field is 0; as you drag, the number increases or decreases, depending on the direction you drag. The resulting number in the Hue field represents the degree of rotation on the color wheel from the original position of each pixel's location on the color wheel. Drag the Saturation slider to vary the depth of the color—dragging to the right enriches the color; dragging to the left creates a lighter tint of the color.

4 | Using the Colorize Option

The Colorize option sets all the pixels in an image or a selection to a tint of a single solid color. Select the Colorize option; all the pixels are set to 0° (red) on the color wheel at 100-percent saturation. As you drag the Hue slider, the number in the Hue field represents the degree of rotation on the color wheel.

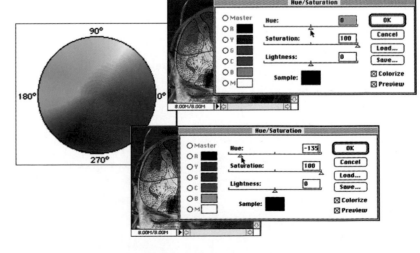

Dorothy Krause

Comments

Many, if not most, photographs contain some degree of color cast. Color casts can be seen in whites that look slightly pink or blue, or in shadows that appear brown.

Studio Usage

A cast can be invisible in an original image and yet be revealed onscreen after you've scanned the image. To see a color cast on your screen, you must be working on a 24-bit color monitor. If you're working with a monitor under 24-bit color, the color cast may not be discernible, but it will appear when you output to a typesetter.

Related Techniques

Adjusting Tonal Ranges   77

Curves 1, 2   81, 82

Adjusting Shadows,
Midtones, Highlights   83, 84
85

Selective Color   90

1 | Open a Document

Open a document that contains a color cast you want to remove. If the color cast is only affecting a certain area of the document, select the region using a selection tool from the toolbox.

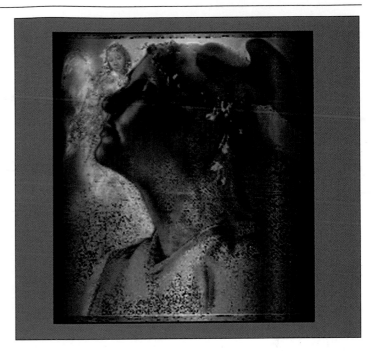

2 | To Remove a Color Cast

Choose Image→Adjust→Curves (⌘-M) to open the Curves dialog box. Depending on the shade of the color cast, choose the appropriate color from the Channel pop-up menu at the top of the dialog box. Make sure that Preview is selected in the Curves dialog box and then drag the point at the lower-left corner to the right along the bottom of the grid. As you drag, you'll notice that the cast disappears. This technique is sometimes referred to as "backing-out" color. When the cast is no longer present, click OK to apply the change and to exit the Curves dialog box.

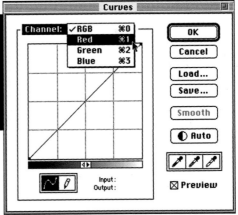

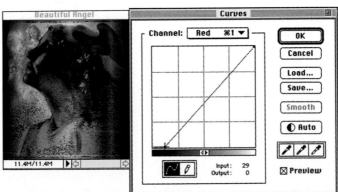

Image and Color Corrections *Using Variations*

Pam Belding

Comments

The Variations command is a simple, visually-oriented color-correction method that lets you click on thumbnails of an image to make color adjustments. You can make color adjustments to the highlights, midtones, and shadows in an image, adjust the contrast in an image, or adjust the saturation of an image.

Studio Usage

If the concept of color correction is new to you, you can use the Variations command to see easily how color adjustments affect opposite colors on the color wheel. In the Variations dialog box, a series of preview thumbnails corresponding with the positions of colors on the color wheel surround a preview of the original image. Each time you click a color thumbnail to add a specific color, an equal amount of the opposite color is subtracted. For example, when you click More Red to add red to an image, an equal amount of cyan (the opposite color on the color wheel) is subtracted from the image.

Related Techniques

Adjusting Tonal Ranges   77

Curves 1, 2   81, 82

Removing Casts   87

1 Open an Image

Open an image in which you want to adjust the color. The Variations command is available for the following image types: Grayscale, Duotone, RGB, CMYK, and Multichannel.

2 Open the Variations Dialog Box

Choose Image→Adjust→Variations. The Variations dialog box appears, containing a number of preview options related to the color mode in which you're working. For example, if you're adjusting a color image, a series of color previews surround the original image allowing you to add color to or subtract color from the preview image.

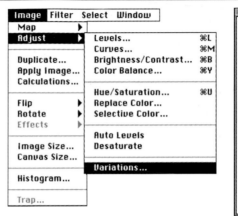

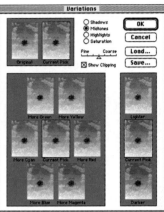

3 Making Adjustments

In the upper-right corner of the Variations dialog box, choose an option to adjust the highlights, midtones, or shadowed areas of the image. Clicking the Saturation option allows you to apply more or less saturation to the image.

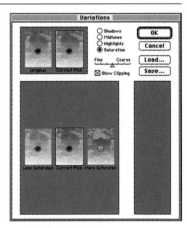

Note: *When you select the Saturation option, areas of the image that will be converted to pure black or pure white are displayed in a neon color. If you don't want to see the neon preview, deselect the Show Clipping option. The Fine and Coarse options control the increments in which adjustments are made. Choosing a finer option adjusts the image in smaller increments; choosing a more coarse option adjusts the image in larger increments.*

4 Applying Changes

If you're not satisfied with the changes you've made, click the Original image preview in the top-left corner of the Variations dialog box to reset the image to the original settings. When you've made the desired adjustments, click OK to apply the changes.

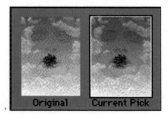

Tip: *If you're working with several images that require the same adjustment, click the Save button to save the Variations settings, which can then be loaded onto the next image to make the same adjustment.*

Peter Martin

Comments

Because each Photoshop image is comprised of separate colors stored in channels, it is possible to affect the density of the ink color in any channel. This technique is used for images that will be printed (CMYK images).

Studio Usage

Images often have color-specific problems when output for color proofs. Perhaps you have seen instructions written on tissue overlays that say something like "reduce cyan 3% in midtone areas." This simple use of the Fill command allows you to make precise adjustments to individual ink colors or to all the colors at once.

Related Techniques

Global Color Adjustments   55

Managing Channels   59

Curves 1, 2   81, 82

1 | Set Info Palette Options

Make sure that the Info window is displayed (Window→Palettes→Show Info). For print projects, set the view to Total Ink and CMYK (the default settings are RGB and CMYK).

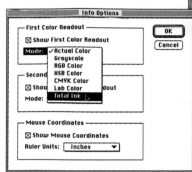

2 | Measure Image Values

Select the Eyedropper tool and measure specific areas of the image. (You may want to write these figures down so that you can check the results later, after you've made the changes and before you've saved the file. When you save the file, the ink density is permanently changed.)

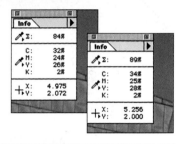

3 | Load the Channel You Want to Affect

Hold down Control, Option, and Command and press the number that corresponds to the channel you want to color correct: 1 for cyan, 2 for magenta, 3 for yellow, and 4 for black. The most common color corrections are applied to the first three channels (CMY), which contain the image colors.

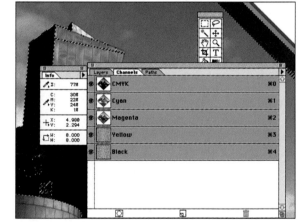

4 | Fill the Channel

Choose Edit→Fill. When the Fill dialog box appears, select White from the Use pop-up menu if you want to increase the density of a specific color; choose Black from the Use pop-up menu if you want to increase (darken) the intensity of a color. Set the opacity of the blending to match the reduction or expansion of the tone. If you want to reduce the cyan by 10%, set the fill to White with an opacity of 10% and click OK to fill only the selected channel. The color values are changed in only the selected channel.

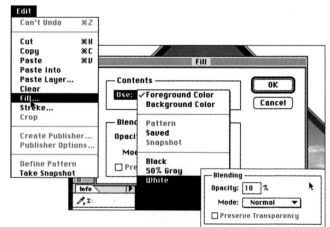

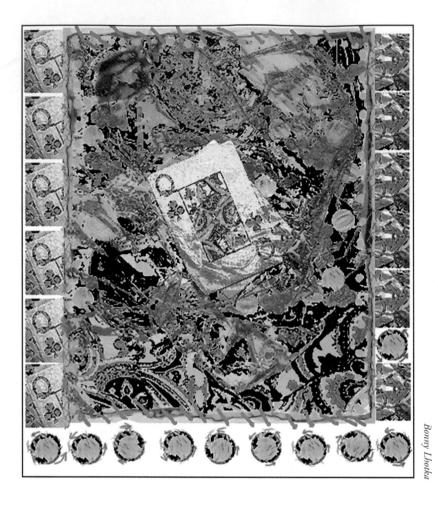

Bonny Lhotka

Comments

Photoshop's Selective Color command is similar to a technique used by high-end scanners—this command enables you to select a range of colors in an image and then adjust the percentages of cyan, magenta, yellow, and black within the color range.

Studio Usage

When a scanner and monitor are properly calibrated, setting the highlight and shadow end points should be enough to accurately reproduce a good original. When you want to adjust a tonal range (for example, all the yellows in an image), using the Selective Color command eliminates the need to first use the Color Range selection method to identify the color range.

Related Techniques

Adjusting Shadows, Midtones, Highlights 83, 84, 85

Using Variations 88

Adjusting Nature's Colors 94

1 | Open the Selective Color Dialog Box

To best view the effects of this technique, open an image with a good range of color. Choose Image→Adjust→Selective Color. Choose a color from the pop-up menu that depicts the color range you want to adjust.

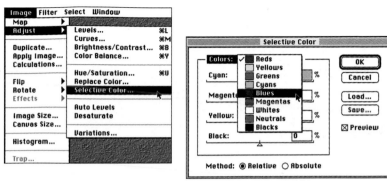

2 | To Adjust Ranges of Color

The CMYK sliders enable you to add or subtract ink colors from the color (or range of colors) that you select from the pop-up menu. Make sure that the Preview box is selected and then drag the CMYK sliders to add to or subtract from the selected color range. Adding magenta to cyan or blue tones

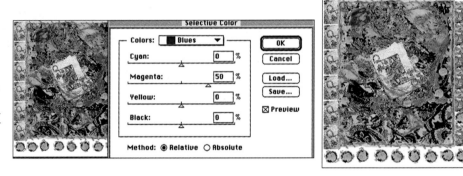

moves the colors toward indigo or purple; adding cyan to yellow tones moves toward green; adding black to blues enriches the blue tones; and adding enough yellow to magenta moves the tones from oranges to reds.

3 | Absolute vs. Relative Adjustments

Two adjustment options are available for color ranges—Absolute and Relative. The Absolute option adds the percentage of the adjustment to the existing color value—adding 15 percent cyan to a region already containing 20 percent cyan creates a result of 35 percent cyan (15%+20%=35%). The Relative option multiplies the percentage of the adjustment by the existing amount and then adds the product to the original amount—adding 15 percent cyan to a region already containing 20 percent cyan creates a result of 23 percent (15%+20%=35%, 20%+3%=23%). Relative is the default adjustment type.

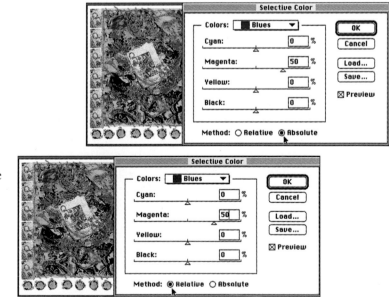

Michael J. Partington

Comments

Images composed of a mix of two ink colors are called *duotones*. Photoshop has a powerful method of utilizing two ink colors to create beautiful images. To create a duotone image, you need to begin with a grayscale image.

Studio Usage

There are two ways to use color halftones in a two-color project: the image can be printed entirely in one ink color, called a *monotone*; or you can use a mix of two ink colors. Using two inks adds tremendous richness to an otherwise ordinary halftone, dramatically improving tonal ranges.

Related Techniques

Curves 1, 2   81, 82

Adjusting Shadows   83

Selective Color   90

Four-Color Black and White   92

1 | Start with a Grayscale Image

Choose Mode→Grayscale. If you are working with a color image, a message box appears to ask if you want to discard the color information when you choose the Grayscale mode. Click OK to discard the file's color information.

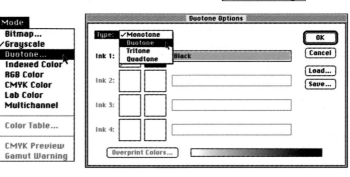

2 | The Duotone Options Dialog Box

After an image has been converted to a grayscale image, the Duotone option becomes available in the Mode menu. Choose Mode→Duotone; the Duotone Options dialog box appears. At the top of the Duotone Options dialog box, a pop-up menu enables you to select an option. The default option is Monotone, which prints the image using one ink color. When Monotone is selected, only the Ink 1 option is available in the dialog box. Choose Duotone from the pop-up menu; the Ink 2 option becomes available. In each ink option area, the left square controls the distribution of color over the image, and the right box displays the ink color.

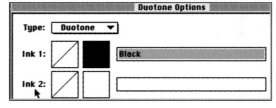

3 | Selecting Ink Colors

Click the Ink 2 color button; the Custom Colors dialog box automatically appears. Select a custom color by clicking it, or by typing the color's number to select it in the color list. If desired, you can also use the Color Picker to create a color. Click Picker in the Custom Colors dialog box to select the Color Picker; then select a color or enter values in the color value fields.

Note: *If you use Custom Colors, make sure that Short Pantone Names is selected in the General Preferences dialog box (⌘-K).*

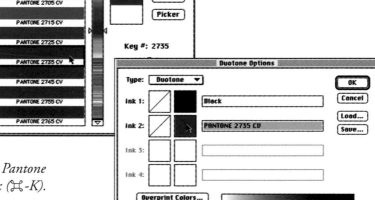

4 | To Adjust Ink Coverage

Click the Curves button (the swatch on the left) next to the ink color you've assigned. By adjusting the curves, you can control the amount of ink that's used in the shadow, midtone, or highlight areas of the image. Generally, you'll want to assign additional inks to boost the depth of a printed piece. If the original image has strong highlights, consider adding color to the midtones.

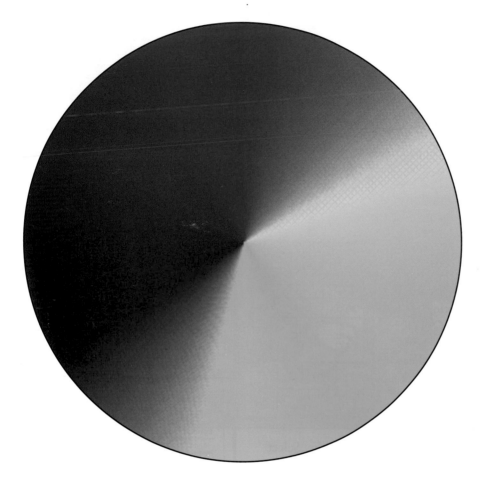

Comments

Most blends are constructed with two colors—one color gradually blends into the other color over the length of the path. You can create blends across a broader spectrum using Photoshop's Gradient Tool Options palette. The Spectrum option allows you to create a transition through a range of colors based on the standard color wheel.

Studio Usage

This technique can be used to create multi-colored blends for a wide range of uses: filling type, backgrounds, complex textures, or creating custom color palettes that can be used in place of the swatch palettes that come with Photoshop. Also, by using the CMYK Preview option under the Mode menu, you can analyze color shifts from your monitor to the output device you're using.

Related Techniques

Selecting Colors   14

RGB versus CMYK   79

Selective Color   90

Gamut Restrictions   120

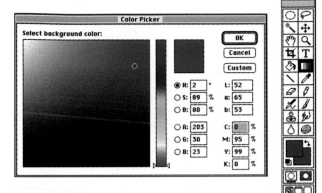

1 | Create a Document

Create a new document with the following attributes: 5 inches square, 72 pixels per inch (ppi), RGB, transparent background. Click OK. These settings create a layered document, with the first layer named Layer 1. (When you choose Transparent as the Contents type, no background layer is created.) Click the foreground swatch in the toolbox to select the Color Picker and then set the values in the CMYK fields to 0% cyan, 96% magenta, 99% yellow, and 0% black. Click OK to exit the dialog box. Click the background swatch in the toolbox and set the CMYK values to 0% cyan, 95% magenta, 99% yellow, and 0% black. Click OK. The foreground and background colors are almost identical.

2 | Create a Color Spectrum

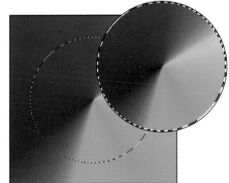

Double-click the Gradient tool to select the tool and its corresponding Options palette. Choose the following settings in the Options palette: Normal, 100% opacity; Clockwise Spectrum; Midpoint 50%; Linear. Deselect the Dither option. In the document window, hold down the Shift key and drag the Gradient tool from the left edge of the window to the right edge of the window. The clockwise setting creates a gradient containing all the colors in the color spectrum. To create a circular representation of the colors, choose Filter→Distort→Polar Coordinates and set the Conversion method to Rectangular to Polar. Click OK.

3 | Cut the Circle

Select the Elliptical Marquee tool from the toolbox (if the tool is currently a rectangle) and Option-click the rectangle to select the ellipsis. Hold down the Option and Shift keys and drag from the center of the wheel outward until you have created a circle of about 3 inches in diameter. Choose Select→Inverse to select the portion of the spectrum opposite the circle; then press Delete. Only the colored circle remains. Choose Select→Inverse again to reselect the circle.

4 | Changing Saturation Levels

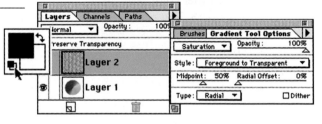

Reset the foreground and background colors to black and white by clicking the small black and white rectangle near the bottom-left of the foreground and background swatches. Open the Layers palette and create a new layer by clicking the new layer icon at the bottom of the Layers palette. (Leave the default name of Layer 2.) Double-click the Gradient tool again to select the tool and its corresponding Options palette and set the attributes to the following: Saturation 100% opacity; Foreground to Transparent; Midpoint 50%; Radial Offset 0%; and Radial. Hold down the Shift key and drag from the center of the circle to the outside edge. The center of the circle darkens accordingly.

Don Morris

Comments

Complementary colors lie directly opposite one another on the color wheel. Besides being important to the painting and creative function, they also contribute to the shape and definition of objects or regions in any image.

Studio Usage

When you're correcting color, it's a good idea to reference complementary colors on the color wheel. When attempting to remove color casts, it is important not to reduce complementary colors too much because they strongly contribute to the opposite color's depth and richness.

Related Techniques

Curves 1, 2

1 | Creating Base Colors

Create a new document using the following settings: 5 inches square, 72 pixels per inch (ppi), RGB, Transparent. In the toolbox, click the foreground swatch. When the Color Picker appears, enter the following settings in the CMYK fields: M=99% and Y=98% (C and K are 0). Click OK. Click the background swatch and enter the following settings in the CMYK fields: M=99% and Y=97% (C and K are 0). Click OK to exit the Color Picker.

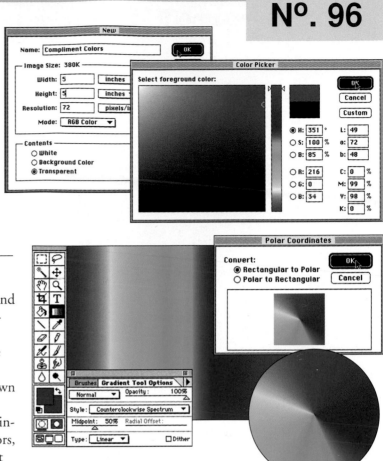

2 | Create a Wheel

Double-click the Gradient tool to select the tool and its corresponding Options palette. Choose the following settings in the Gradient Tool Options palette: Normal, 100% opacity; Counterclockwise Spectrum; Midpoint 50%; Linear. Deselect the Dither option. In the document window, hold down the Shift key and drag the Gradient tool from the left edge of the window to the right edge of the window. To create a circular representation of the colors, choose Filter→Distort→Polar Coordinates and set the Conversion method to Rectangular to Polar. Reset the foreground and background colors to black and white. Create a circular selection with the Elliptical Marquee tool. Invert the section and press Delete to clear the area around the circle.

3 | To Create a Selection Grid

Create a New layer (Layer 2). Click the Brush tool in the toolbox; then click the Brushes tab to display the available brushes. Choose a small brush and click on a red portion of the color wheel and then hold down the Shift key and click in a blue area of the wheel. A line appears between the two points. Continue holding down the Shift key and click a green area to create a second line; then close the area by Shift-clicking the starting point. Change the foreground color to a gray shade. From each of the three corners, create a line by Shift-clicking from the corner to the opposite side of the wheel.

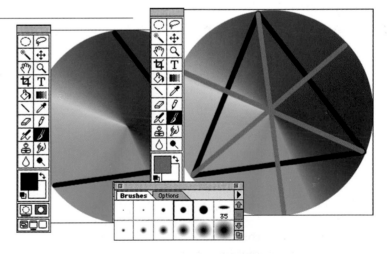

4 | To Select Complementary Colors

The color lying directly opposite one of the corners is its complementary color—defined by the gray lines. To choose the complement of any color, choose Select→All (⌘-A) on the grid layer (Layer 2), choose Image→Rotate→Arbitrary, and then enter a value to determine how much you want to rotate the grid to move one of the corners to the appropriate location. (You can move the grid one degree at a time, so you don't have to be perfect on the first attempt.) Save this file in Photoshop format (to maintain the layers) and use it whenever you need it.

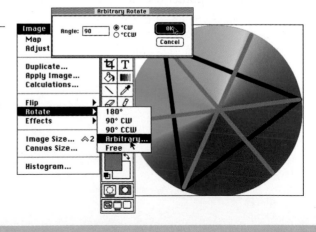

©95 M. Anthony

Mitchell Anthony, MADworks®

Comments

No matter how diligently you work, there's still a chance that some colors may shift when your image is output to a particular imagesetter and run on a specific press. Accurate color is a hallmark of fine design. This technique shows you how to make use of color targets to help you achieve the color results you want.

Studio Usage

The only way to be certain that colors reproduce within an acceptable range of color is by using color targets. All the artwork from MADworks® made use of color targets. Using this solution, you can begin to test the results of your vendor's equipment before you output color-critical projects.

Related Techniques

RGB versus CMYK   79

Enriching CMYK Colors   93

1 | Using Color Targets

This artist routinely includes color targets directly inside the images. Using this method, you can simply use an electronic device to measure the results of the target strip found at the right side of the artwork when the image is output. (A ColorTron is a good example of such a device.) If discrepancies occur between the targeted values and the output values, inks and densities can be adjusted on press to accommodate for differences.

2 | To Create Target Strips

Using a drawing program that can save files in EPS format, create a grid of squares. Fill some of the boxes with standard mixes of CMYK colors and leave some of the squares blank. The blank boxes can be used to accommodate custom-created colors directly in Photoshop. Save the file as an EPS file.

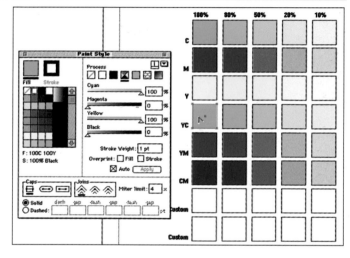

3 | To Open the EPS File

In Photoshop, choose File→Open, select the file from the file list, and open the image directly into a Photoshop window. Choose a resolution equivalent to an average project. (You may also want to consider creating several files at different line screens—266 dpi for 133 line screen; 300 dpi for a 150 line screen; 350 dpi for a 175 line screen.)

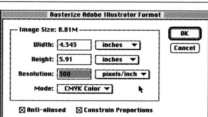

4 | To Add Custom Colors

Add any custom colors found in your document into the blank grid spaces at the bottom of the standard colors. You can also choose to sample colors directly from the image using the Eyedropper tool. After you sample a color, use the Paint Bucket (fill) tool to drop the colors into the appropriate spaces.

Illustration: Jeff Yesh, Cover Design: Tim Amrhein

Comments

Each image contains a specific range of colors—some of which you may want to use in other applications. You can create your own custom paint swatch palettes to save the colors from specific images.

Studio Usage

You can save color characteristics from an image by storing the image's colors in separate paint swatch palettes. After you've saved the colors, you can use them to create color themes in other images or add the colors to existing swatch palettes.

Related Techniques

Selecting Colors   14

Selective Color   90

Creating Color Wheels   95

1 | Create an Empty Palette

First, make sure that the Swatches palette is displayed. If it is not displayed, choose Window→Palettes→Show Swatches. Move the cursor onto the palette; then hold down the Command key. The cursor becomes a scissors icon—click each color swatch to cut all the colors from the palette.

Tip: Position the scissors icon over the first swatch at the top-left corner of the palette and click the mouse button repeatedly. Each time you click, the color at the top-left corner is deleted and all the remaining colors shift one space to the left.

2 | Select Colors for the Custom Palette

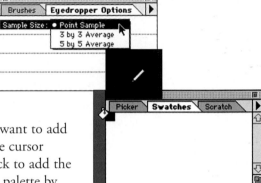

Open the document in which you want to select colors for the custom swatches palette. Double-click the Eyedropper tool to select the tool and its corresponding Option palette. Select the Point Sample option from the Sample Size pop-up menu in the Eyedropper Options palette. The Point Sample option selects a single pixel directly under the pointer. Using the Eyedropper tool, click a color you want to add to the swatch palette (which becomes the foreground color). Position the cursor within the blank swatch palette; the cursor becomes a paint bucket. Click to add the color to the palette. Add all the colors you want included in the custom palette by selecting each color and clicking the paint bucket within the swatch palette.

3 | Save the Palette

Choose Save Swatches from the Swatches sub-menu. The Save Swatches dialog box appears. In this example, a folder named Custom Swatch Books was created, and the swatch palette was saved using the name Monster Swatches. If you're going to use many different custom paint swatch palettes, it's a good idea to organize them in a single folder for easy retrieval. To return to the default swatches, choose Reset Swatches from the Swatches submenu. To combine several swatch palettes, choose Append Swatches from the Swatches submenu and select each palette that you want to add to the existing swatches.

4 | Save a Palette Model

In order to create new custom swatch palettes, cut all but one color from the default palette and then save the palette with a unique name. (Completely blank swatch palettes cannot be loaded using the Load Swatches option in the Swatches submenu.) Each time you want to create a new palette, open the palette containing the single color, save the palette under a new name, and then add colors to the palette.

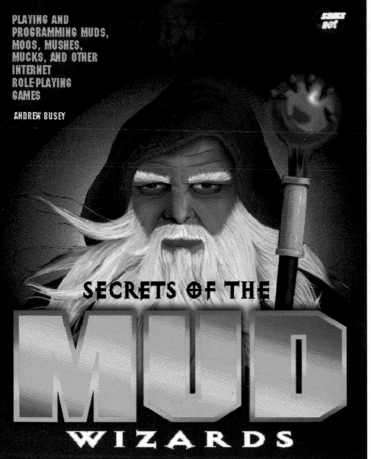

Illustrator: Jeff Yesh; Cover Design: Tim Amrhein

Comments

Adobe Photoshop enables you to open or place Adobe Illustrator files, or to copy and paste selections from Adobe Illustrator into Adobe Photoshop.

Studio Usage

When working with projects that contain large amounts of type or when you want type to appear along a path, you should create the type in Adobe Illustrator and then import or paste it into the Photoshop document. The extensive type functions available in Adobe Illustrator allow you to create and modify type in ways that are not available in Adobe Photoshop.

Related Techniques

The Pen Tool   110

Importing and
Exporting Paths   115

EPS   122

1 | To Place Type from Illustrator

In Adobe Illustrator, save the file in EPS format by choosing File→Save As and then choosing EPS from the Format pop-up menu at the bottom of the Save As dialog box. To place the artwork in an Adobe Photoshop document, choose File→Place, select the EPS file from the file list, and then click OK. A rectangular selection box appears in the Photoshop document. To scale the artwork before placing it, drag the squares at the corners of the selection box; to place the artwork, click the gavel within the rectangular selection area, and then deselect the artwork.

2 | To Create a Path for Type

In Adobe Photoshop, choose Window→Palettes→Show Paths. Select the pen tool and draw a path in the shape along which you want type to appear. When you have completed the path, click the selection tool in the Paths palette, hold down the Option key, and click the path to select the entire path. Choose Edit→Copy to copy the path onto the Clipboard.

3 | To Create Type on the Path

Open a new, blank document in Adobe Illustrator, choose View→Artwork (⌘-E), and then choose Edit→Paste. The path from the Photoshop image is pasted into the Illustrator document. Choose the Path Type tool from the toolbox and click the path to position the type cursor on the path. Type the desired text; it appears along the shape of the path. To adjust the type on the path, drag the I-beam that appears at the beginning of the type using one of the selection tools.

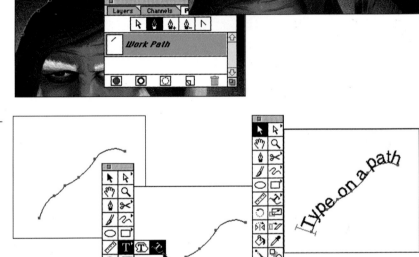

4 | Paste the Type into the Photoshop Image

When you have completed the type in Adobe Illustrator, choose Edit→Copy (⌘-C), return to the Adobe Photoshop document, and choose Edit→Paste (⌘-V). The type appears and is selected. Choose a selection tool from the toolbox and drag the type onto the path in the Photoshop image. When the type is positioned where you want it, select the Paths palette and delete the Workpath by dragging it to the trash icon.

Greg Simsic

Comments

When creating type, it's best to work in a vector-based application such as Adobe Illustrator, rather than a raster-based application such as Photoshop. Vector images retain their crisp, clear lines when they are scaled and resized. Raster images, because they're resolution-dependent, can appear jagged and lose detail when they are scaled. Import the type into Photoshop when you're ready to add the special effects.

Studio Usage

Neon or glowing type, a very interesting and popular effect, is easy to create in Photoshop by using paths and brushes. Neon type works well against dark backgrounds and can be used in a variety of ways—for example, to simulate signs or neon art. The number of possible creative variations is limited only by your imagination.

Related Techniques

Selecting Colors   14

Custom Brushes   16

Defining Layers   50

Importing and
Exporting Paths   115

1 | Create and Import the Type

Create the type in a drawing or illustration application (Adobe Illustrator was used in this example). Select the type and choose Type→Create Outlines to convert the type to paths. Choose Edit→Copy or press ⌘-C to copy the paths to the Clipboard. In Photoshop, choose File→New (or open the file you want to use as the background) and choose Edit→Paste or press ⌘-V. In the Paste dialog box, select the Paste as Paths option and click OK.

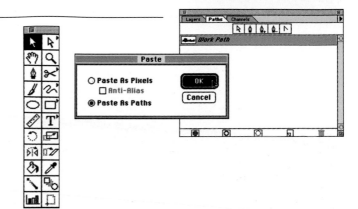

2 | Stroke the Path

Display the Paths palette. Choose Save Path from the Paths pop-up menu and save the Work Path as Path 1. Select a color for the glow and a large, soft brush. Select a paint tool in the toolbox and click the stroke path icon (the second icon from the left at the bottom of the Paths palette). Alternately, you can choose Stroke Path from the Paths palette pop-up menu, choose a tool in the Stroke Paths dialog box, and click OK. Select a second color and a smaller, harder brush. Stroke again. Repeat this procedure several times, each time using a different color and a smaller, harder brush.

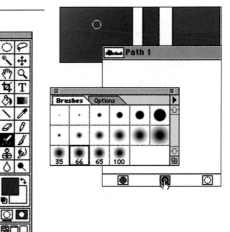

3 | Experiment with Brush Shapes

Choose New Brush from the Brushes palette pop-up menu and create a new, angled brush. You can experiment using variations on the brush specifications shown here. As the brush turns curves on the path, it provides a calligraphic effect.

4 | Delete the Path

When you're finished creating the neon glow, choose Delete Path from the Paths palette pop-up menu. Although paths don't increase the file size as much as layers, it's a good idea to eliminate them when they're no longer needed.

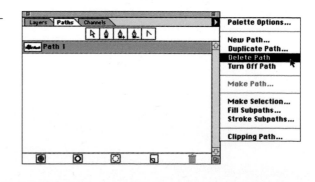

Gary Poyssick

Comments

Two factors determine how much an object reflects its surroundings—the reflective properties of the surface in which the reflection occurs, and the distance of the reflected object from that surface.

Studio Usage

Shiny objects reflect what's around them—and sometimes even parts of themselves—if their surfaces face each other. By using channels, you can reproduce this effect by placing one image inside another.

Related Techniques

Wave and Zigzags   27

Managing Channels   59

Metallic Type   102

1 Create the Channels

Create the type in an illustration program. Choose File→Open and open a Photoshop image. Display the Channels palette and click the page icon at the bottom of the palette. Name the channel type. Choose File→Place to import the type into the Type channel. Choose Image→Map→Invert (⌘-I) to invert the type from black to white. Drag the Type channel over the new channel icon (the page) at the bottom of the Channels palette to create a copy of the channel. Follow the directions in Tip Number 102 (Metallic Type) to create metallic highlights for the type and then save the results in a third channel.

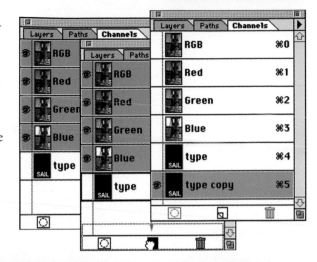

2 Copy a Grayscale Selection

If the reflection is blurred and indistinct, you can use almost any image to simulate the reflection. Choose File→Open and open a grayscale image. Click the Marquee tool and select an area that's approximately the size of the reflective object (in this case the type). Choose Edit→Copy or press ⌘-C to copy the selection to the Clipboard. A landscape is used in this example. In general, horizontal images work well for creating reflections.

3 Paste the Reflection into the Type Channel

Click the Type copy channel (#5) and load the selection by dragging the channel to the load selection icon. Choose Edit→Paste Into and paste the landscape into the type selection. Choose Filter→Blur→Gaussian Blur and blur the selection. The less you blur, the more distinct the reflection is—that means, the closer the object appears to be to the reflecting surface, the shinier the reflection. You can also apply Wave or other filters to distort the selection. When you've finished modifying the selection, choose Edit→Copy (⌘-C) to copy the selection to the Clipboard.

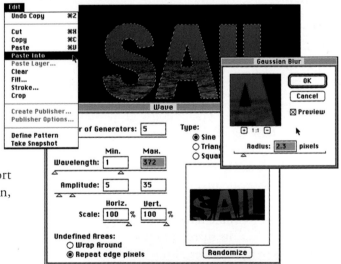

4 Paste the Results into the Composite Channel

Click the composite channel to make it the target channel. Drag the Type channel over the load selection icon (the rectangle containing the dotted circle) at the bottom of the Channels palette to load the contents of the channel. Choose Edit→Paste Info to paste the reflection into the type. Drag the Metallic channel over the load selection icon to load the metallic highlights and then press the Delete key. The highlights appear, making the reflection look more realistic.

Bill Morse

Comments

Metallic and other highly-polished surfaces have unique highlight and shadow reflective patterns. You can achieve extremely realistic metallic effects by following this simple step-by-step procedure that makes use of Photoshop's channels and filters.

Studio Usage

This technique is useful for any kind of type that you want to appear as metallic or shiny. The procedure also produces interesting effects when applied to artwork depicting glass, crystal, liquid, or any other reflective material.

Related Techniques

Managing Channels   59

Reflections in Type   101

Smoked Glass   104

1 | Create or Load the Type

Create the type in an illustration program. Choose File→Open to open the Photoshop document you want to use as the background. Display the Channels palette. Click the page icon at the bottom of the Channels palette to create a new channel. Choose File→Place to import the type into Channel #4. Choose Image→Map→Invert (⌘-I) to make the type white. Drag Channel #4 over the page icon to create a copy of the type in Channel #5. (To rename the channels, double-click the channel and enter the name in the Channel Options dialog box.) Choose Filter→Other→Offset. Enter values in the Offset dialog box. Use higher values for higher-resolution images and to produce more shine.

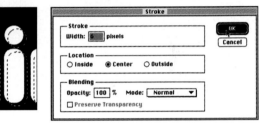

2 | Stroke the Channel

Make sure that white is the foreground color. With Channel #5 as the target channel, drag Channel #4 to the load selection icon to load Channel #4. Choose Edit→Stroke. In the Stroke dialog box, enter 6 for the Width, click the Center option, set Opacity at 100%, and set Mode at Normal. Click OK to stroke the selection with white.

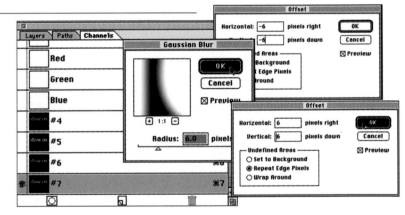

3 | Duplicate and Offset Channel #4

Select Channel #4. Drag Channel #4 over the page icon to create a copy of the type in Channel #6. Repeat the procedure to make a copy in Channel #7. Click Channel #6 to make it the target channel. Choose Filter→Blur→Gaussian Blur and blur the selection. Choose Filter→Other→Offset to offset the type. Repeat these two steps for Channel #7. (Offset the channels in the opposite directions—for example, enter -6 pixels for both axes for one channel and +6 for both axes for the other channel).

4 | Combine the Channels

Choose Image→Calculations. Combine Channels #6 and #7 using the Difference Blending mode, as shown in the dialog box. Save the results in a new channel (#8). Choose Select→None or press ⌘-D to deselect. Choose Image→Map→Invert or press ⌘-I to invert the channel, turning black into white and white into black. Look at the image. You can see that the highlights are very similar to the reflective properties of real-world metallic objects.

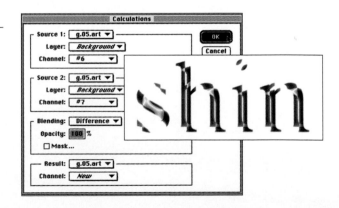

Comments

This technique shows the power of Photoshop's channels to create a realistic engraving effect in combination with filters. By adjusting the width of the text and the amount you "cut" into the surface, you can produce an amazing number of variations on this theme.

Studio Usage

When you have created the type in an illustration program, Photoshop has a capacity to build type effects that far outstrip applications that are more type-intensive—such as Illustrator, Freehand, Pagemaker, Quark, or Frame. You might consider doing your headlines, pull-quotes, or other type treatments in Photoshop, and then exporting them for use in other applications.

Related Techniques

Managing Channels   59

Metallic Type   102

Smoked Glass   104

1 | Create the Type and Cut Channels

Create the type in an illustration program, and then open the Photoshop document you want to use for the background. Display the Channels palette. Click the page icon at the bottom of the Channels palette to create a new channel and name it Primary. Choose File→Place to import the art. Drag the Primary channel to the page icon at the bottom of the Channels palette to duplicate it. Double-click the new channel to display the Channel Options dialog and name the duplicate channel Outside Edge. Choose Filter→Other→Maximum and enter a low value to "fatten" the type slightly. Choose Image→Map→Invert or press ⌘-I to invert the Outside Edge channel.

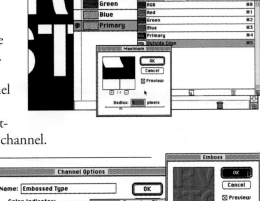

2 | Create an Embossed Channel

Drag the Primary Channel to the page icon to make another copy. Double-click the new channel and name it Embossed Type. Choose Filter→Blur→Gaussian Blur. In the Gaussian Blur dialog box, enter a Radius of about 5; you don't want the blur to be extreme. Choose Filter→Stylize→Emboss. In the Emboss dialog box, enter a negative value for the Angle; then adjust the Height (to throw the shadow) and the Amount. The more you emboss the type, the deeper the "cut."

3 | Create the Shadows Channels

Drag the Embossed Channel to the page icon and name the duplicate channel Highlights (if you're working in an RGB document, this is channel #7). Choose Image→Adjust→Levels or press ⌘-L. In the Levels dialog box, click the black eyedropper and then click any gray area in the image. This turns all the gray areas black, leaving only the highlights visible. Duplicate the Embossed Channel again and name the second copy Shadows. Choose Image→Map→Invert or press ⌘-I and invert the Shadows channel. Press ⌘-L and, using the black eyedropper, click the gray in this channel leaving only the shadows visible.

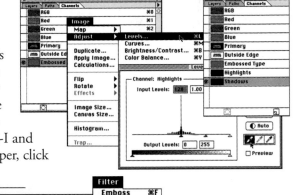

4 | Make the Cut

The Shadows channel is the target (as shown by the eye icon to the left of the channel name and the gray highlight). Shift-click the eye column for the Highlights channel, so both channels are the target (both names have eye icons and are highlighted). Load the Cut Edge channel by dragging it to the load selection icon (the icon on the far-left at the bottom of the Channels palette). Press Option-Delete. Drag the Primary Channel to the load selection icon to load the original type and then press Option-Delete again. Finally, make one last copy of the Primary Channel and name it Lower Surface. Press ⌘-I to invert this channel. Choose Filter→Other→Offset and enter identical values of 4 into the Horizontal and Vertical options in the Offset dialog box. This moves the selection down and to the right slightly.

5 | Shading the Cut

Click the RGB channel or press ⌘-0 to make the color channels the target. Drag the original Primary channel to the load selection icon. Choose Image→Adjust→Levels or press ⌘-L. In the Levels dialog box, drag the black Input Levels triangle to darken the selection. If you prefer, you can choose Image→Adjust→ Brightness and Contrast or press ⌘-B and drag the Brightness slider to darken the selection. Drag the Shadows channel to the load selection icon and use the Levels command or the Brightness and Contrast command to darken the selection.

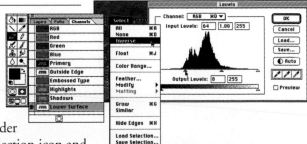

Comments

There are so many amazing effects that you can achieve using type, backgrounds, and various opacity and density settings, that the sky is literally the limit. This technique demonstrates how simple type against a patterned background can produce a striking effect.

Studio Usage

Text techniques can be used for presentations, banners, posters, book covers, or anywhere that you want to creatively emphasize text. It's always best to import type from an illustration program. You will usually want to place the imported type in a channel, so that you can manipulate it before adding it to the Photoshop image.

Related Techniques

Creating Lighting Effects   22

Textures on Layers   38

Managing Channels   59

1 | Create a Type Channel

Create the type in an illustration program and import it into Photoshop using the File→Place command. When the type appears, click the gavel within the rectangle to position the type in the document. Choose Select→Save Selection. In the Save Selection dialog box, click OK to save the type in a new channel. Press delete to delete the original type from the window—you will only use the saved outline of the type for the technique.

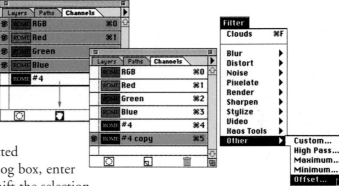

2 | Duplicate and Offset the Channel

Click the Channels palette tab and then click Channel #4 to select the new channel. To duplicate the channel, drag Channel #4 to the new page icon at the bottom of the palette. The new channel (#5) is named #4 copy. To load the type outline selection, drag the #4 copy channel to the load selection icon at the bottom of the Channels palette (the rectangle containing the dotted circle). Choose Filter→Other→Offset. In the Offset dialog box, enter the same value in the Horizontal and Vertical boxes to shift the selection by the amount you enter.

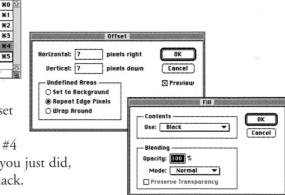

3 | Cut Shadow Masks

Select Channel #4. Load #4 copy (the offset channel) by dragging it to the load selection icon at the bottom of the Channels palette. Choose Select→Inverse or press ⌘-I to reverse the selected areas. Choose Edit→Fill. In the Fill dialog box, choose Black from the Use menu. Leave the Opacity at 100% and set the Mode to Normal. Click OK to fill the selection. Now, select #4 copy (Channel #5) to make it the target channel and load Channel #4 by dragging it to the load selection icon (you're doing exactly what you just did, but in reverse), choose Select→Inverse and fill this selection with black.

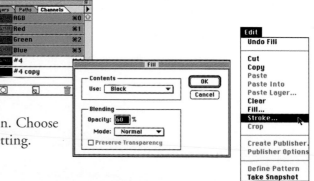

4 | Load and Fill the Masks

Click RGB to return to the composite channel or press ⌘-0. Drag Channel #4 to the load selection icon. Choose Edit→Fill and fill the selection with black at an Opacity setting of 60%. Choose Edit→Stroke. In the Stroke dialog box enter a small value in Width and Stroke. Put a black rule around the channel. Drag #4 copy to the load selection icon. Choose Edit→Fill and fill this selection with black at a 70% Opacity setting.

Phil Howe

Comments

In the Neon Type technique, the appearance of neon type was simulated using stroked paths. You can also add a glow around type by using channels.

Studio Usage

Slightly different from neon type, glowing type or objects have a sharper definition but similarly soft lighting. You can use this technique to put a glow around an object or a piece of line art.

Related Techniques

Managing Channels   59

Reflections in Type   101

Metallic Type   102

1 Create a Channel for the Type

Choose File→Open and select the Photoshop document you want to use as the background. Display the Channels palette. Click the page icon at the bottom of the Channels palette to create a new channel. In the Channel Options dialog box, name the channel Type. Choose File→Place to place the art (if it was created in an illustration program) and then choose Image→Map→Invert (⌘-I) to invert the type from black to white. You can also select the Type tool in Photoshop and enter the type directly into the channel.

2 Create a Channel for the Glow

Drag the Type channel to the page icon at the bottom of the Channels palette to duplicate the channel. Double-click the new channel to display the Channel Options dialog box and name the second channel *Glow.*

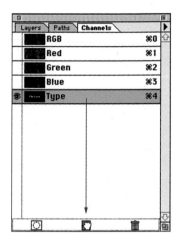

3 Create the Glow

Click the default colors icon in the toolbox to return to a white foreground color. Choose Edit→Stroke. In the Stroke dialog box, enter a value for the Width (the wider the stroke, the bigger the glow). Select the Outside location to start the stroke from the outside edge of the selection. Set the Opacity to 100% and the Mode to Normal and then click OK. Click anywhere outside the selected area to deselect the type.

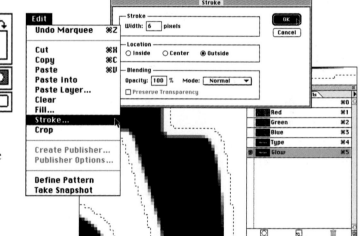

4 Adjust the Glow

Choose Filter→Blur→Gaussian Blur. Drag the Radius slider in the Gaussian Blur dialog box to diffuse the glow. Use higher values to make the glow softer. Click the RGB channel. Drag the Glow channel to the load selection icon (the dotted circle icon at the bottom left of the Channels palette) to load the selection. Adjust the color of the glow by choosing Image→Adjust→Color Balance (⌘-Y) or Image→Adjust→Hue/Saturation (⌘-U). Glows usually look best when they're filled with very saturated colors. Drag the Type channel to the load selection icon to load the type. Adjust the color of the type until you get the effect you want.

Comments

Photoshop provides an Emboss filter; however, this filter has limited capabilities and doesn't produce a totally realistic effect. To create embossed surfaces with more dramatic impact, try this technique using channels to emphasize the embossed surfaces.

Studio Usage

True embossing creates a plateau of the embossed graphic. The plateau has a definite top and sides and the height determines the shadows that the object casts. Embossing can be used to add an extra dimension to type when more than a simple shadow effect is required. Almost any logo, sign, or poster can benefit from this technique.

Related Techniques

Managing Channels   59

Reflections in Type   101

Metallic Type   102

1 | Create a Channel for the Type

Create the type in an illustration program. In Photoshop, open the document you want to use as the background. Display the Channels palette. Click the page icon (the middle icon at the bottom of the Channels palette) to create a new channel and name it Top Surface. Choose File→Place to import the type. Choose Edit→Fill and choose White from the Use pop-up menu to fill the type with white. Duplicate the Top Surface channel by dragging it to the page icon. Deselect the text and choose Filter→Other→Maximum. Enter a value that expands the edges of the type by a noticeable amount, but doesn't distort it. Click OK.

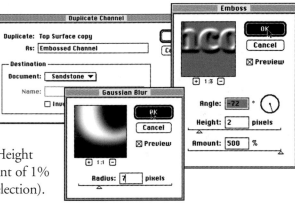

2 | Duplicate the Top Surface and Emboss

Duplicate the Top Surface copy channel and name it Embossed Channel. Choose Filter→Blur→Gaussian Blur. In the Gaussian Blur dialog box, drag the Radius slider to enter a value slighter higher than the Maximum value you entered in Step #1. Click OK. Choose Filter→Stylize→Emboss. In the Emboss dialog box, set the Angle by entering a negative value. (A positive value raises the surface and a negative value stamps the surface.) Drag the Height slider to about 2 and enter a high percentage for Amount. (An amount of 1% produces the least color; 500% retains the color at the edges of the selection).

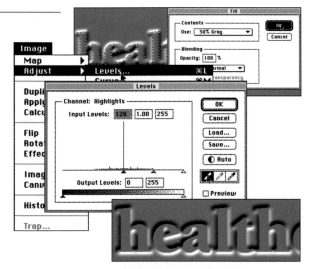

3 | Create the Flat Surface

With the Embossed Channel as the target, drag the Top Surface channel to the load selection icon. Choose Edit→Fill. In the Fill dialog box, choose 50% Gray from the Use pop-up menu. Click OK to fill the selection. Deselect the text. Duplicate the Embossed channel and name the new channel Highlights. Choose Image→Adjust→Levels or press ⌘-L. Select the black eyedropper in the Levels dialog box and click anywhere in the gray area of the channel. The image turns black—except for the highlights. Click OK. Duplicate the Embossed channel again and name this channel Shadows. Choose Image→Map→Invert or press ⌘-I to invert the Shadows channel. Repeat the Levels command; only the shadows remain white. Click OK.

4 | Use Channels to Emphasize the Embossing

Click the RGB channel and drag the Top Surface channel to the load selection icon. Press ⌘-L and drag the black Output Levels slider to the right to lighten the text. Click OK. Drag the Highlights channel to the load selection icon. Adjust the channel's brightness using the Output Levels sliders in the Levels dialog box or by choosing Image→Adjust→Hue/Saturation (⌘-U) and dragging the Lightness slider. Click OK. Finally, drag the Shadows channel to the load selection icon. Use the Levels command or the Hue/Saturation command to darken the shadows. Click OK and deselect the mask to see your emboss.

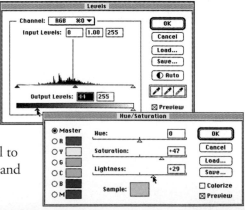

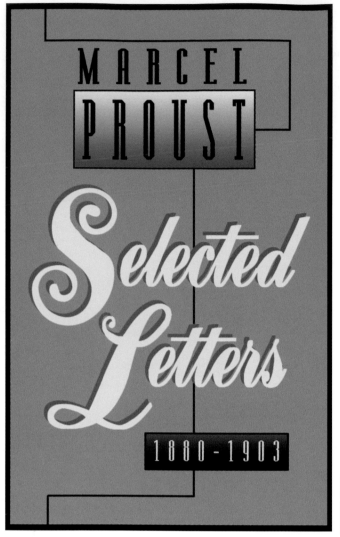

Mike Pantuso

Comments

Before computers could display color or grayscale images, all images had "jagged" edges where the pixels changed from black to white. This effect wasn't so noticeable in high-resolution images, but at lower resolutions, edges had a definite stair-step appearance. Anti-aliasing eliminates harsh transitions from one color to another by only partially filling edge pixels. This creates a smooth blend where one color flows into another. No detail is lost because only the edge pixels change.

Studio Usage

Most type and high-contrast line art benefit from anti-aliasing. You can apply anti-aliasing to type in several different situations—when you open an Adobe Illustrator file, when you're creating text objects, or when you're converting paths to outlines. Unless you're seeking a special effect, it's best to always use anti-aliased type.

Related Techniques

Managing Channels   59

Metallic Type   102

Importing and
Exporting Paths   115

1 | Create a New Document

Choose File→New or press ⌘-N to create a 2.5-inch square, 300 ppi, RGB document with a white background.

2 | Create a Type Element

Select the Type tool and click the document. In the Type Tool dialog box, choose a serif font from the Font pop-menu (Berkeley Black is used in this example). Enter a large size and type an uppercase O in the text box. Deselect the Anti-Aliased option and click the center icon in the Alignment options box. Click OK to display the text. Select the Zoom tool and zoom in on the text edge. You can see that the edge is very hard with no blending from the black to white pixels.

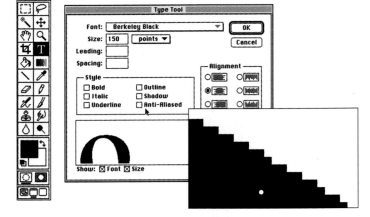

3 | Create Anti-Aliased Type

Press the Delete key to clear the type you just created. Use the Type tool to click the document again. In the Type Tool dialog box, select the Anti-Aliased option. Click OK to display the type. Choose Select→Hide Edges or press ⌘-H to hide the Selection marquee. Zoom in again and examine the edges. You can see that applying anti-aliasing results in the edge pixels being partially filled, creating a soft transition from the black to the white pixels. Delete the text.

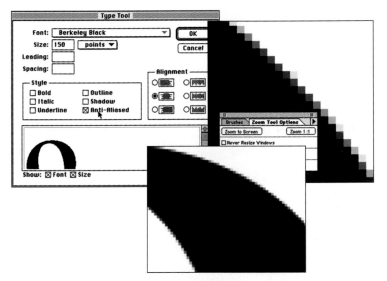

4 | Use an Anti-Aliased Brush

Select a medium brush in the Brushes palette and double-click. In the Brush Options dialog box, drag the Hardness slider all the way to the right until it reads 100%. Select the Paintbrush tool and stroke. Even though the brush is at maximum hardness, the stroke edge is still anti-aliased. When you use most of the painting tools—such as the Paintbrush tool, the Rubber Stamp tool, or the Airbrush tool—anti-aliasing is on by default. Select the Pencil tool and draw a line. Zoom in, if necessary, so that you can see the stroke edge. The Pencil tool draws without anti-aliasing.

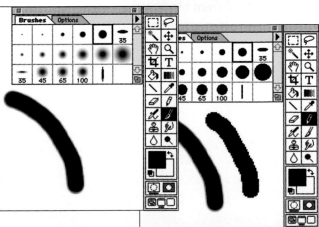

Comments

Photoshop provides many ways to produce worn-looking type. This effect uses channels and filters to create a broken effect in type.

Studio Usage

This technique simulates the appearance of burned-in type, and works well for putting type on wood surfaces. The effect is equally successful using serif or sans serif fonts. Vary the opacity of the type color to let more or less of the background surface show through the letters.

Related Techniques

Managing Channels   59

Reflections in Type   101

Cut Stone   103

1 | Create Type in a Channel

Open the Channels palette, click the new channel icon to create a new channel, and name the channel Type channel. To type in the channel, select the tool from the toolbox, click the tool in the channel to open the Type dialog box, enter the type, and then click OK.

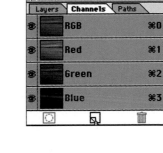

2 | Paint the Type

In a channel, black is opaque and white is transparent, and any color between black and white is converted to a shade of gray. When you type directly into a channel, it's important to paint the type outline white, so that it is interpreted as transparent when it is loaded back onto an image as a selection. Make sure that the foreground color is set to white, choose Edit→Fill, and fill the type with 100% white. Click OK.

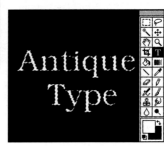

3 | Create Texture in Type

While the type selection is still active, choose Filter→Noise→Add Noise, select the Gaussian option, and drag the slider to a value above 100. After you've applied noise, choose Filter→Stylize—>Diffuse to blur the noise. Choose Select→None (⌘-D) to deselect the type, and then apply the Diffuse filter to the entire channel two more times. (To repeat the last filter using the same settings, press⌘-F).

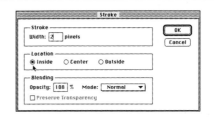

4 | Edit the Type in the Channel

Click the Magic Wand tool, click in the black area of the channel, and then choose Select→Inverse to reselect the type. Choose Edit→Stroke. In the Stroke dialog box, enter a Width of 2 or 3 pixels, select the Inside option (so the stroke starts from the inside edge of the text), set the Opacity to 100% and the Mode to Normal, and click OK.

5 | Place the Type in the Background

Click RGB in the Channels palette (⌘-0) to return to the composite channel. Drag the Texture channel to the Load Selection icon. Select a foreground color and choose Edit→Fill. In the Fill dialog box, choose Foreground Color from the Use menu and adjust the Opacity setting. The lower the opacity, the more the background shows through and the more worn the type appears. To see the effect more clearly, choose Select→Hide or press (⌘-H) to temporarily hide the selection marquee.

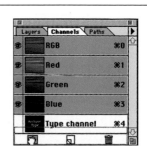

Judith J. Moncrieff

Comments

Filling type with images is a frequently used design function that produces many interesting and unexpected combinations. This technique is quick and easy to use in Photoshop.

Studio Usage

Posters, logos, and any project that demands a dramatic headline or copy element lends itself well to this effect. The possibilities for using this technique are so unlimited that you might soon find it to be one of your favorite expressions of creative vision.

Related Techniques

Managing Channels   59

Metallic Type   102

Importing and
Exporting Paths   115

1 | Create a New Document

Choose File→New or press ⌘-N to create a new document that is appropriate to the project you're designing. This example uses an oblong RGB document that is 5 by 2 inches with a resolution of 300 ppi.

2 | Create a Channel for the Type

Display the Channels palette. Click the page icon at the bottom of the Channels palette to create a new channel and name it Type. Select the Type tool and click the document. In the Type Tool dialog box, choose a font from the Font pop-up menu (Berkeley Black is used in this example), and a font size. Type the text in the text box and click OK. The type appears in white on a black background.

3 | Copy the Image and Paste into the Type

Choose File→Open or press ⌘-O to open the image you're going to use to fill the type. Select the Marquee tool and make a rectangular selection, roughly proportional to the size of the type. Choose Edit→Copy or press ⌘-C to copy the image to the Clipboard. Return to the document that contains the type. Click the RGB channel or press ⌘-0 to make it the target channel and choose Edit→Paste Into. A portion of the image appears in the type.

4 | Cleaning Up

Select the Move tool and drag the image until the portion you want is showing through the type. A selection rectangle indicates the edges of the pasted image. When the type is in position, choose a foreground color to form a border around the type. Choose Edit→Stroke. In the Stroke dialog box, enter a small value in the Width option and click Center in the Location options. Click OK to stroke the type. The stroke increases the contrast between the type and the image and emphasizes the type edge.

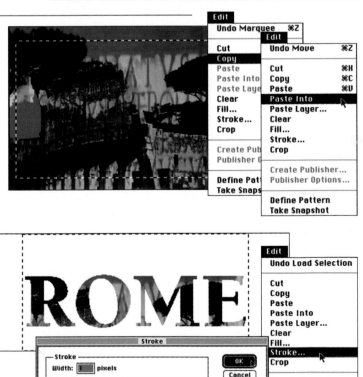

Drawing *The Pen Tool*

Lucas Deaver

Comments

You use the Pen tool to draw straight or curved lines, called *paths*. After you have drawn a path, you can fill or stroke the path with any of the painting tools. You can also turn a path into a selection. For certain types of objects, it is easier to draw a path using the Pen tool and then turn the path into a selection. You can save, edit, and delete paths without affecting any underlying pixels in an illustration.

Studio Usage

The Pen tool works well when you must draw outlines around objects that combine straight and curved lines. You can also use the Pen tool to create paths for designs, later painting or stroking the paths to color the design.

Related Techniques

Converting Paths
and Selections   113

Importing and
Exporting Paths   115

1 | To Draw Straight Lines

Open a new document. Choose Window→Palettes→Show Paths to select the Paths palette. Click the Pen tool in the Paths palette. To draw a straight line, click the Pen tool and then click again on another point on the page to create a line between the two points. Each time you click the Pen tool another line is drawn between two points. To end a path, click the Pen tool in the Paths palette. To close a path, click the Pen tool over the starting point of the path.

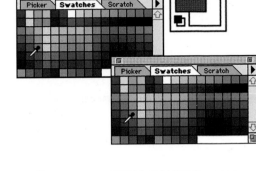

2 | To Draw Curved Lines

To draw curved lines, double-click the Pen tool to select the Pen Tool Options palette. Click the Rubber Band option. The Rubber Band option displays a preview of the shape of the line before you actually place the point by clicking again. To draw a curved line, select the Pen tool, click and drag the mouse to establish the direction of the first curve, and then click and drag again to create a curved path between the two points. After you have finished drawing the path, click the Pen tool in the Paths palette to end the path. Each time you complete a path, you *must* click the Pen tool to end the path; otherwise, the Pen tool connects the points to form a continuous path.

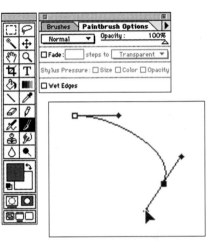

3 | To Combine Straight and Curved Lines

To alternate between drawing straight lines and curved lines, click where you want straight segments and then click and drag where you want curved lines. To establish the direction of a curved line, hold down the Option key, position the Pen tool on the point from which the curve will be drawn, and then drag in the direction you want the next curve.

4 | To Convert a Path to a Selection

To turn a path into a selection, make sure that the path is selected in the Paths palette. Click the Selection icon at the bottom of the Paths palette (the rectangle with the dotted circle). The path becomes a selection, which can then be edited or saved. To delete a path that you are no longer using, drag the path to the Trash icon at the bottom of the Paths palette.

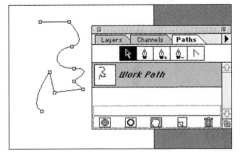

Drawing *Planning Paths*

Paul Watson

Comments

The Pen tool requires more practice to master than any other tool in your Photoshop repertoire. Each time you click the Pen tool, you set an anchor point. When you click the Pen tool, the line between two anchor points is straight. When you click and drag the Pen tool, the line between two anchor points is curved. This tip shows you how to best position anchor points for straight and curved lines.

Studio Usage

The types of images with which the Pen tool works best usually combine straight lines and curves—like the scissors in this image. Getting your paths to perfectly align with curves in an existing document requires practice.

Related Techniques

The Pen Tool   110

Managing Paths   112

Converting Paths
  and Selections   113

Exporting Outlines   114

1 | Positioning Anchor Points

Open a piece of artwork that contains several curves and select the Pen tool from the Paths palette. Click the Pen tool at the start of a curve. Click and drag at the midpoint of the curve and then click and drag at the end of the curve. Press the Delete key twice—the first time you press Delete, the last anchor point you drew is erased; the second time you press Delete, the entire path is deleted. Then draw the curve again, this time using only two anchor points. Click and drag at the start of the curve; then click and drag again at the end of the curve. Notice that the curve is the same shape, and was drawn with fewer anchor points. As a general rule, the fewer anchor points you use, the smoother the curve is.

2 | To Add and Delete Points to a Path

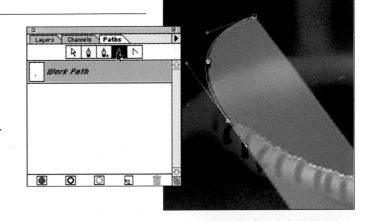

You can add and delete anchor points to adjust paths you've already created by using the Pen tool. To delete points, click the Pen tool directly on the anchor point that you want to remove. To add points, click the Pen tool on the existing path where you want to add points.

3 | To Adjust Anchor Points on a Path

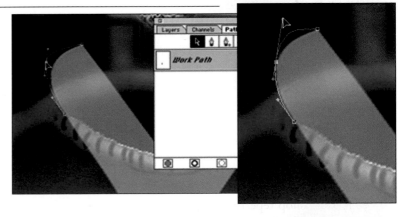

When a path requires an adjustment, use the Selection tool. To move a segment, choose the Selection tool and drag the anchor point to move the segments on either side of it. To adjust the shape of a curve, click the Selection tool on the anchor point—the two lines that emanate from the anchor point are called direction lines and have direction points at the ends. With the Selection tool, drag the direction points to adjust the shape of the curve. (Straight lines do not have direction lines and direction points.)

4 | To Change the Direction of a Curve

To change the direction of a curve while you're drawing, Option-click the anchor point where you want to adjust the direction of the curve; then drag from the anchor point in the direction you want the new curve to appear.

Drawing *Managing Paths*

Jacqueline Comstock

Comments

Documents can contain an unlimited number of paths. After you've mastered drawing paths, it's helpful to learn to manage them in your images. You can name, save, copy, and delete paths. You can also hide the paths you're not currently working with.

Studio Usage

When creating intricate selections, the Lasso tool often creates jagged edges. The Pen tool enables you to draw perfectly smooth paths, which can then be turned into a smooth-bordered selection.

Related Techniques

The Pen Tool   110

Importing and Exporting Paths   115

Photoshop 3.0 File Format   121

1 | To Name and Save Paths

While you're developing a path, it's called a *Work Path*. To name and save the path, choose Save Path from the Paths palette submenu, located in the upper-right corner of the palette. The Save Path dialog box appears. Enter a name and click OK to save the path.

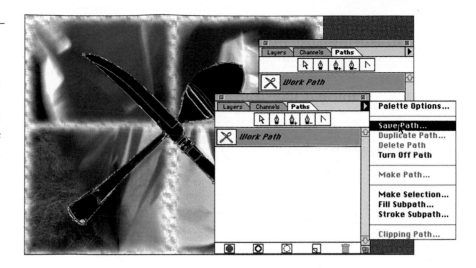

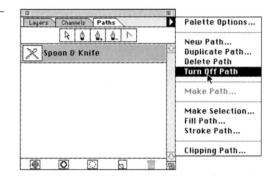

2 | To Hide a Path

Select the path you want to hide and then choose Turn Off Path from the Paths palette submenu or Shift-click its name in the Paths palette. To display the path, simply click its name in the Paths palette.

3 | To Create a Copy of a Path

Select the path in the Paths palette and drag it to the new path icon (the page icon) at the bottom of the Paths palette. A copy of the original path is created and added to the list of paths displayed in the palette. To rename the path, double-click the path name in the Paths palette, enter a name in the Rename Path dialog box, and click OK.

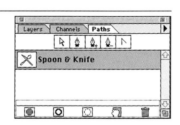

4 | To Delete a Path

To delete a path no longer in use, drag the path from the Paths palette to the Trash icon in the lower-right corner of the Paths palette.

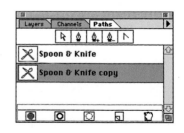

Drawing *Converting Paths and Selections*

Oko & Mano

Comments

As you develop complex outlines, selections, and composite images, you will need to convert paths to selections and vice versa. The Paths palette enables you to complete both conversions by using commands from the submenu or by choosing icons that correspond with the desired function.

Studio Usage

Some of the more complex selection functions allow you to create selection areas more quickly than you could with the Pen tool. If you need a path in a very complex shape, you might consider using the Color Range command to create the selection before you turn the selection into a path. You might also choose to convert a path into a selection before performing functions such as color-correcting or applying a gradient to a path.

Related Techniques

Adding to and Subtracting
   from Selections 6

Managing Paths 112

Exporting Outlines 114

1 | To Convert a Path to a Selection

To convert a path to a simple selection, drag the path from the Paths palette onto the make selection icon (the dotted circle inside the square) at the bottom of the palette. The path becomes a selection. The original path is hidden (deselected), but not deleted. You can now save the selection or make other color adjustments to it.

2 | Selection Options

To apply options to a selection, select the path in the Paths palette and choose Make Selection from the Paths palette submenu. The Make Selection dialog box appears. Enter a value in pixels for the Feather Radius. The number indicates how many pixels on either side of the selection edge are feathered. Select the Anti-aliased option for a smoother selection. You may also select an Operation option. The Operation options enable you to convert the path to a new selection, add to or subtract from an existing selection, or create a new selection consisting of the area where the path and the existing selection intersect.

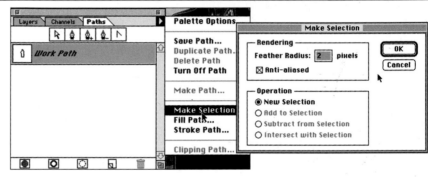

3 | To Convert a Selection to a Path

Before converting a selection to a path, it's a good idea to save the selection (in case you make an error and want to start the process again). Save the path using the Select→Save Selection command. With the selection still active, choose Make Path from the Paths palette submenu. The Make Path dialog box appears. Enter a value in the Tolerance field to indicate how sensitive the path should be to slight changes in the selection border. The higher the tolerance value, the less sensitive the path to the changes in the selection is, resulting in a path created with fewer anchor points (and potential distortion).

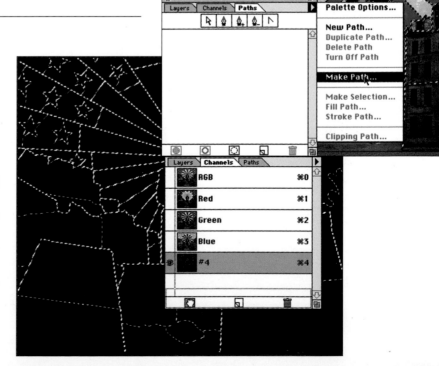

Drawing *Exporting Outlines*

Greg Vander Houwen

Comments

When you place a Photoshop image into another program, the illustration appears inside a solid white square. To eliminate the solid background surrounding the desired portion of the image, you can create a special path, called a clipping path. Clipping paths exclude (make transparent) the area outside the outline of the object.

Studio Usage

A clipping path cuts the background away from the selection border—making the background transparent to page layout and drawing programs. By using this technique, you won't have to import images surrounded by white boxes.

Related Techniques

The Pen Tool   110

Managing Paths   112

Converting Paths
and Selections   113

EPS   122

1 | Create an Outline for the Clipping Path

From the Paths palette, select the Pen tool and create the outline around the area that you want to export. Double-click the Work Path in the Paths palette to select the Path dialog box and then enter a name for the path.

2 | Create a Clipping Path

A clipping path is actually a specialized set of PostScript instructions that act to eliminate the area outside of the path. Choose Clipping Path from the Paths palette submenu; then select the path name from the Paths pop-up menu in the Clipping Path dialog box. Click OK. The path's name is displayed in hollow type in the Paths palette to indicate that it has been defined as a clipping path.

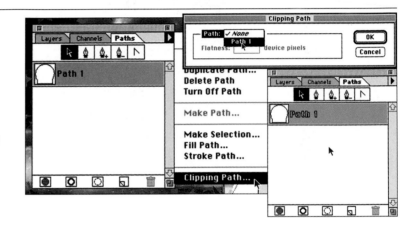

3 | Save the File in EPS Format

In order to save a clipping path with a file, you must save the document as an EPS (Encapsulated PostScript) file. Choose File→Save As and then choose EPS from the Format pop-up menu at the bottom of the Save Dialog box. Click Save and the EPS Format dialog box appears.

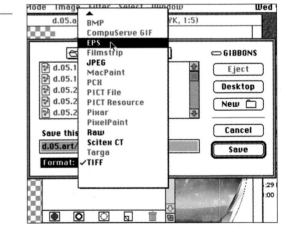

4 | Save the Clipping Path with the File

In the EPS Format dialog box, select the desired clipping path from the Path pop-up menu. You *must* select the path name for the path to be saved with the document. To import the clipping path, open the program you want to place the clipping path in, choose the appropriate command for importing images, and then select the file name from the list and click Open. The area outside the clipping path is transparent.

Drawing *Importing and Exporting Paths*

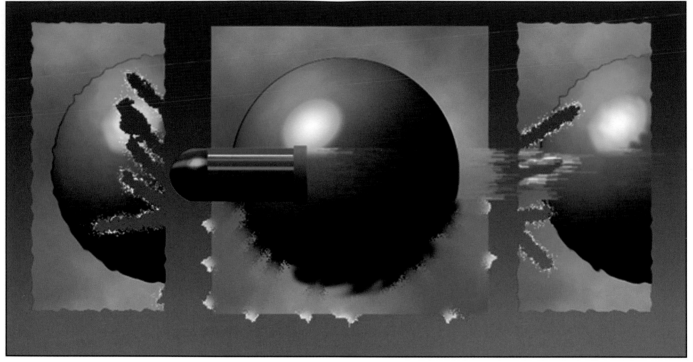

Victor Claudio

Comments

You can export paths from Photoshop to Illustrator, and import paths from Illustrator into Photoshop. The Photoshop Pen tool and the Illustrator Pen tool function almost identically.

Studio Usage

Much of the artwork you see in this book was created using several programs. To achieve certain effects, you'll need to use more than one program. For example, to check the size and alignment of objects between two programs, you could export a path to Illustrator, size and align type along the path in Illustrator, and then import the correctly sized type back into the Photoshop illustration.

Related Techniques

Importing Custom Masks 63

The Pen Tool 110

Managing Paths 112

Converting Paths
and Selections 113

1 | Select the Path

In Photoshop, create a path using the Pen tool or select an existing path by clicking its name in the Paths palette.

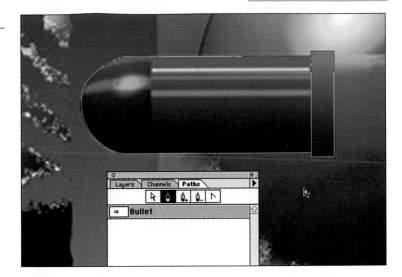

2 | Export the Path

Choose File→Export/Paths to Illustrator, name and save the file, and then click OK.

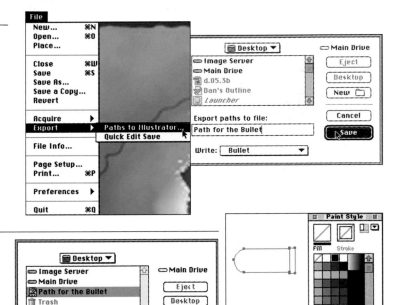

3 | Open the Path in Illustrator

In Illustrator, choose File→Open (⌘-O), select the file name from the file list, and click Open. When the file opens in Illustrator, a set of crop-marks appear that indicate the size of the selection. However, the path is not visible because no fill or stroke options have been applied. Choose View→Artwork (⌘-E) to display the outline of the path; then select the path and apply the desired options. Choose View→Preview (⌘-Y) to see the results.

4 | Paste the Illustrator Path into Photoshop

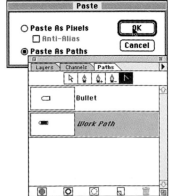

Choose Edit→Copy (⌘-C) to copy the edited path to the Clipboard. (You can copy and paste PostScript objects between Illustrator and Photoshop.) Select the desired Photoshop image and choose Edit→Paste (⌘-V). The Paste dialog box appears. The Paste as Pixels option pastes the path with all the paint attributes; the Paste as Paths option pastes only the edited path and adds the path to the document and to the Paths palette as a Work Path.

Don Morris

Comments

Any image that consists of shades of gray or color—such as a photograph or illustration created in a paint program—is considered a continuous tone image. These images are raster-based and are made up of a collection of pixels versus lines or objects. To reproduce these images on a printing press, they must be converted to various sized dots, called the halftone screen. In a process or four-color image, the dots' colors are cyan, magenta, yellow, and black (CMYK).

Studio Usage

The most common halftone screening process takes place when the file is saved in EPS format or printed to an output device. Pay close attention to the final output resolution when selecting the halftone frequency.

Related Techniques

Line Screen Angles
and Dot Shapes   117

Dot Gain and
Transfer Functions   118

UCR and GCR   119

Gamut Restrictions   120

1 | Examine a Continuous Tone Image

Open a continuous tone image. Select the Zoom tool and drag a small marquee (rectangle) onto a dark or colorful section of the image to magnify it. If necessary, repeat until you can clearly see the individual pixels. Notice how each pixel has its own color or gray value. The density of the pixels depends on the resolution of the image when it was created or scanned.

2 | Examine a Printed Image

As a simple example, locate a photograph in your newspaper and examine it with a magnifying glass. You will be able to clearly see the halftone dots that make up the image. The areas of shadow, midtones, and highlights (even the very white areas) are filled with distinct dots. These dots, arranged in a specific pattern, are responsible for the illusion of continuous tone achieved in printed halftones.

3 | Determining the Halftone Dot Size

The tonal values of a continuous tone image are converted to various-sized halftone dots. The smaller the dot, the brighter the tone appears to the eye. The larger the dot, the darker a specific tone appears. You can see this tonal difference in bright and dark areas of a printed image by examining the areas with a magnifying glass or a loupe.

4 | Determining the Halftone Screen Frequency

Halftone screen frequency, or screen ruling, refers to the grid or lines of dots used to produce an image on film or on paper. Lines per inch (lpi) is the measurement for screen ruling and determines how fine or coarse the image appears on final output. The higher the screen ruling, the better the illusion of continuous tone is.

Gary Poyssick

Comments

Photoshop gives you greater control of your output quality by allowing you to set specific screen angles and different dot shapes. These options can produce different effects that can improve your design. You can then save this information with your file to eliminate problems in pre-press and printing.

Studio Usage

Different dot shapes produce different results. Elliptical dots, for example, often prove superior when outputting duotones with lots of shadow details. Before selecting a specific dot shape, check with your printer. Experimentation is vital if you intend to manipulate screens and dot shapes, but the rewards can be worth the effort.

Related Techniques

Resolution and Image Size   65

Gamut Restrictions   120

1 | Halftone Screen Angles

Process color separations print at different angles to form a pattern that the eye merges into continuous tone color. Before determining screen angles, check with the prepress and print vendor for the frequency, angle, and dot pattern settings that work best with their output and printing devices. Select Page Setup from the File menu and click Screen. To have Photoshop select the correct screen angles for the output resolution you plan to use, click the Auto button, select the output resolution, and click OK. To use the output device's default screens, select the Use Printer's Default Screens option. To customize the screen angles, choose the color for the screen from the Ink menu and enter a frequency and angle.

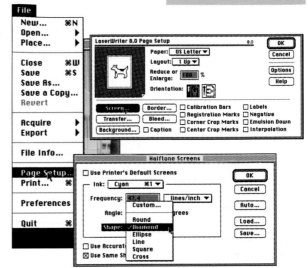

2 | Moiré Patterns

When outputting or printing a multicolor image, incorrect screen angle values create a moiré pattern. This pattern disrupts the continuous tone of the image. Save the screen angle values that correspond with the output device; each output device has its own screen angle values. When printing spot or custom color with black, the default screen angles for both are 45 degrees. To avoid moiré patterns, change the spot color setting.

3 | Dot Shapes

You can select a dot shape from the Shape menu, located in the Screens dialog box. These shapes have a profound effect on the image. The options are Diamond, Round, Line, Ellipse, Cross, and Square. Using a sample image, select a different dot shape and save it with your file. Print the result to see the result on your image. You can have the same dot for all colors or specify differently-shaped dots for each color. Choosing different dots for different colors can sometimes help to eliminate moiré patterns.

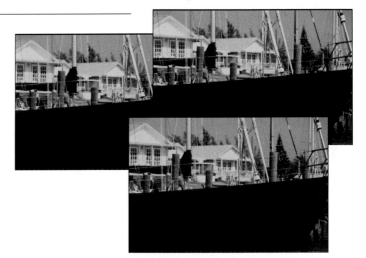

4 | Saving the Screen Settings

To save the file with the screen settings, save the file in EPS format. If necessary, choose File→Save As and select EPS from the pop-up Format menu. Click OK. The EPS Format dialog box appears. Select the Include Halftone Screen option in the dialog box and then click OK. (Only an EPS file can store this information.) Saving your file in this format ensures that the screen angles you entered will override the settings of the output device.

Don Morris

Comments

Many factors can contribute to a halftone dot's loss of integrity. The absorbency of the paper determines how much a dot of ink can spread on the paper. The more porous the paper, the greater the spread will be. For example, newsprint has a much greater spread factor than a coated, glossy paper stock does. This spread factor is called Dot Gain. Dot gain can also be a result of a miscalibrated imagesetting device. Photoshop allows adjustments for dot gain in Printing Inks Setup and Transfer Functions.

Studio Usage

In the Printing Inks Setup, the default setting is Standard White Offset Paper (SWOP). Check with your printer to determine the correct setting for the paper stock you are using. If you use recycled paper, which adds significantly to dot gain, you must be careful to determine the correct attributes. To check imagesetter calibration, test the film output with a densitometer. Transfer functions are used to compensate for any miscalibrations in the imagesetter.

Related Techniques

Adjusting Tonal Ranges   77

Creating a Scale of Grays   78

Curves 1, 2   81, 82

UCR and GCR   119

EPS   122

1 | The Printing Inks Setup Dialog

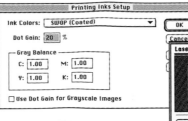

Open an RGB image and choose File→ Preferences→Printing Inks Setup. In the Printing Inks Setup dialog box, make sure that Use Dot Gain for Grayscale Images is selected. The default setting for Ink Colors is SWOP (Coated). With this choice selected, the dot gain is set to a standard 20%. This dot gain only works for a specific paper under very controlled conditions. Select Ad-Litho (Newsprint) from the pop-up menu. Notice that the dot gain assumed for this more porous paper is 30%. Choose Canon Color Laser Copier. The dot gain for this device, which utilizes toner, is 33%. Click cancel to exist the dialog box.

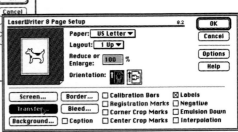

2 | To Measure Differences

You may have noticed the density changing in your image as you made different Ink Colors selections in the Printing Inks Setups dialog box. With an RGB image open, open the Printing Inks Setup dialog box again. Set the dot gain to 30% by entering the figure directly into the Dot Gain field. Next, open the Info palette and measure a specific area of the image, noting the location of the measurement in the palette. Set the dot gain to 33% and measure the same area again. You will notice a change in the RGB data (the CMYK data doesn't change; the percentage of inks stays the same, but the dot size changes to adjust for the gain). Set the dot gain to 0%. The image changes dramatically.

3 | Transfer Function Adjustments

Open an RGB file and select File→Page Setup; then click the Transfer button. Transfers are a series of adjustments made to the output (using the curve graph on the left) that affect the density range of the halftone. If densitomer readings taken from the output device generate a curve that is different from perfect neutral, transfer functions create adjustments to the file to offset those differences.

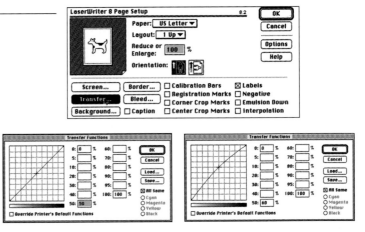

4 | Adjusting and Measuring Transfer Functions

Each of the hatch marks displayed on the grid represents a ten percent adjustment to the tonal range. Click the middle of the diagonal curve to place a point—this point represents a perfectly neutral tone. Drag the point upward to the first hatch mark. This represents a ten percent adjustment to the midtones—a 50% tone will now output at 60%. Adjusting the end point in the lower-left will affect highlights and upper-right affects shadows. Click on different sections of the line and look at the (transferred) values that appear in the numeric grid. You can also enter percentages directly into the fields to the right of the grid.

5 | Saving the Results

Only Photoshop native format and EPS are capable of storing transfer functions as part of the image file. Select Save As and select EPS as the file format. Select the Include Transfer Function box. The adjustments become part of the saved file.

Richard Smyth

Comments

Under Color Removal (UCR) and Gray Component Replacement (GCR) are two styles of color translation used when converting images from RGB to CMYK. Each method controls the amount of ink used to reproduce images. UCR adds black ink to shadow areas and neutral colors to create greater depth, and GCR adds black ink over a wider range of colors, resulting in darker, more saturated tones.

Studio Usage

Three important factors must be discussed with your printer before determining which style of translation you should use: Total Ink Coverage, Gray Balance, or Black Generation Limits. UCR and GCR reduce the effect of dot gain in shadow areas. If you convert your images from RGB to CMYK before sending your work to a prepress or print vendor, consider adjusting UCR or GCR.

Related Techniques

RGB versus CMYK   79

Dot Gain and
Transfer Functions   118

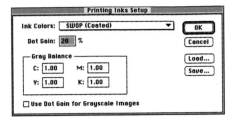

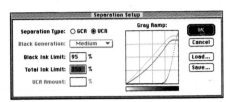

1 | Preparing an Image for Separation

Open an RGB image and choose File→Preferences→Printing Inks Setup. When the Printing Inks dialog box appears, select the appropriate device profile from the pop-up menu. If your printer has supplied you with specific Gray Balance figures, enter them in this dialog box and then click OK. Choose File→Preferences→Separation Setup→UCR. An average total ink coverage would be 350%, but this figure will vary depending on the intended output—from as low as 240% for newspaper, to as high as 375% for extremely high-quality, sheet-fed presses. Black at 95% works well for most images because printers do not like to print solid black in shadow areas. Again, check with your printer for exact figures specific to the printing press you're using to output your work.

2 | Creating the Black Plate with UCR

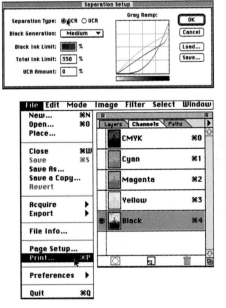

Open an RGB image and choose File→Preferences→Separation Setup. In the Separation Setup dialog box, select UCR and click OK to accept the default values. Choose Mode→CMYK to convert your RGB image and then click the black channel to select it in the Channels palette. All the channels, with the exception of the black channel, are hidden. Choose File→Print (⌘-P) to print the channel. (You'll print another channel in the next step to make a comparison between UCR and GCR.) Click the CMYK channel at the top of the Channels palette to display all the channels when you've finished printing the black channel.

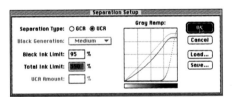

3 | Creating the Black Plate with GCR

Using the same RGB image you opened in Step #2, choose File→Preferences→Separation Setup, select GCR, and then click OK to accept the default values. Choose Mode→CMYK to convert your RGB image and then click to select the black channel in the Channels palette. All the channels, with the exception of the black channel, are hidden. Choose File→Print (⌘-P) to print the channel. Compare the differences in the printouts of the two channels.

Mitchell Anthony, MADworks®

Comments

A gamut is the range of colors a device can display or print. RGB, a color model based on light, has a larger range of hues than CMYK, a color model based on ink. Photoshop's Gamut Warning command notifies you when a color is not printable in the CMYK gamut.

Studio Usage

While you're editing images, you should work in the RGB color model—RGB files are smaller than CMYK files and contain a broader range of color information. Additionally, repeated conversions between RGB and CMYK modes cause a loss in color information that can't be restored. In order to work in RGB mode and see a CMYK preview of your image, use the CMYK Preview command.

Related Techniques

Curves 1, 2 81, 82

Hue and Saturation 86

Adjusting Shadows, Midtones, Highlights 83, 84, 85

1 | CMYK Preview

To see how your image will look in printable color without changing the color model, use CMYK Preview. Open an RGB image and choose CMYK Preview from the Mode menu. The program builds the color separation tables that it will use to convert the image. Notice the shift in the color. In some cases the color will appear dulled. An effective way to use this feature is to have two windows open, one in RGB and one in CMYK Preview. You can adjust your RGB image and preview the effects simultaneously on your CMYK image.

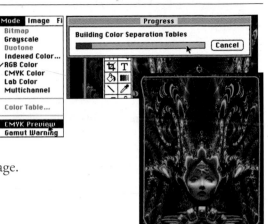

2 | Gamut Warning

Turn on Gamut Warning from the Mode pop-up menu. The program warns you of colors that are outside the gamut of your output device by displaying them in gray. You can change the gamut warning color and opacity in the Preferences→Gamut Warning Preferences dialog box.

3 | Selecting the Out-of-Gamut Ranges

Open an RGB image and choose Color Range from the Select menu. Choose Out of Gamut from the Select pop-up menu. The dialog box displays the areas that are out of the CMYK color gamut. The selection can be previewed as Grayscale, Black Matte, White Matte, or Quick Mask.

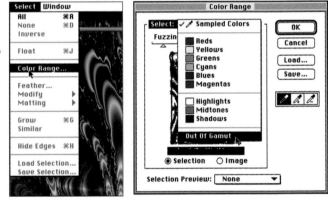

4 | Adjusting the Area

To adjust large out-of-gamut areas of color, choose Select→Color Range→ Out of Gamut and click OK. This selects only the out-of-gamut colors that require editing. Press ⌘-H to hide the edges of the selection. Select Mode→ Gamut Warning to preview your edits. Use color-correction features under the Image→Adjust menu (Levels, Curves, or Hue/Saturation) commands until the Gamut Warning fails to display any non-printable regions.

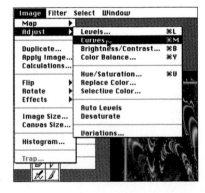

Don Morris

Comments

Adobe Photoshop lets you save documents in many file formats. Each format has a specific use. For example, you might save a file in EPS format in order to use it in an illustration or page layout program, or you might save a file in TIFF format if you're going to use it on another computer platform. The format determines which image modes will be preserved in the file (such as RGB, CMYK, Duotone, Indexed Color and so on), and the type of data that will be saved (such as channels, paths, and layers). Only Photoshop 3.0 format supports all the color modes and data types.

Studio Usage

Photoshop 3.0 format provides excellent file compression (the files are smaller than compressed TIFF files but not as small as JPEG compressed files). During the creation phase of a project, you should *always* save your files in Photoshop 3.0 format. This allows the most flexibility for editing and image manipulation because you keep all channels and layers intact. For comps and layout, you can make a smaller, flattened version of the file in another format by using the Save a Copy command.

Related Techniques

Grouping, Merging, and Flattening Layers   57

Managing Channels   59

1 | Make a Selection

Open a Photoshop 3.0 file or choose File→New
to open a new document. If necessary, choose
Window→ Palettes→ Show Layers to display the
Layers palette. Click the page icon at the bottom
of the Layers palette to create a new layer. Click
the Channels tab at the top of the layer group to
display the Channels palette. Click the page icon
at the bottom of the Channels palette to create a
new channel.

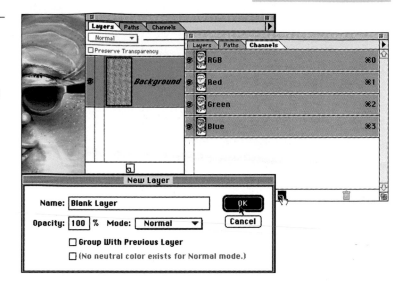

2 | Select a File Format

Choose File→Save As. Click to display the Format pop-up menu
and look at your choices. When you're working in a Photoshop
3.0 document containing multiple layers, only the Photoshop 3.0
file format is available. This feature prevents you from accidentally
losing your layers by saving a layered document in another format. When working with other file formats, such as JPEG, more
file formats are available when you choose the Save As command.

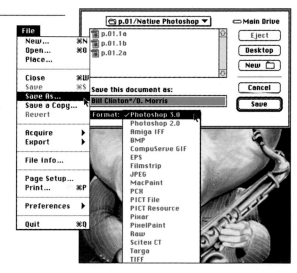

3 | Format Options

Choose File→Save a Copy; then hold down the mouse button on
the Format submenu. In this case, you can select from a wide variety of file formats. Select TIFF. Unless you select the Don't Include
Alpha Channels option at the bottom of the dialog box, TIFF
saves the alpha channels in a file, but doesn't save the layers. After
you select TIFF and release the mouse, the Flatten Image option at
the bottom of the dialog box is selected, indicating that the saved
copy won't contain layers. When you use the Save a Copy command, the file is saved to disk but does not replace or affect the
active file.

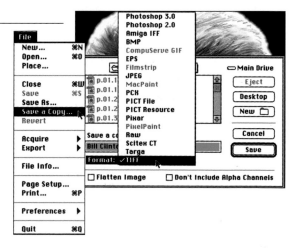

File Formats *EPS*

Rhoda Grossman

Comments

EPS (Encapsulated PostScript) format is specifically designed for saving object-oriented graphics that will be printed on a PostScript output device. EPS is supported by most illustration and page layout programs. In this technique, you use the Save a Copy command to save several versions of your file. When you use the Save a Copy command, the file is saved to disk but does not replace or affect the currently active file.

Studio Usage

To use a Photoshop image in Adobe Illustrator, you must save it in EPS format. EPS files have several useful features: only EPS files can store pen paths as clipping paths, which you can use as a mask in an EPS image; only EPS files can store halftone screen attributes and transfer functions that you set in Photoshop; and EPS files provide an image preview you can use to place an image on a page.

Related Techniques

JPEG   67

Importing and Exporting
Paths   115

DCS (Desktop Color
Separations)   123

1 | Create Several Comparison Files

In the Finder, create a new folder and name it EPS Comparison. Choose File→Open and select an image stored in a file format *other* than EPS. Choose Image→Image Size and note the current file size. Then save three versions of the file. First, Choose File→Save a Copy, choose JPEG from the Format pop-up menu, and click Save. Select Maximum in the JPEG Options dialog box. Next, choose File→Save a Copy and choose TIFF in the Format menu. Click Save and select LZW Compression in the TIFF Options dialog box. Finally, choose File→Save a Copy and choose Photoshop 3.0 in the Format menu.

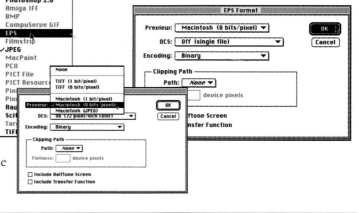

2 | Save a Copy in EPS Format

Choose File→Save a Copy and choose EPS from the Format pop-up menu. Click Save. In the EPS Format dialog box, select Macintosh (8 bits/pixel) as the Preview type. This is the most commonly used EPS preview format. The preview is the version of the image that you see in a layout program, and it gives you an idea of what the image will look like when it's printed. When you're going to use the image with an IBM-compatible PC application, save the preview in TIFF format.

3 | Compare File Sizes

Return to the Finder and open the folder containing the files you saved in steps 1 and 2. Compare the file sizes. The original file was 12.0 MB. The largest file (over 15 MB) is the EPS file, and the smallest is the file saved using JPEG compression. Because EPS always produces the largest file, use it only when you need the unique capabilities that the EPS format offers.

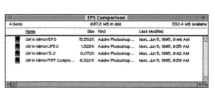

4 | Combining EPS with JPEG Compression

In Photoshop choose File→Save a Copy, choose EPS from the Format menu, click Save, and then select JPEG (maximum quality) from the Encoding pop-up menu in the EPS Format dialog box. Return to the Finder and check the file sizes again. Combining the two formats results in an almost 1500% decrease in the file's size. Before making your final file format decision, contact your service bureau to see if they support the use of EPS/JPEG. Many vendors are converting to this space-saving file format.

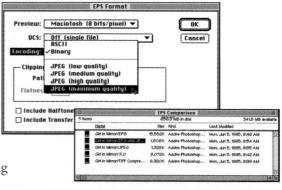

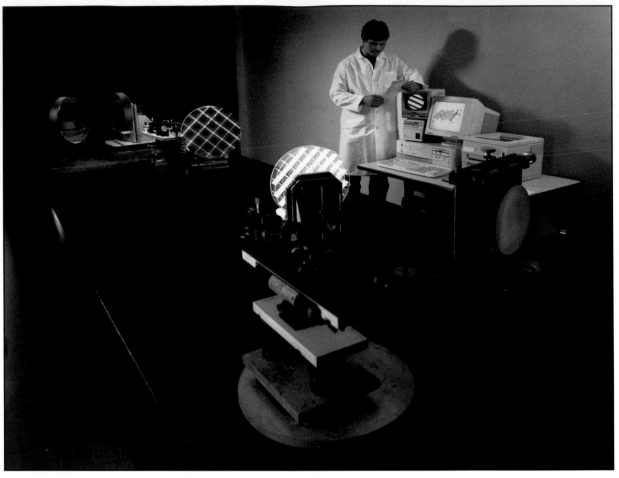

Bob Hamor

Comments

Desktop Color Separations (DCS) file format, developed by Quark, Inc., is an extension of the EPS format. When you're working in a page layout program, DCS lets you print color separations directly to film. The format contains five files; one master file and four files that contain color information for the C, Y, M, and K plates.

Studio Usage

When you save a file in DCS format, you have the option of saving a low-resolution Postscript preview of the image. This composite preview is different from the standard bitmapped preview, which you can also include in an EPS file. Use this composite Postscript preview when you want to print a DCS file to a low-resolution printer for proofing. Select the composite preview option only if you're going to output to a printer because it increases the size of the DCS file significantly.

Related Techniques

Resolution and Image Size   65

JPEG   67

Resolution and Screen
Frequency Requirements   68

1 Convert the Image to CMYK

In the Finder, create a new folder and name it DCS Folder. In Photoshop, choose File→Open and open a color image. If the file isn't in CMYK format, choose Mode→CMYK to convert the file.

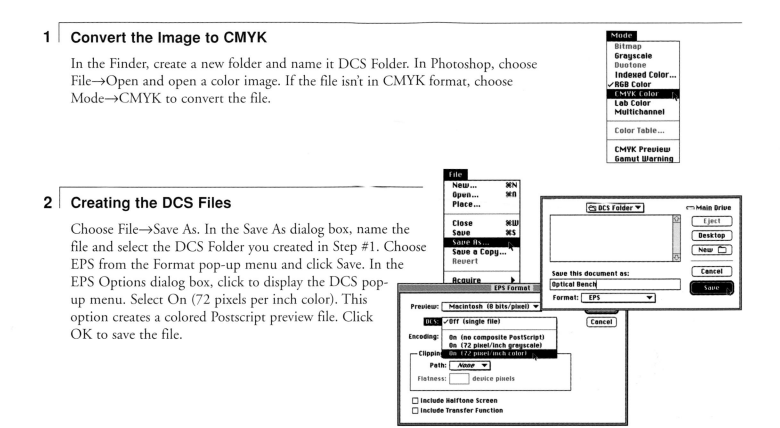

2 Creating the DCS Files

Choose File→Save As. In the Save As dialog box, name the file and select the DCS Folder you created in Step #1. Choose EPS from the Format pop-up menu and click Save. In the EPS Options dialog box, click to display the DCS pop-up menu. Select On (72 pixels per inch color). This option creates a colored Postscript preview file. Click OK to save the file.

3 Looking at the DCS Files

Return to the Finder and open the DCS Folder. Inside are five files: one with the name you entered and four with the name plus a suffix. The file without a suffix is the master file, which contains the color Postscript preview. This preview image is sometimes called an FPO (For Placement Only) because it's used to place the EPS image for proofing. It is not, however, the high-resolution file that is printed to film. The files with suffixes contain the color information from the cyan, magenta, yellow, and black channels that are used to generate the color plates.

4 Using the Preview File

Open your page layout program and choose File→New (Adobe PageMaker is the application used in this example). Choose the File→Place or File→Get Picture command and import the master file (the file without the suffix). Notice that the image appears quickly. Drag to change the placement of the image and again notice that the move response time is relatively fast. Using a small composite preview file can save you a lot of time during the production process. When you print to film, the page layout application substitutes the four high-resolution files for the preview file.

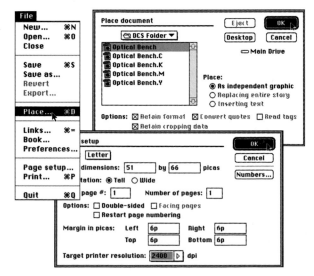

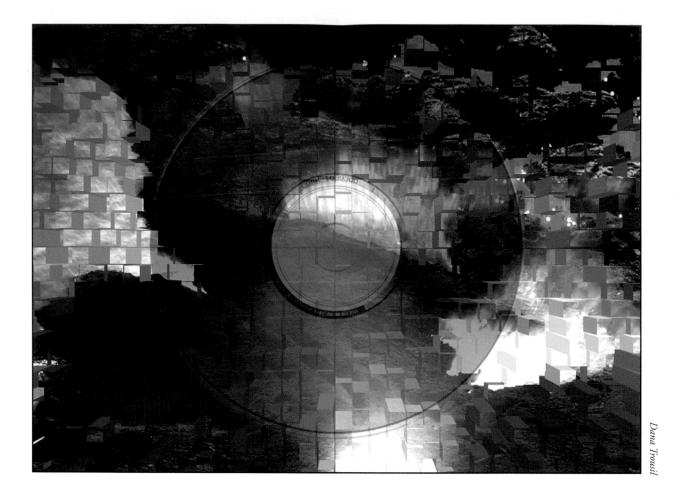

Dana Trousil

Comments

Kodak's PhotoCD format provides a convenient way to obtain scanned images of your own work. The scans on a PhotoCD disk come in a range of resolutions and arrive ready for use in Adobe Photoshop.

Studio Usage

With the exception of very large, high-quality projects, most other jobs can be done using PhotoCD scans. Because of their relatively low cost, they are often used as preliminary art and as place holders during the development phase of a project. When you're using PhotoCD scans, your first step is to move the images you want to use from the CD-ROM disk to your hard disk.

Related Techniques

Resolution and Image Size   65

Opening Photo CD Images   126

1 | The Disk Contents

Insert and open your PhotoCD disk. All PhotoCD disks have the same generic CD icon. When you double-click the icon, three items appear in the window: the Slide Show Viewer, which is an application developed by Kodak that allows you to browse the images on the disk; the Slide Show file, which contains pointers about the contents of the Photos folder; and the Photos folder. You may or may not see an additional folder named PHOTO_CD.

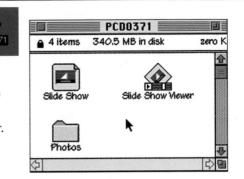

2 | The ImagePac

Within the Photos folder is a set of folders, each representing a specific image size measured in pixels. The icons in this folder aren't the actual images. The actual images are stored inside the PHOTO_CD folder in a folder called Images. Double-clicking an individual size file starts a decompression program that opens the image at the indicated size. It's much easier to use Kodak's plug-in Acquire module to open the images from within Photoshop than it is to open images from these files. The Photos folder is best used for viewing the slide show.

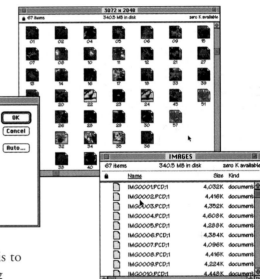

3 | Using the Slide Show Viewer

Double-click the Slide Viewer icon to browse through the images on the disk. You can resize the viewing screen, but when you resize the image, the resolution doesn't change. If you make the screen too large, your image appears blurry and you begin to see individual pixels. To use a larger viewing screen, choose File→ Preferences. In the Preferences dialog box, select one of the Slide Show Size options.

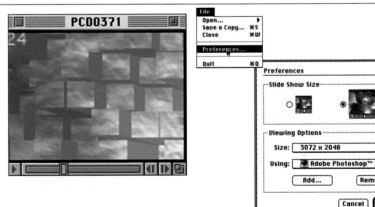

4 | Setting the Application Preference

The Preferences dialog box also allows you to set the application and default image size. After you set this preference, double-clicking an image in the Slide View opens the image in Photoshop at the default image size you choose.

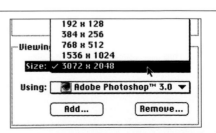

Michael J. Partington

Comments

There are several ways to open PhotoCD images in Photoshop. You can use the Kodak CMS PhotoCD plug-in module, or you can use a third-party plug-in such as the Kodak Acquire Module or the CD-Q module from Human Software. This technique explains how to use the Kodak CMS PhotoCD plug-in module, which is shipped with Photoshop 3.0. The other plug-in modules are available directly from their vendors.

Studio Usage

Kodak PhotoCD images come in five different resolutions (the resolutions are represented as image sizes measured in pixels). Use the larger files for graphic design because they have the necessary resolution for editorial and advertising images. Use the smaller files for databases, image libraries, and multimedia projects. If your image requires color-correction, sharpening, or retouching, start with a larger file than you'll need for the final image. When you've finished editing, use the Image Size command (with the File Size option selected) to crop the image and increase the resolution.

Related Techniques

Resolution and Image Size   65

Resolution and Screen
Frequency Requirements   68

Using the Photo CD Disk   125

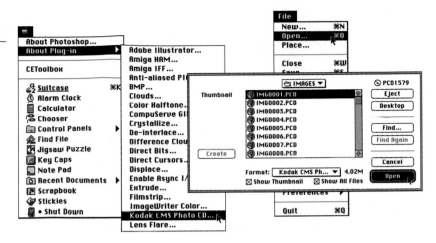

1 | Open the Photo CD File

To open a PhotoCD file, the Kodak CMS PhotoCD plug-in must be installed on your system. To make sure that the plug-in is available, choose Apple menu→About Plug-In and see if Kodak CMS PhotoCD appears in the pop-up menu. If it isn't there, you need to install it (it's located in the application's File Format folder within the Plug-ins folder). Insert the PhotoCD disc in your CD-ROM drive and switch to Photoshop. Choose File→Open. Locate the IMAGES folder inside the PHOTO_CD folder on the PhotoCD disk, select the image you want to use, and then click Open.

2 | Choose the Resolution

In the PhotoCD dialog box, click to display the Resolution pop-up menu and choose a resolution. The default size of 512 pixels by 768 pixels opens an image that is 7 inches wide by 10 inches high with a resolution of 72 ppi. The file size is about 1.13MB. The higher the number of pixels, the larger the image size. For example, if you choose 1024 pixels by 1536 pixels, Photoshop opens an image that is 21 inches wide by 14 inches high with a resolution of 72 ppi. This larger file is about 4.5 MB.

3 | Select the Source

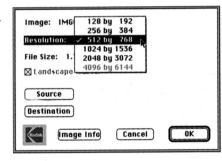

Click the Source button to display the Source Precision Transform dialog box. In this box, you indicate the original document's type. The first time you open a PhotoCD file, no source profile is selected. Choose an option from the Source Device pop-up menu (Kodak PhotoCD may be the only choice if you don't have any other profiles installed). Select a description from the source list. After you determine the source profile, it remains selected until you choose a different one. Click OK to return to the PhotoCD dialog box.

4 | Select the Destination

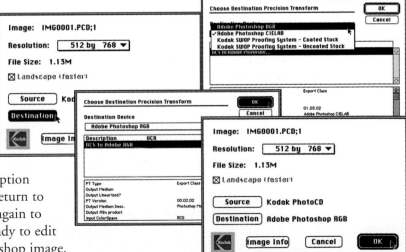

Click the Destination button to display the Destination Precision Transform dialog box. In this box, you indicate the Photoshop mode that you want to work in (RGB or CIELAB) or the proofing system (SWOP Coated or SWOP Uncoated). Select an option from the Destination Device pop-up menu. The description changes to match your choice. Click OK to return to the PhotoCD dialog box and then click OK again to open the image as a TIFF file. Now you're ready to edit this image just as you would any other Photoshop image.

Glossary

8-bit color. A color model that provides a palette of 256 colors—the minimum amount of colors displayed on a color monitor.

24-bit color. A color model that provides 256 shades of color for each color channel (red, green, and blue). When the shades from all three channels are combined, more than 16 million colors can be generated.

32-bit color. A color model that provides 256 shades of color for each color channel (red, green, and blue) and also provides a mask channel that contains 256 possible shades. Thirty-two-bit color provides the most precise color matching between a color monitor and printed output.

Additive color. *Additive color* refers to red, green, and blue light. When red, green, and blue light are combined in various percentages, the visible range of colors is produced. When 100 percent of red, green, and blue are combined, white light is produced.

Adobe Systems. The company responsible for writing the Postscript Language, Adobe Illustrator (the program this book discusses), Adobe Photoshop (an image editing program), a wide range of typefaces, the Adobe Acrobat program (a method of creating platform-independent documents), and other tools designed for the professional graphic artist and communicator.

Anti-aliasing. The softening effect produced by mixing pixels. To create a soft edge around an object, for example, the pixels at the edge of the object gradually mix into the color of the surrounding pixels.

Assembly. In traditional graphic-arts terms, the stripping or combining of disparate components to create a set of final film, which is used to create printing plates; in Adobe Photoshop, the merging or combination of digital images and/or drawings into a single composite image.

Balanced screening. A term used by AGFA to describe its proprietary halftone-dot or screen rendering methods.

Bézier curves. A curve that is mathematically defined using four control points. The Pen tool in Photoshop creates Bézier curves.

Bitmap mode. A *bitmap* is an image comprised of pixels, each of which has a specific value. In Adobe Photoshop, Bitmap mode refers to a black-and-white image; each pixel is either black (on) or white (off). Converting an image to a bitmap discards any color information in the file.

Bleed. When ink (a portion of the image) extends to the final trim size of a page, it is called a bleed. In a *full bleed*, ink extends to all the trim marks, placing color all the way to the edge of the page.

Brightness. In printing terms, brightness refers to the reflective nature of the paper. In Adobe Photoshop, brightness refers to the amount of light in each pixel.

CCD (Charged Coupler Device). A CCD is a light-sensitive electronic component used to measure light in devices such as scanners and digital cameras.

CD. An abbreviation for *compact disc*. Many stock photographic images are available in this format—for example, Kodak's PhotoCDs.

CEPS (Color Electronic Publishing System). This term is usually used to describe proprietary image correction and/or retouching systems, such as those available from Scitex, Linotype/Hell, Crosfield, and others.

Chrome. A slang term for a transparency.

Clipboard. The area of memory reserved for sequential temporary storage. Each time an item is copied to the Clipboard, the preceding contents are discarded.

Cloning. The duplication of individual pixels or regions of pixels. In Adobe Photoshop, the Rubber Stamp tool performs cloning functions.

CMYK (cyan, magenta, yellow, and black). CMYK refers to the four process inks used to output to a printing press.

Color correction. The process of correcting undesirable color or color casts in an image.

Color gamut. The range of colors that can be perceived on a specific device. Monitors display the RGB color gamut, which is based on light, and printed material displays the CMYK color gamut, which is based on ink colors. The RGB gamut is larger than the CMYK gamut.

Color separation. The process of converting an image to the four process ink colors (CMYK) for reproduction on a press.

Color space. The way a color image is being described and stored. RGB, CMYK, and Kodak YCC are examples of color space.

Composite. A composite image displays all the color elements of an image simultaneously. When you work in Adobe Photoshop, you can view individual channels or all the channels at the same time.

Compression. The method by which a file is condensed to create a smaller file, or the method by which certain pixels are discarded to store color data.

Halftone. An image created by converting a continuous-tone image to a series of dots of various sizes.

High-key image. An overexposed, washed-out image or an image whose highlight details were lost during scanning.

High-resolution image. An image whose resolution is at least twice as much as the line screen at which it will be reproduced. A 300-dpi image printed at a line screen of 150, for example, is a high-resolution image.

HSL (hue, saturation, and lightness). Hue is color; saturation is the degree, or shade of color; and lightness is how much white is in the color.

Hue. Color. Red and blue are two hues.

Imagesetter. An output device that is capable of achieving very high resolutions when rendering computer images. Typical resolutions of today's imagesetters range from around 1,200 dpi to more than 5,000 dpi.

Importing. The process of reading an image created in one application into another application.

Jaggies. Jagged edges, usually found in high-contrast art elements, in type, or in line-art illustration.

JPEG. A compression method, created by the Joint Photographic Experts Group, that reduces the original file size.

Layer. The method by which objects can be placed and edited on separate planes without affecting the entire image.

Leading. The vertical space between lines of type, measured in points. Originally, strips of lead of varying widths were placed between lines of type—hence the term *leading*.

Lightness. A measurement of the brightness of a color or shade.

Line art. High-contrast artwork, usually created in a drawing program (such as Adobe Illustrator).

Linearization. An adjustment made (usually with software) to an imagesetter or scanner in an attempt to adjust the input or output so that it matches factory specification.

Local color correction. An adjustment made to a selected area of an image, as opposed to the entire image.

Luminance. A measurement of a tone's brightness or lightness, with no consideration of its color or saturation.

Mask. An object created to protect or remove a portion of another object. You can think of a mask as being a stencil.

Memory colors. Colors that are easily recognized in nature, including skin tones, blue (sky), and green (grass); also called *reference colors.*

Metamerism. A term that describes the phenomenon in which a color appears different under varying lighting conditions. Metamerism affects proofing and viewing conditions, and is the reason why professional printing shops rely on measured lighting for viewing and client approval.

Midtones. The tonal values approximately halfway between black and white.

Moiré. An unsightly and undesirable pattern caused by improper alignment of halftone screens.

Monochrome. Usually refers to a black-and-white monitor but also can indicate a black-and-white image.

Negative. An image whose tonal values have been reversed (black areas are white and vice versa), or the image used to create a positive print.

Neutrals. Gray tones that have no apparent hue (color).

Opaque. A tone that blocks all light (100 percent black).

Pantone™. A commercial color-matching and ink-mixing system that ensures consistency in matching or attaining specific colors.

PICT. A file format used by several programs. Many multimedia applications rely on PICT format to display graphics on-screen.

Pixel. An individual (pic)ture (el)ement; a single dot on the screen or in a continuous-tone image.

Pixelization. A special effect achieved by lowering the resolution of an image in an attempt to make individual pixels visible.

PMS (Pantone Matching System). See *Pantone.*

Press proof. The method of determining how a job will look when it is printed. The proof (meant for client approval) is a sheet pulled from a press that uses the actual paper, ink sets, and images used for final reproduction.

Primary colors. Red, green, and blue (additive primary colors); cyan, magenta, yellow, and black (subtractive primary colors).

Process color. One of the four primary colors used for offset printing (cyan, magenta, yellow, and black).

Resolution. The height and width of a digital image, measured in pixels.

Retouching. Modification of a digital image with tools designed to adjust pixel values.

RGB (red, green, and blue). The three primary colors used to display images on a color monitor.

Rosette. A pattern formed when screen angles are overlayed to create a multicolor halftone, duotone, or four-color image. You can see a rosette by examining an image with a magnifying glass.

Saturation. The measurement of a color's intensity. Pink is less saturated than red, for example, and sky blue is less saturated than royal blue.

Scanner. A device that uses one of several methods to capture (digitize) artwork.

Screen. A process whereby a continuous-tone image is converted to halftone dots for reproduction on a conventional printing press.

Screen angle. The angle at which halftone dots are positioned on a page. In conventional color separations, the four screens (CMYK) are placed 30 degrees apart. Software allows for variable screen-angle placement.

Screen ruling. The measurement that indicates the number of halftone dots per inch. Newspapers normally are printed at a line screen (ls) of approximately 80, whereas high-quality magazines may be printed at 133 ls to 175 ls.

Shadows. The darkest portions of an image that still contain detail.

Sharpening. Sharpening, which increases the edge contrast of an image, reduces the halftone-dot size in an effort to improve details in an image.

Silhouette. An image that is isolated from its background, or the removal of a background in an effort to isolate a key element of a photograph.

Spot color. A color achieved by the addition of a specific ink color and not defined by using CMYK process inks. Also called *custom color*.

Stripping. The act of manually assembling page elements on a light table.

Substrate. The material on which an image is printed or imaged.

Subtractive color. The color system based on the four process ink colors (cyan, magenta, yellow, and black).

SWOP. A set of specifications, established by the GATF, that describes how colors output on standard white opaque paper. SWOP standards exist for newsprint, gloss, and uncoated paper. SWOP inks are inks that meet the established standard for reproduction on those substrates.

TIFF (Tagged Image File Format). A standard file format, created by Aldus Corporation, for storing bitmapped images.

Tint. A percentage of a given color at less than 100 percent opacity.

Tonal range. The number of tones between black and white in a given image.

Tone. The measurement of a color independent of its hue; a measurement of brightness or lightness.

Tone curve. The relationships of tones in an image displayed on a chart.

Transparency. A photographic image on a material that enables light to pass through its surface; the capability of a digital image to enable underlying images to show through.

Trapping. Adjustments made to overlapping or abutting images that compensate for slight shifts in the substrate during the printing process.

Tritone. A halftone comprised of three printing plates.

UCR (undercolor removal). The removal of varying amounts of cyan, magenta, and yellow in areas where black values are sufficient to achieve the desired level of gray.

Unsharp mask. A filter that sharpens an image by creating "halos" at the edges of objects. The human eye isn't sensitive enough to recognize very slight gradations in tone; this process increases these gradations to make them more visible.

Vector images. Images in which objects are mathematically defined, as opposed to raster or continuous-tone images, in which objects are defined in pixels.

Listing of Artists

Anne S. Barrett
10 Ledyard Lane
Hanover, NH 03755
603-643-6073

Anne Barrett is a graphic artist, cartoonist, and award-winning animator who recently moved from New York City to Vermont. Her cartoons are featured in a magazine in Hawaii and have appeared in publications in New York. She has worked in commercial animation and multimedia production for several years. In addition, she has performed with her cartoons in clubs in downtown Manhattan, and her performances and animations have appeared on cable and public television. Her email address is: /annimation@aol.com.

Melissa C. Beckman
68-35 Burns St.
Suite A3
Forest Hills, NY 11375
212-967-7711 x4544

"Though most of my personal work is figurative in nature, I occasionally work on other themes. The advent of the computer provides me with more than a tool to explore alternative variations of an idea, but a new way of seeing.

I generally prefer high-resolution imaging for my personal work. But I also enjoy the challenge of low-res files. All is based on my own photography. I work on more than one platform (SGI, Mac, Shima Seiki, DOS) as an artist/trainer for print and game development."

Pam Belding
235 Byrondale Ave. North
Wayzata, MN 55391
612-476-1338

Minneapolis artist Pam Belding began working on Paintboxes in 1983. Trained as an animator, Pam worked for a number of years in broadcast animation/graphics and direction of special effects for television, but since 1990, has been independently working as an animator and illustrator. She combines painterly technique, original photography, found objects, and graphics in collage form for expression, preferring a mixture of effects created inside and outside the digital realm for a more organic image.

Robert Bowen
Robert Bowen Studio
137 West 25th St.
New York, NY 10001
212-206-0848

Robert Bowen is an artist and principal of Robert Bowen Studio, a high-end facility for creating computer visual effects, photo-design, and retouching for print media. He works directly with advertising agencies as well as with many well-known photographers. He is an instructor in the graduate programs of computer art and photography at the School of Visual Arts. Robert is also a former director of RGA Print.

"I'm also involved in the production of fine artwork, which is always there to inform my commercial projects. I usually consider my advertising work to be a collaboration with art directors from advertising agencies and photographers. When I work on these projects, I'm often brought in at the concept stage, or at least before the photography begins. In doing this, someone once referred to me as a 'hired gun' for the advertising trade. Agencies hire me to solve their visual problems in an unique, elegant, and timely fashion. I can really do anything, given the appropriate time frame and budget, but my real specialty is combining 3-D computer graphics effects with 2-D photography."

Victor Claudio
12329 Glenfield Ave.
Tampa, FL 33626
813-891-6188

"I have been illustrating on the Mac since 1988. My illustrations are strongly influenced by my painting background and incorporate a wide range of techniques."

Victor is a Pratt Institute graduate; worked as Art Director for Norman, Craig & Kummel; was Graphic Creative Director for Grey Advertising in Puerto Rico; and is presently Art Director for AAA Auto Club South's Marketing Department in Tampa, FL. Victor can be reached at AOL through the user name Madcirq.

Jacqueline Comstock
17 Oakland Ct.
Warwick, NY 10990
914-987-8314

Trained as a designer, Jacqueline's career was profoundly affected by the advent of the Macintosh computer and Adobe Photoshop. This combination of hardware and software enabled her to find her niche—a style of illustration that encompasses photography, found objects, and painting. When she isn't creating illustrations, Jacqueline also writes magazine articles on design and computer graphics.

Lucas Deaver
Creative Freelancers Management, Inc.
25 West 45th St.
New York, NY 10036
212-398-9540

Lucas Deaver is a graduate of the New England School of Art and Design in Boston, MA, where he majored in illustration and graphic design. Although he is a traditionally trained illustrator, he now does all of his art on the Macintosh. Lucas incorporates a variety of drawing, painting, and 3D programs into his work, but Adobe Photoshop handles the crux of most of his projects. "I found the computer to be the most powerful tool in elevating my art to levels impossible before."

Ellie Dickson
185 West End Ave.
Apt. 3L
New York, NY 10023
212-724-3598

Ellie Dickson has been freelancing as an illustrator, designer, and instructor in New York City since 1989. Her clients include Young & Rubicam, Grey Direct, The U.S. Postal Service, Bantam Doubleday Dell, McGraw Hill, Peachpit Press, and such magazines as *Newsweek*, *Sports Illustrated*, and *MacUser*.

Ellie studied art at Boston University, SUNY at Purchase, and SUNY at Binghampton. Her illustrations are featured in *The Photoshop WOW Book*, *The Best of Business Card Design*, *The Guerrilla Marketing Handbook*, *The Painter Wow Book*, and *The Macintosh Handbooks for Designers*, among others.

Anne Farrell
VideoGraphicArts
131 Huddleson
Santa Fe, NM 87501
505-983-5126

Anne Farrell pursues computer graphic arts in the combined genres of still images, 3-D animation, and digital video. After graduating with honors from St. John's College in Annapolis, MD, Anne went to New Mexico to find a painting teacher. She also studied print-making at the University of Colorado. In 1980, she entered the world of computer graphics with an Apple IIe. She continues to do her own work today while heading the Electronic Graphics Department at Santa Fe Community College.

Frog Publications
Victor Bruha
P.O. Box 280096
Tampa, Florida 33682
813-935-5845

Our Tampa based company writes, designs, publishes, advertises, and sells educational games to elementary level schools across the United States. We also create custom designs, illustrations, and layouts for an expanding clientele looking for fresh looks in their advertising and promotions. With this much to do, high-quality and effective design is the key. I have a philosophy with the Mac. If I don't learn something new from every job I do, I haven't worked to my potential and eventually that could ruin me as a desktop designer.

Skip Gandy
Gandy Photography
4006 North Ola
Tampa, FLA 33603
813-253-0340

We do a lot of stock business, magazine photography, and aerial photography.

Rhoda Grossman
216 Fourth St.
Sausalito, CA 94965
415-331-0328

"My background in cartooning and life drawing influences my electronic paintings. I work rapidly (whether at the easel or at the digitizer), mixing classical drawing, contemporary illustration, and playful sensuality. It is exciting to work with live models at the computer. Or I may scan pencil sketches and rework them electronically. My current 'commercial' style involves photo-collage blended with painterly techniques, using 'natural media' software. I plan to continue exploring various combinations of high-tech and low-tech art—I must be 'bi-tech'!"

Rhoda is represented exclusively by Salzman International (415-285-8267).

Bob Hamor
The Hamor Group
2308 Columbia Circle
Merrimack, NH 03054
800-274-2656

A successful commercial advertising photographer for nearly 30 years, Bob Hamor has been providing clients with electronically enhanced photography since it became available on the desktop. Recently, Bob added a digital camera to his "all-format" studio. He estimates that nearly 50 percent of his photography will be totally digital. He is past president of the NHPPA and ASMP NE and has taught advanced color photography at the Franklin Institute in Boston, MA.

Richard Hommell
Tampa, Florida
813-546-5408

Phil Howe
Creative Freelancers Management, Inc.
25 West 45th St.
New York, NY 10036
212-398-9540

Phil Howe is a Photoshop pro as well as an excellent conventional artist. He also uses Painter, Premiere, Live Picture, and QuickTime. Phillip taught advanced illustration courses at the Art Institute of Seattle. His work merges traditional illustration and photography with high-end digital manipulation. He has a complete system capable of taking any project from initial scans through to high-res transparency output, allowing illustration, retouching, and complex design work at a much higher level with movable design elements of graphics and type. Some of Phillip's major clients include Hewlett Packard, Microsoft, Nintendo, *Reader's Digest*, Caterpillar, and the Seattle Symphony. He recently completed an annual report for Silicon Valley Bank.

Scott Kelby
Kelby Creative Services, Inc.
2194 Main St.
Suite K
Dunedin, FL 34698
813-733-6225

Scott Kelby is Editor-in-Chief and Publisher of *Mac Today* Magazine, as well as principal of Kelby Creative Services, Inc. (a Florida-based ad agency that specializes in print media). Scott was on Adobe's Beta team for Photoshop 2.5 and 3.0. Scott is one of 12 designers in the country to be chosen to participate in Adobe's "Design To Print" project, and he is on Adobe's Certified Instructor Advisory Committee. Scott has trained thousands of Photoshop users nationwide through his work as an instructor and training director for the Adobe Photoshop Conference Seminar Tour (sponsored by *Mac Today* Magazine), and he is featured in a series of Photoshop video training tapes.

Sanjay Kothari
130 West 25th St.
New York, NY 10001-7403
212-647-9743

Upon earning his degree in engineering at Mysore University, India, Sanjay Kothari changed course and pursued his strong interest in the visual arts by attending the New England School of Photography. In 1984, he discovered photomontage. This crucial discovery enabled expression of his irreverence for the unaltered photograph, to circumvent its singularity of time and space, enabling him to dismantle the photograph's factuality. According to Kothari, a photograph that includes the process of documentation and transformation allows for greater artistic expression than does documentation alone. Kothari's vision of photography integrates the documentary possibilities inextricably with the possibilities of transformation for a complete and integrated approach to using photography as an artistic medium.

Dorothy Krause
32 Nathaniel Way
Marshfield Hills, MA 02051
617-837-1682

In the past three years, the work of Dorothy Krause has been featured in eight solo shows: Gallery 911, Indianapolis, IN; Wellesley College, Boston, MA; The Center for Creative Imaging, Camden, ME; IRIS Graphics, Inc., Bedford, MA; The New England School of Photography, Boston; The University of Massachusetts, Lowell; Salem State College, Salem, MA; The University of Southern Maine, Portland; and Digital Equipment Corporation, Marlboro, MA. During the same time, her work has been in more than 30 group shows, including The Computer in the Studio at the DeCordova Museum in Lincoln, MA and the Boston Computer Museum; Digital Dialects at the Creiger-Dane Gallery in Boston; the Digital Salon at the School of Visual Arts in New York; Pixel Pushers Exhibition of Digital Art in Vancouver; SIGGRAPH 94 in Orlando; Fractal Design's Art Expo 94 and 95; and more.

Current and upcoming publications with her work include *Computer Graphics 2: The Best of Computer Art and Design, Fractal Design Painter, Inside Fractal Design Painter 3, The Painter WOW! Book, Great Photoshop Techniques, Kai's Power Tools: An Illustrated Guide,* and *MacWorld, Publish, On-Line Design, Digital Imaging, DIGI, Creativity, IdN, MacArt and Design,* and *Step by Step* magazines.

Dorothy Krause is a Professor of Computer Graphics at the Massachusetts College of Art, Corporate Curator for IRIS Graphics, Inc., and a member of the tradigital artists' collaborative Unique Editions™.

Bonny Lhotka
5658 Cascade Place
Boulder, CO 80303
303-494-5631

Bonny Lhotka graduated from Bradley University in 1964, where she majored in painting and printmaking. As an experienced artist, she has become known as a true innovator, creating such media as her new MonoGraphic Transfer process. In 1992, she added a Macintosh computer to her studio tools and continues to innovate new approaches in her work. Her paintings have been commissioned by or are included in over 100 corporate collections, including United Airlines, Johns Space Center, Jones Intercable, Microtek Labs, the U.S. Department of State, Charles Schwab, MCI, and McDonnell Douglas. Her work appears in numerous books and articles featuring experimental media. Bonny is listed in *Who's Who in American Art* and *Who's Who is American Women*.

Rich Lovato
Advanced Concepts
4864 Valley Hi Dr.
Sacramento, CA 95823-5155
916-429-2655

Rich Lovato is an award-winning illustrator living in Sacramento, CA. Rich offers a wide range of services including technical illustration, artistic renderings, 3D modeling, rendering, and animation. Advanced Concepts utilizes a Power Mac workstation, Illustrator, Painter, Photoshop, Director, Studio Pro, Hash Animation Master, and other applications. Rich's work has appeared in *MacArtist*, *Digital Video* Magazine, *Computer Artist*, *AV Video*, and *California Computer News*.

MADworks® the 3D studio
Contact: Mitchell Anthony
Email: madworks@aol.com
Web Site: http://www.madworks.com

"MADworks was originally built in 1978. As the times changed, so did MADworks. What were once pencils and airbrushes eventually became computers (really nice Mac computers). We've spent the better half of the last 17 years working on some interesting projects for a variety of people (most of them being of the Fortune 500 flavor). We continue to ply our trade with technology and creativity. Some of our renderings in this book came from "BioFractals®," our limited edition poster series. Want more info? Come visit our "Cyber HeadShop" Web site: http://www.madworks.com. You can also email us.

Peter Martin
PM Foto
1849 Rome Ave.
St. Paul, MN 55116
612-699-7198

Peter Martin is an artist/educator with a background of fine art/photography and digital imaging for personal expression. He is currently working on a suite of portraits and a series of sequential, digitally combined panoramics. He is also a teacher of photography and digital imaging at the University of Minnesota.

Marylu Miller
5130 La Jolla Blvd.
San Diego, CA 92109
619-488-1286

Marylu Miller, a San Diego-based computer graphic designer and teacher, enjoys creating conceptual collage using Photoshop 3.0. Her extensive background in publications includes monthly magazines, sales/advertising collaterals, brochures, and book and CD covers. Proficient with QuarkXPress, Photoshop, and Illustrator, Marylu is presently exploring Painter, RayDream Designer, and Elastic Reality.

Judith Moncrieff
4543 SW Water Ave.
Portland, OR 97201
503-294-9947

Judith Moncrieff received her MFA from The Massachusetts College of Art in Boston in 1991. Her studies included Design and Fine Art in London, Ireland, Paris, and New York. At present, Judith is an Assistant Professor at The Pacific Northwest College of Art in Portland. She manipulates digital images and transfers them to Fabriano, BFK Reves, and Windsor & Newton watercolor papers, where they are further manipulated with traditional techniques such as gold leaf, water colors, colored pencils, and inks. Judith refers to her work as Tradigital™ art.

Judith has recently shown her work through the Urban Digital Color Gallery in San Francisco, CA; The Art Council Gallery in Fayetteville, NC; The Wentz Gallery in Portalnd, OR; The Museum of Visual Arts in New York; and the Sandy Carson Gallery in Denver, CO.

Don Morris
The *St. Petersburg Times*
110 60th Ave. South
St. Petersburg, FL 33705
813-864-4349

As an illustrator and designer working for the *St. Petersburg (FL) Times*, a large daily newspaper, and as a children's book illustrator and freelance illustrator, Don has developed a versatility of style and technique. The foundation of his skills are based on his ability to conceptualize and invent different ways to illustrate stories. Don's favorite subject is zany characters and settings that provoke laughter and fond recognition. Don is the creator of "Blahville Middle," a cartoon based on the life of middle schoolers and those affected by them, including teachers, parents, bus drivers, janitors, etc. The cartoons are scanned into the Mac and colorized using FreeHand. Don is represented by Alexander/Pollard of Atlanta, GA (800-347-0734).

Bill Morse
173 18th Ave.
San Francisco, CA 94121
415-221-6711

Bill Morse has been producing graphics since the late 70s. Before Photoshop existed, Bill designed a computer-controlled camera system that enabled him to composite photographs and add special effects, such as glows and motion trails, textures, and airbrush simulation. He works primarily in Illustrator, Photoshop, and Painter. Bill's clients include Pepsi, Visa, Disney, Nintendo, Apple, Sharper Image, Pacific Bell, and Bank of America. His work can be seen in the *Creative Illustration* workbook and online at the Design Link graphics BBS at 415-241-9927.

Oko & Mano, Inc.
10 East 2nd St.
New York, NY 10003
212-387-9209

Partners Alejandro (Alex) Arce and Mirko Ilic´ founded Oko & Mano in 1993 to design 2-D and 3-D computer graphics and animation. Combining a focus on the creative side of computer graphics with their widely varied backgrounds, they have distinguished themselves through their ability to create interesting visual stories rather than simply computer special effects.

Both partners began in New York as freelancers, Mirko earning fame as a scratchboard illustrator while Alex specialized in computer graphics. Later, both worked for *Time* magazine, where Alex served as a Technology Consultant and Mirko as Art Director in charge of the magazine's International edition.

While still at *Time*, Alex cofounded Square Design to product animation for interactive media projects and educational and music videos. He went on to build a television graphics studio and put together the art department for Medical News Network, where he subsequenty created graphics and animation for medical and promo spots.

Mirko has received medals from the Society of Illustrators, the Society of Publication Designers, and the Art Directors Club for his design and illustration work.

Mike Pantuso
240 Union St.
Doylestown, PA 18901
215-340-0158

Much of Mike Pantuso's work is done for preschoolers and can be seen daily on *Sesame Street*. Though substantial recognition has been through *Sesame Street* (earning him three Emmy Awards and the AIGA Design Leadership Award), he also does print illustration. Mike's work has appeared in publications such as the *LA Times* Magazine, *Business Week*, *Bride*, *Seventeen*, *Sports Illustrated for Kids*, *The Philadelphia Daily News*, *Mademoiselle*, *Nickelodeon* magazine, and *Disney Adventures*. He has also done ads and products for Kool-Aid, Sunkist, Warner Bros., and Comedy Central.

Michael J. Partington
Partington Design
P.O. Box 20391
Indianapolis, IN 46220
317-259-4415

Michael Partington is primarily a fine artist, specializing in acrylic on canvas and digital fine art. He uses various media for his digital works, including the durable Cibatrans transparency films, which are displayed in a backlighted fashion to replicate the intense color display of a computer monitor.

"I don't necessarily use the computer to complete each work, but when used, even partially, my creativity seems to flow more naturally and easily."

Gary Poyssick
Against the Clock
6126 Schooner Way
Tampa, FL 33615
813-855-5067

Lisa Rivard
507 Wood Rd.
Indpls., IN 46216
317-541-1349

Lisa Rivard is a nationally-based freelance illustrator currently working out of Indianapolis, Indiana. She received a BFA in illustration from the Art Institute of Chicago in 1980, with studies in Hawaii and Rome. Since then, Lisa has worked in Europe and the US, with 16 years of experience as an art director and illustrator. For the past six years, she has managed her studio as a specialist in oil, pastel, and watercolor for several national clients, including four permanent exhibits in the world-renowned Children's Museum of Indianapolis, The Discovery Channel, and others. She is also fluent in the Macintosh environment, specifically in Photoshop and Adobe Illustrator.

Javier Romero
Javier Romero Design Group
24 East 23rd St.
3rd Floor
New York, NY 10010
212-420-0656

Javier Romero Design Group has been in the business of communications design for nearly ten years, serving a variety of clients with creative and marketing ideas. From corporate identity and logo development to trade video, collateral, advertising, and electronic media, JRDG fills a variety of needs. Working as a partner, JRDG's purpose is the development and design of effective and impactful creativity in marketing tools, no matter what the medium.

Denise Salles
709 Sutter Ave.,
Palo Alto, CA 94303
415-328-6033

Karin Schminke
5803 Norteast 181st St.
Seattle, WA 98155
206-402-8606

Mary Sillman
2515 Northwest Flanders
Portland, OR
503-226-1945

Mary Sillman is an artist/designer living in Oregon. She teaches in the Visual Design program for the University of Oregon.

Richard Smyth
Airbrush Arts
1235 Glenview Rd.
Glenview, IL 60025
708-998-8345

Born and educated in the United Kingdom, Richard Smyth has owned his own business since 1975. During this time, he has worked with such major accounts as Coca Cola, Scott, Foresman, and Chris Craft.

Gordon Studer
1576 62nd St.
Emeryville, CA 94608
510-655-4256

Gordon Studer is a designer who has worked out of his Emeryville studio for the past four years. His clients include Apple, *MacWorld*, *MacWeek*, *Time*, and *Newsweek*. Not one to rest on his laurels, Studer's current projects incorporate photography, 3D modeling, and multimedia, as well as his recognizable illustration style.

"Working fast—seeing many variations of an image—brings me into an intuitive flow. I use the computer like I used to paint, lining up many canvases, going down the line, working very quickly on each one until one hits the mark. I don't like my work to be calculated."

Dana Trousil
Atelier Graphics
532 North Civic Dr.
Suite C
Walnut Creek, CA 94596
510-938-8496

Dana Trousil is an artist émigré who has lived and worked in California since 1986. Originally a painter, illustrator, and a fine print maker, she switched to computer graphics and established Atelier Graphics in 1987. Since that time, her award-winning works have been published in national magazines, books on digital imaging, and CD-ROM publications (*HOW* Magazine, *EDI World* magazine, *Getting Started in Computer Graphics*, The Virtual Portfolio CD-ROM, etc.). Currently, Dana is also an art director for a leading electronic commerce company, DistriVision Development Corporation, specializing in electronic catalogs and EDI solutions.

Frances Valesco
135 Jersey St.
San Francisco, CA 94114
415-648-3814

Frances Valesco is President of the California Society of Printmakers and Vice President of the American Print Alliance. She trained at UCLA and California State University, and has taught at the Academy of Art College, San Francisco Art Institute, and the University of California, Berkeley. She has had over 150 group and solo exhibits, including the Biennale, Sao Paulo, Brazil; Bronx Museum, NY; Computer Museum, Boston, MA; Ars Electronica, Linz, Austria; and many SIGGRAPH exhibitions. Her work can be found in collections at the New York City Public Library, NYNEX, and the Fine Arts Museum in San Francisco.

Greg Vander Houwen
Interact
P.O. Box 498
Issaquah, WA 98027
206-999-2584

Greg Vander Houwen is a principal in the computer graphics firm Interact. He has a background in video, computers, photography, and apple farming.

As one of Adobe's Digital Masters, his fine artworks have been shown internationally and are featured on the Photoshop 3.0 CD-ROM. His clients include Apple Computer, Adobe Systems, Microsoft, and others. Greg is an artist by nature, an illustrator by trade.

Victoria Vesna
University of California, Santa Barbara
Santa Barbara, CA 93106
805-893-8545
Web Site: http://www.arts.ucsb.edu/~vive

Victoria Vesna is an installation and performance artist working with new technologies. She has exhibited internationally, including the Venice Biennale, the P.S.I Museum in New York, the Ernst Museum of Budapest, and the Long Beach Museum, where she briefly served as media council chair. She is a regular contributor to the SIGGRAPH art show. Currently, Victoria teaches Electronic Intermedia at UC Santa Barbara, where she initiated a collaboration with the College of Engineering and has received numerous awards and sponsorships.

Victoria is interested in exploring new tools and techniques in both art and education. The images reproduced in this book are from her interactive CD-ROM/WWW project, "Computers & the Intuitive Edge" (sponsored by the UCSB Department of Instructional Development). Victoria can be reached via email at vesna@humanitas.ucsb.edu.

Paul Watson
225 Sterling Rd.
Unit #9
Toronto, Ontario M6R2B2
416-535-2648

"I am a graduate of Sheridan College in Oakville, Ontario Canada, where I studied for four years. My commercial work is entirely computer-based while, to stay sane, I do some traditional pieces in my spare time. In both areas, my work is collage-based with multiple layers and leans heavily on design."

Jeff Yesh
9312 Jutland Ct., Apt. B
Indianapolis, IN 46250
317-849-6647

Jeff Yesh graduated with a degree in graphic design from Indiana State University. He has been an illustrator with Macmillan Computer Publishing for the past two years, specializing in computer illustration.

Hayden Books

WANT MORE INFORMATION?

CHECK OUT THESE RELATED TOPICS OR SEE YOUR LOCAL BOOKSTORE

Adobe Press

Published by Hayden Books, the Adobe Press Library reveals the art and technology of communication. Designed and written by designers for designers, best-selling titles include the Classroom in a Book (CIAB) series for both *Macintosh* and *Windows* (*Adobe Photoshop CIAB, Advanced Adobe Photoshop CIAB, Adobe PageMaker CIAB, Advanced Adobe PageMaker CIAB, Adobe Illustrator CIAB, and Adobe Premiere CIAB*), the Professional Studio Techniques series (*Production Essentials, Imaging Essentials, and Design Essentials, 2E*), and *Interactivity by Design.*

Design and Desktop Publishing

Hayden Books is expanding its reach to the design market by publishing its own mix of cutting-edge titles for designers, artists, and desktop publishers. With many more to come, these must-have books include *Designer's Guide to the Internet, Photoshop Type Magic, Adobe Illustrator Creative Techniques, Digital Type Design Guide*, and *The Complete Guide to Trapping, 2E.*

Internet and Communications

By answering the questions of what the Internet is, how you get connected, and how you can use it, *Internet Starter Kit for Macintosh* (now in 3rd ed.) and *Internet Starter Kit for Windows* (now in 2nd ed.) have proven to be Hayden's most successful titles ever, with over 500,000 Starter Kits in print. Hayden continues to be in the forefront by meeting your ever- popular demand for more Internet information with additional titles, including *Simply Amazing Internet for Macintosh, Create Your Own Home Page for Macintosh, Publishing on the World Wide Web, World Wide Web Design Guide, World Wide Web Starter Kit, net.speak: The Internet Dictionary*, and *Get on the Internet in 5 Minutes for Windows and Macintosh.*

Multimedia

As you embrace the new technologies shaping of multimedia, Hayden Books will be publishing titles that help you understand and create your own multimedia projects. Books written for a wide range of audience levels include *Multimedia Starter Kit for Macintosh, 3-D Starter Kit for Macintosh, QuickTime: The Official Guide for Macintosh Users, Virtual Playhouse, Macromedia Director Design Guide*, and *Macromedia Director Lingo Workshop.*

High-Tech

Hayden Books addresses your need for advanced technology tutorials and references by publishing the most comprehensive and dynamic titles possible, including *Programming Starter Kit for Macintosh, Tricks of the Mac Game Programming Gurus, Power Macintosh Programming Starter Kit, FoxPro Machete: Hacking FoxPro for Macintosh, 2E*, and *The Tao of AppleScript: BMUG's Guide to Macintosh Scripting, 2E.*

Orders/Customer Service **800-763-7438**   Source Code **HAYB**

Hayden Books   201 West 103rd Street ◆ Indianapolis, Indiana 46290 USA
Visit our Web page at http://www.mcp.com/hayden/